Analyzing Operations in Business

Analyzing Operations in Business

Issues, Tools, and Techniques

Michael R. Summers

QUORUM BOOKS
Westport, Connecticut • London

Library of Congress Cataloging-in-Publication Data

Summers, Michael Roger, 1947–
    Analyzing operations in business : issues, tools, and techniques /
by Michael R. Summers.
        p.   cm.
    Includes bibliographical references and index.
    ISBN 1–56720–126–1 (alk. paper)
    1. Operations research.   2. System analysis.   I. Title.
T57.6.S86   1998
658.4'034—dc21   97–41005

British Library Cataloguing in Publication Data is available.

Library of Congress Catalog Card Number: 97–41005
ISBN: 1–56720–126–1

First published in 1998

Quorum Books, 88 Post Road West, Westport, CT 06881
An imprint of Greenwood Publishing Group, Inc.

Printed in the United States of America

The paper used in this book complies with the
Permanent Paper Standard issued by the National
Information Standards Organization (Z39.48–1984).

10 9 8 7 6 5 4 3 2 1

To Ann and Adam with all my love
For time and all eternity.

Contents

Figures

Analyzing Operations
in Business

CHAPTER 1

Introduction to Operations Management

OVERVIEW OF OPERATIONS MANAGEMENT

The ''operations'' of an organization are all of the activities directly related to accomplishing the main purpose of the organization, whether it be producing some product or providing some service. In either case the operations system will provide the conversion of certain inputs, such as materials and labor, into certain outputs, either products or services. Thus, the operations function can be distinguished from the other main functional areas of an organization, such as marketing, finance, personnel, and accounting, which are no less vital for the firm's success but which are less directly related to the organization's day-to-day pursuit of its main business. Of course, all main functional areas of an organization are intricately entwined; all interact with and provide support for the others, and the boundaries are not always clear between them.

''Operations management,'' then, refers to performing the traditional managerial functions (planning, organizing, directing, and controlling) on the organization's operations. Operations managers include those with traditional line authority (the chain of command from the Vice President of Operations down through supervisors and foremen, for example) and those in staff positions (production planning, inventory control, and quality control, for example). Staff personnel are responsible mainly for preparing recommendations regarding the planning, organizing, and control of operations, while line personnel have the actual authority to direct the operations.

Goals of Operations Management

What is the goal of all this managerial activity in the operations area? Obviously, the goals of operations management must be supportive of the goals of the overall organization, but what specifically are the goals relevant to the operations function? Perhaps the most obvious goal is *productivity*. Productivity simply refers to the ratio of a firm's outputs to its inputs. Typical inputs to an operations system would include capital, raw materials, labor, and money. Increasingly, information is also being thought of as a resource. Outputs would include the organization's products and services. Of course, organizations produce many less obvious and sometimes undesirable outputs, such as pollution and traffic congestion. Generally, though, the operations manager is striving to maximize the system's outputs relative to its inputs. In other words, the goal is to produce the most products and services for the least cost, to the extent that this goal doesn't interfere with the other goals of the organization.

This goal of productivity has become more important lately because of the increased worldwide competition. A company with a high cost of production will have difficulty competing unless it has some other distinctive competitive advantage. To compete in price with lower-cost producers, a company will need to reduce its profit margins until it too can improve its productivity. Because of differentials in labor cost, raw material cost, and shipping cost, as well as trade restrictions and tariffs imposed by various countries, a company today is compelled to do all it can to improve its productivity in order to compete with efficient companies in Japan, Germany, Korea, Taiwan, and so forth.

Thus, the quest for increased productivity has become a hot topic in today's business world. While in the past the areas of marketing and finance might have appeared more glamorous to business students, today it is increasingly obvious that operations management is "where the action is." It is here that a manager can make a real difference in the success or failure of the organization.

A company that strives for productivity to the exclusion of all other concerns, though, will surely fail. Another important basis of competition is *quality*. This also has become a hot topic because of competition from firms that have drastically increased the quality of their products while simultaneously keeping production costs down. Japanese automobile companies are a good example of this emphasis on quality as a means of competing. It is remarkable that, by taking seriously the well-known theories of quality control, Japanese firms have made their products synonymous with high quality where a generation ago they were just as universally associated with shoddiness.

All of this is not to say, though, that all firms should produce only products of the highest quality. Not everyone can afford a $100,000 Rolls-Royce or a $500 camera. Certainly, there is a market for less-expensive, lower-quality products. Today even disposable cameras are available for little more than the cost of the film. The point is that the customer has the right to expect a consistent level of quality, regardless of the product's position in the overall quality continuum. This brings us to another goal of the operations manager—*dependability*. Whether regarding delivery times of a product, the willingness of the company to make good on its own mistakes, or the accuracy of information given to a customer in a service-oriented organization, the customer demands that the organization maintain consistency and dependability. It is the operations manager's job to maintain a smoothly running, predictable yet flexible operation as much as possible.

The challenge of the operations manager, then, is to use both technical and behavioral skills to manage the organization's operations, to achieve the goals of productivity, quality, and dependability. It is this challenge that makes the job of the operations manager one of variety, excitement, and importance. For this reason more and more of today's business students are eager to "get their hands dirty" and get into the action.

THE SYSTEMS APPROACH TO OPERATIONS MANAGEMENT: LOOKING AT THE WHOLE PICTURE

Systems theory seeks to treat human organizations as systems of interrelated components, similar in many ways to more physical systems such as the solar system or the human body. The idea is to take a broad view of the system and its relationships with other systems in the environment. That is, a system is considered "open" when there are interactions between the system and its environment. A system is studied, then, by observing the flows into, out of, and within the system.

The operations system can be seen as a system which converts inputs from outside the system, such as raw materials, money, people, and information, into outputs, such as goods and services. The operations system, though, is but a subsystem of the overall organization, along with other subsystems such as marketing, finance, personnel, and accounting.

The structure of a system and its subsystems depends upon the actual functions of the components and the resulting flows between components. There is no necessary connection to the organization chart of the company. For example, a company may have a department called "Shipping and Receiving." In the systems view, however, the "shipping" function is separate from the "receiving" function. The value of the systems approach, then, is that it can give a much clearer picture of what actually goes on in a system, as opposed to the very limited and often misleading picture given by an organization chart. It also enables us to appreciate the effects that a decision made in one part of the system may have on other parts.

A Generalized Operations System

Figure 1.1 shows a very general view of an operations system. For simplicity, the example used is a manufacturing system. The diagram includes some of the major components of the operations system, as well as other major systems within the overall organization. Probably the easiest flow to trace in a manufacturing system is the flow of materials. This flow is included in the diagram, as are some of the flows between other major systems in the organization and

Figure 1.1
A Generalized Operations System

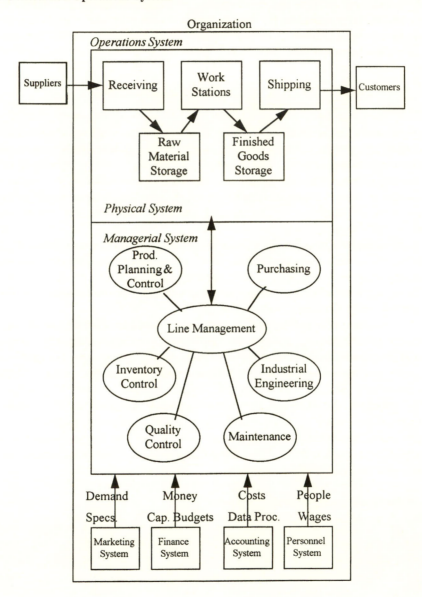

the operations system. Informational flows between components of the operations system itself are far too numerous even to approximate in such a diagram, so they will be discussed later.

The material flow begins with raw materials being sent from outside suppliers into the company and then into the operations system to a component we have called "Receiving." From there the materials might go to a storage area, called "Raw Material Storage," and from there into the actual manufacturing system. The manufacturing system has been greatly simplified, with the materials shown progressing through a few work stations. Obviously, in real companies this flow can be quite complex. After the manufacturing process we show the materials going to a "Finished Goods Storage," then to a "Shipping" component, and finally outside the company to the customers.

This is all fine as a gross generalization, but the interesting part of the operations system is the other supporting components and the informational flows within the operations system. These again are highly generalized, but they give the flavor of typical operations subsystems.

We have identified a component called "Line Management," which consists of the chain of command down from such positions as Vice President of Operations to Plant Manager to Supervisor to Foreman to workers on the production line. This can be thought of as the decision-making component of the operations system, while other components perform advisory, or staff, functions. There are obvious flows of information between the top line managers and the workers at the work stations.

Next we consider what types of staff groups might typically be present in the operations system to help plan and keep things under control. One might be called "Production Planning and Control." This component would be responsible for helping to plan the schedule and to collect information on the progress of the operations. This group would then send information to the line managers to make the actual assignments or to take corrective action when something goes wrong.

"Inventory Control" would be another essential component of the system, charged with keeping track of inventory and planning the optimal amounts to order and to produce. They again would report to the line managers, and they would also interact with the two storage components shown on the diagram, "Raw Material Storage" and "Finished Goods Storage," as well as with work-in-process inventories between the work stations on the line.

The "Quality Control" component would interact with components along the material flow line at several points, to measure quality and then report to the line managers. These interactions would generally take place with the raw materials coming in, checking for quality before putting them into use, and with the finished goods, checking them before shipping them out. There might very well be other critical points along the production line where quality would be checked.

The "Maintenance" component would interact mainly with the physical facilities of the system, such as the machines at the work stations. As with the other advisory groups, they would also communicate with the line managers any major problems requiring decisions.

"Industrial Engineering," as described earlier, is in charge of studying methods, motions, and equipment. Besides interacting with the line managers, they would mainly be involved with the workers and machines at the actual work stations.

The "Purchasing" function might well be considered as a subsystem of the organization that is not entirely a subsystem of the operations system. That is, the same group might be responsible for purchasing such things as office supplies as well as production materials. For simplicity, we have shown it here as a component of the operations system. Besides the line managers, this group would interact with the Receiving, Shipping, and Inventory Control components, and perhaps to some extent with Quality Control.

It is apparent that if we were to show all of these informational flows on the diagram, it would be quite a mess. However, it is important to realize how one component of the system affects others. Also, by identifying some of the major components within a general operations system, we can see what some of the main problem areas are. These components are there because they are necessary to solve certain types of problems and keep the system running smoothly. In fact, it would be fairly easy to construct a course syllabus simply by looking at the components included in the operations system diagram.

It is also useful to consider the flows, or interactions, between the operations system and the other major subsystems of the overall organization. Here again we must be aware that decisions are not made in a vacuum, that what is decided in the marketing system, for example, has a great effect on the operations system. The marketing system, in fact, provides the crucial information to the operations system regarding what and how much to produce. The demand forecast, possibly prepared by marketing or possibly jointly between marketing and operations, is the single most important piece of information for the operations system. From this forecast flow all the decisions on how much to produce and when, how many workers and machines will be needed, when to order materials, and so on. Besides providing the *numbers* of products demanded, the marketing system provides information on the *specifications* for those products, as well as feedback on the market's acceptance of the products. In return, the operations system provides the marketing system information on what is possible as far as product features and delivery times are concerned.

In a sense, we can think of the finance system as providing a flow of money to the operations system. Certainly, major projects must be approved and funded by the finance system. Thus, the finance system provides the operations system with return-on-investment standards for its capital budgeting, and the operations system communicates its needs to the finance system.

Similarly, we can visualize the flow of people from the personnel system to the operations system. Typically, the personnel system would be responsible for recruiting, testing, and possibly providing some training, while the operations system would do the final selecting and training of the new workers. For existing workers the personnel system also has many interactions with the operations system. Personnel would be in charge of wage and salary administration, benefits, health and safety programs, and maintaining employee records.

The accounting system provides feedback to the operations system on how well it is doing regarding efficiency, cost, and profitability measures. In many organizations accounting is also responsible for the data processing function, which would interact with the operations system's inventory control and quality control components.

From this brief overview of the relationships between other major subsystems of the company and the operations system, we can see an intricately interrelated system of components. It is worthwhile for any organization to understand in a much more specific way their own flows and interrelationships.

Kinds of Operations Systems

The most obvious distinction between operations systems is between manufacturing systems and nonmanufacturing, or service, systems. Within the general category of manufacturing systems we can also make some distinctions.

At one extreme of the manufacturing systems spectrum we have the *job shop*. This type of operation is very nonrepetitive and produces very nonstandard products. That is, every job is basically different. The system doesn't know what to produce until a customer provides an order. Obviously, such a system doesn't lend itself to an assembly line system, but rather would consist of a number of work centers, each providing one particular function but able to be quite flexible in its exact output. Examples of job shop operations would include machine shops, print shops, and custom woodworkers.

At the other extreme would be the *mass production* system. This system is characterized by very repetitive work and very standard products. Each product would be produced on its own assembly line. In the extreme mass production system, materials would flow in, be processed in exactly the same way each time, and then flow out. Chemical plants and oil refineries would be examples of extreme mass production systems, while automobile and electronics plants would represent less extreme systems where there is some variability between products.

A middle category of operations system could be called *intermittent production*. In this type of system, products are produced in batches; that is, a fairly large quantity of one product is produced, then another, and so on. A good example of intermittent production would be the clothing industry, where one type of garment might be produced for half a day, then a different one for half a day, and so on.

It should be apparent that operations systems do not fall nicely into these three categories, but rather that these categories represent points along a continuum of operations ranging from the extreme job shop system to the extreme mass production system. A company could fall anywhere along this continuum. The reason for distinguishing operations along this dimension, though, is that the type of system we have can indicate which of the problem areas that we have mentioned are most crucial for that particular system's success.

In a job shop system, for example, we have no particular production line. Each job requires slightly different treatment. Therefore, the scheduling and control functions are crucial in maintaining profitability. It is imperative to do a good job of utilizing the system's facilities, both machines and workers, so as not to waste money. Since jobs may come in at any time and require various operations, there is a constant juggling of the schedule. The objective is to avoid idle time on our facilities and at the same time to get the job done quickly for our customer.

In a mass production system, however, there is really no scheduling to speak of. Once the system is designed, we simply turn it on and keep doing the same thing over and over. Therefore, the crucial problem to be solved is the design of the system. It must be designed efficiently in order to compete, since we are going to be stuck with it for a while. As an example, the steel industry in the United States must try to compete using plants that are much older than those of its competitors in West Germany and Japan, whose plants were built after World War II. The cost of new plants is prohibitive, so U.S. companies must constantly fight for any efficiency improvements they can find.

There are other problem areas where job shops differ from mass production systems. Inventories are important in both types of system, but for different reasons. A job shop is forced to carry a large and varied inventory of parts and components because they don't know what the next job will require. For example, in a service station you will often see a whole wall full of different sizes of fan belts because no one knows which will be needed next. This large investment in inventory becomes very expensive for a job shop, and it must be carefully controlled to protect the company's profitability. But since job shops generally operate under a make-to-order system rather than a make-to-stock system, a job shop would not usually have a large finished goods inventory.

In mass production, raw material and in-process inventories can be smaller and should be much more predictable. However, to the extent that there is some variability in demand or in supply, inventories must still be watched closely. If one work station were to run out of materials, for example, the whole line might have to shut down, at great expense. Mass production systems tend to be rather large, and any shutdown will represent a large loss of production. Also, to the extent that a mass production system uses a make-to-stock system, there will be an expensive finished goods inventory that must be controlled.

Likewise, quality control is important in both types of systems, but for slightly different reasons. In a job shop, quality control is often a major marketing tool. Future demand may well depend on the company's reputation for quality. Also, labor expense tends to be rather high in a job shop because of the skilled labor required and the lack of continuous production. Therefore, any rework of products is also very costly. In mass production, the very quantities involved make quality control important. If a machine starts producing poor products, a large quantity of items might be affected before a correction can be made. It is important, then, to catch any defects quickly and ascertain their cause.

Finally, let's consider a service operation. While there may be some physical flow of materials and even "products" in such a system, the main output in these systems is some kind of service. Some service systems, however, such as those in the transportation, communication, and utility industries, are just as capital-intensive as large manufacturing operations. Such systems have similar concerns regarding methods improvement and the efficient use of capital resources.

Other service systems, such as retailers, banks, hotels, restaurants, hospitals, and government agencies, are more labor-intensive systems. We can see that the organization and operation of such systems are really quite similar to those of job shops. There is no one flow of materials or customers through the system; each customer has slightly different needs. As in a job shop, labor efficiency is a major concern. Because of the great similarity between these systems and job shops, many of the same analytical techniques that have long been used in job shops are now being applied to service systems.

Because of the large expansion of the service sector in recent years, service systems are receiving much greater consideration in the operations management field. In labor-intensive systems it is obviously more difficult to increase productivity than in capital-intensive systems where technological breakthroughs are possible. Therefore, improving efficiency is a great concern in service systems, and they are justly receiving much more scrutiny. Automation is increasingly seen in previously labor-intensive systems, such as the use of automated teller machines in banks. In California there is discussion of a massive change in the insurance system where customers will in effect pay for insurance at the gas pump. It is apparent that service systems will continue to receive much more attention in the future.

OPERATIONS MANAGEMENT AS A STRATEGIC WEAPON

How does a company succeed in today's business world? For all types of firms, large and small, manufacturing and service, the answer given today might very well be different than that given just a few years ago. Today the area of operations management is receiving more attention as a way to compete in the world arena, where recently such areas as marketing and finance were considered more important. Similarly, the types of managers who rise to the top positions of a company seem to run in cycles. When those managers from the ranks of marketing, for example, reach the top, they naturally give that area a greater weight in decision-making. Conversely, if a company feels that marketing is crucial to its success, this belief would tend to produce top managers from that field.

Traditional Strategic Weapons

Some of the areas traditionally emphasized in successfully competing would include:

Product Innovation and Entrepreneurship

The "better mousetrap" approach is a tried and true way to capture a market. Fad items would be included here, such as hula hoops and Rubik's Cubes. However, in most stable industries it is also important to continue innovating. Computer companies are continually working to make faster, smaller products and to find new applications for their products. Even food producers continually strive for an edge through more convenient products. Finally, of course, there are those companies that take a leap by introducing entirely new products, such as copy machines, videocassette recorders, fax machines, and the whole array of products now taken for granted that didn't exist a generation ago. It is apparent that the strategic weapon of innovation will continue to be a powerful one in worldwide competition.

Marketing, Advertising, and Distribution

Marketing is an essential part of converting an innovative idea into a profitable product for a company. Also, in those industries where innovation comes more slowly, marketing has been necessary to differentiate one's product from those of competitors. Indeed, to some extent it has been accepted that marketing can make up for deficiencies in other aspects of a company, resulting in continuing suboptimal results in these other areas.

Marketing can be used as a strategic weapon in several ways. Marketing research can help to discover existing demands and to develop market segments that can then be pinpointed. Advertising can be used to differentiate products, to promote awareness of new products, and to provide information on the benefits of products. It can sell politicians as well as products and services. The distribution system can enhance the marketing effort by making it easy for customers to find and to purchase products and services. The location of retail outlets and the use of mail order are examples of distribution strategies for products. Mobile car washes and veterinarians are similar examples in service industries.

Finance

By providing an infusion of money for capital and for operating expenses, the finance area is also a strategical weapon. For example, a company may decide that it can enjoy certain economies by expansion. A company can ensure reliable supplies through vertical integration (i.e., by buying their suppliers). Horizontal integration or simply building new facilities can provide for increased volume. Even without expansion a company can compete by purchasing more sophisticated or more efficient equipment. In any of these endeavors there are many financing avenues that must be explored. The 1980's were known as the age of high-flying financiers who used such instruments as junk bonds and leveraged buyouts to gain an advantage. While not all such attempts proved beneficial, such companies as banks, retailers, fast-food companies, and a variety of manufacturers did manage to strengthen their positions through mergers and acquisitions.

Price

Other things being equal, price is still probably the main competitive weapon available. In order to compete through price, a company must either keep its costs lower than its competitors or reduce its profit margin and make it up through high volume. The costs of providing a product or service are materials, labor, and overhead. Traditionally, companies have focused on improving their methods of producing a product or service, through automation, for example, and on reducing their labor costs, through such strategies as motivation, more efficient procedures, or finding a source of less expensive labor. Automobile plants are good examples of the use of improved methods to contain costs, while the clothing and electronics industries are examples of those that locate their plants in areas where wages are low. As opposed to the previously mentioned strategic weapons, these cost-cutting strategies do fall under the province of operations management. Along with the other strategies, they will continue to be important means of competing.

Competing through Operations Management

As indicated earlier, the current trend is toward the awareness that operations management is increasingly where the action is. While only a few of the traditional strategic weapons mentioned above fell under the area of operations management, recent developments in the field have provided several more competitive options for a company in the general area of operations management.

Some writers have called these strategies collectively the "new" operations management, or "world-class" manufacturing or service. In reality, as will become apparent, these strategic tools represent not revolutionary new ideas, but rather new emphases. Taken as a whole, they can radically change a company's strategic approach. We will discuss these strategies under the following categories—demand-flow manufacturing, emphasis on quality, flexibility, automation, decentralization, worker responsibility, and speed of decision-making.

THE "NEW" OPERATIONS MANAGEMENT

The strategic weapons of operations management mentioned above for the most part represent natural evolutionary changes in the theory and practice of operations management. Taken together, though, they also represent a change in philosophy that is rather significant. Further, a combination of several of these tools can have a synergistic effect on a company's operations. That is, they share several philosophical threads, such as doing things correctly and efficiently in the first place, goal-directedness, and unleashing human resources; thus, one of these strategic tools can build upon and support another for even greater benefit. In fact, even though we necessarily discuss each separately, it is not always clear where the boundaries are between them (and different writers will describe these differently). For example, Just-in-Time (JIT) systems have much in common with the idea of Total Quality Management (TQM), even though the original impetus was in reducing inventories rather than quality. Therefore, it will be apparent that a company used as an illustration of one technique will also be using several of the others, and the discussion will necessarily overlap.

Demand-Flow Manufacturing

This strategy, which represents the central concept of JIT, bases production on what is called the "pull" of demand. Rather than produce items for inventory, a work center produces only when items are demanded by subsequent work centers or, ultimately, the customer. Thus, each demander pulls items from the previous work center only as needed. As opposed to a very sporadic movement through a plant, interrupted by long waiting times in inventory, products flow through the plant virtually continuously. If such a system is perfected, a company can gain a competitive advantage by being extremely responsive to a customer's demands in terms of quantity and speed of delivery. At the same time, a company can save on many of the costs of operating, such as floor space, inventory holding costs, rework costs, scrap costs, setup costs, maintenance costs, and idle labor costs from work stoppages. These cost savings can then be used to compete on the basis of price. An added benefit is the attendant increase in quality, another strategic advantage that will be discussed below.

Emphasis on Quality

Everyone says that quality is primary in importance, but relatively few companies have been willing to make the necessary commitment from the top to the bottom of the organization chart. Working against this commitment have been the fear that quality is too costly, the belief in planned obsolescence, and the lack of real competition on the basis of quality. However, more and more companies are now discovering quality as a strategic weapon, and they find that they can still keep costs low to compete on price as well. Once a car manufacturer, for instance, shows that it can build cars that last longer, have fewer repairs, and perform better without a huge cost increase, other companies must follow suit or be left behind.

There are several aspects to employing quality as a strategic weapon. First is the simple-sounding principle of giving customers the products or services that they really want. However, this often means changing an old mind-set about what things are actually possible to provide at competitive prices; creativity and a real willingness to listen are essential. Second is the idea that real quality means designing it right and producing it right the first time rather than trying to go back and fix mistakes (which can be very costly). Finally, a company must involve everyone in the quality effort and give them the necessary responsibility and resources to make quality happen.

Quality is certainly just as important in service operations as in manufacturing operations; however, the definition may change. Quality in a service operation may involve speed of service, accuracy of service, and the perceived helpfulness of the server.

Flexibility

A challenge for modern manufacturing systems is to be able to react quickly to changing customer demands, switching from production of one product to another, while still enjoying the efficiencies of repetitive production. Flexible manufacturing systems (FMS) seek to take advantage of whatever parts of a process are repetitive by putting them into mini-assembly lines, or cells. Along with demand-flow manufacturing principles, such a system can cut flow-through time significantly in order to respond to changing demands.

Companies with less flexible manufacturing systems can provide quick response times only by maintaining costly finished goods inventories. Thus, the capital investment and possible increased training required for workers in a flexible manufacturing system can be a less expensive way of obtaining the competitive advantage of quick response. As discussed below, the increased automation has advantages of its own.

Automation

There is certainly nothing new in the replacement of human workers by machines where machines can do repetitive jobs more quickly, accurately, and cheaply than humans. The strategic advantage of automation can be seen, then, in its effects on cost, quality, and speed of response to customers. However, the cost of the investment in expensive new equipment has always been a deterrent to automating. Now, though, it seems that exploding technological advances have created a new surge in automation. In some modern Japanese automobile plants, for instance, the traditional sight of workers along an assembly line has been replaced by the sight of workers at their computers guiding the robots on the assembly line. Besides the strategic advantages mentioned above, such plants benefit workers through better safety and decreased physical demands.

Increased automation raises several related issues. For instance, parts may need to be designed in such a way that they facilitate quick, inexpensive setups and greater interchangeability. In this area, too, technology has surged recently, with Computer-Aided Design (CAD) and Computer-Aided Manufacturing (CAM). Another issue that must be addressed is the displacement of workers, possibly resulting in morale problems and the need for retraining.

Service industries can also benefit from automation where it allows them to serve their customers more quickly and accurately. For instance, automatic teller machines have taken over several banking functions from humans because of their convenience for customers.

At any rate, it is clear that technological advances will continue to change the jobs that workers do in a company. New operations systems will continue to reshape jobs to have more responsibility and decision-making, more variety, and less repetitive physical labor.

Decentralization

Decentralization refers to spreading the decision-making authority away from top management to lower levels much closer to the point of impact of the decision. Thus, actual production may be decentralized by distributing the work among many autonomous plants. Similarly, the information system can be decentralized by the use of small computers controlled by lower-level groups. The theory is that those persons most directly involved in a decision will generally do a better job of making the decision than some higher-ranking manager. They have better information, and they have more of a stake in the outcome of the decision.

The disincentive to decentralize has been the perception of economies of scale—surely large, high-speed computers must be more efficient than a lot of small ones; large, high-volume plants must be cheaper than small shops. While such centralized systems may in fact be physically more efficient, they lack the flexibility, speed, and quality of decision-making of decentralized operations. These latter benefits may provide a competitive advantage that the centralized systems can't match.

Worker Responsibility

The trend in all of these new strategies is toward greater responsibility for individual workers at lower levels than before. Under JIT, workers are responsible for performing their own preventive maintenance, speeding up setup times, and coming up with ways to improve the general efficiency of their work center. Under TQM, workers are given the responsibility of checking their own items for quality, making suggestions for designing products for easier quality, and stopping production when defects are produced. Under FMS, each worker is trained to operate several pieces of equipment rather than being tied to one repetitive process forever. Organizations that decentralize their operations necessarily pass along greater decision-making responsibility to the workers.

The benefits of all of these programs have been discussed. However, the strategic benefit of having committed, involved, and motivated workers is hard to quantify. Having greater responsibility and more variety on the job will almost certainly increase a worker's satisfaction with the job and lead to higher performance. Cost savings may result from lower turnover, reduced absenteeism, and fewer accidents, as well as from generally higher productivity. Companies are discovering that their workers represent a largely untapped resource that can constitute a huge competitive advantage when utilized better.

Speed of Decision-Making

Recent experience shows that even huge companies are feeling the need to be able to move quickly in the competitive arena. When it takes American automobile companies 6–8 years to develop and introduce a new model, Japanese companies that can do the same thing in 3–4 years have a distinct advantage. This was the situation through the 1970's and 1980's when the Japanese companies rode the wave of consumer demand for more efficient cars with higher quality.

Again, the strategies already mentioned can combine to provide this increased speed. JIT and FMS create the speed of production that can offer the possibility of quick changes in direction. Decentralized organization structures can enhance the quality of such decisions, while also providing higher managers a greater opportunity to pursue strategic planning. Technological improvements in product design, resource planning software, and manufacturing itself also reduce the time it takes to institute strategic changes.

PART I

Long-Run Decisions

We will be considering the problems of operations management based on the expected duration of the decisions made. It seems logical to work our way from those decisions expected to last for a long time down to those made for more immediate problems.

Long-run decisions can be described as those made when starting up a new operation or when making major changes in an existing operation. We will be planning and designing the operations system to last for at least several years under normal conditions. The exact duration of the system depends, of course, on the volatility of the industry that we are in, and in any case we can expect to make some minor alterations to the system as we go along. Basically, though, we want to design an efficient, dependable, flexible system that will enable us to be competitive and to meet the goals of our organization.

American managers in general have been criticized for their lack of attention to long-range planning, and increasing attention is now being devoted to this important aspect of management. In the field of operations management especially, it is apparent that the design of the system is extremely important, for the great expense of creating a new operations system precludes us from doing it very often. In other words, we are going to be stuck with whatever system we create for a long time, so we had better create a good one.

When setting up a new system, we first need to know what products or services we want to produce and in what quantities. Such quantitative tools as long-range forecasting methods, linear programming for product-mix decisions, and break-even analysis for capacity decisions would be useful in this early analysis. Some operations management texts include discussions of these techniques. However, these decisions would most likely be made by the top management of an organization rather than by operations managers. Therefore, such topics seem more appropriate for, and are typically covered in, several other courses in accounting, economics, statistics, and quantitative methods. For these reasons, then, we will take the product mix and long-run capacity decisions as inputs into the long-run decision-making process of operations managers.

To set up the operations system, then, operations managers need to decide the location of the system, the layout of the facilities, and the exact production process or method of providing service. Obviously, these decisions are not made in isolation but are quite dependent on each other. For example, the facility layout depends on the location decision if an existing building is purchased and the production layout must be designed to fit that building. On the other hand, if a new facility is built, it will certainly be built to the size and specifications needed to fit the desired facility layout. Similarly, the layout decision is intricately connected to the design of the production process itself.

This section, then, will discuss the problems of facility location, facility layout, and process planning in a sequence of chapters, but with the realization that many of these decisions are really simultaneous or sometimes in reverse order. Finally, we will look at the time studies that we have taken as given in our analysis of facility layout and process planning, but which in actuality had to be performed prior to this analysis.

CHAPTER 2

Location of Facilities

OVERVIEW

Choosing a facility location is an important but complicated decision. Because of the significant cost involved in starting up an operation or in moving operations from one place to another, the location chosen will probably be with us for a while. In a large company such as General Motors the decision to close a facility and shift operations elsewhere or to open a new facility is a long, painstaking process, often taking many years. Even small, relatively mobile operations such as fast-food outlets tend to stay in one location for a long time. McDonald's, for example, uses a sophisticated computer analysis of sites before selecting one.

The location chosen can have a great impact on many of the costs of operating, resulting in either an efficient or inefficient operation overall. These costs will be examined in some detail. However, an equally important aspect of choosing a location in many cases is the effect that the location has on the firm's marketing efforts. This is a good example of the interrelationship between the marketing and the operations functions of the organization.

A facility that is primarily a retail or service operation will certainly be located largely through marketing considerations. It is necessary to locate near large concentrations of customers and in such a way that customers have easy access to the facility. Also, the visibility of the facility can serve as an advertising mechanism to draw even more customers. For example, a service station often depends a great deal on its visibility from the highway.

Another marketing aspect to consider is the relative location of competitors. Some operations, such as hospitals, would prefer to be fairly far from competitors in order to claim their own cluster of customers without competition.

Others, though, such as fast-food outlets and automobile dealerships, are increasingly locating near each other. The volume of customers generated by the convenience of having several facilities close together outweighs the chance that some customers will be lost to competitors. The firms grouped together in such a manner typically have enough distinguishing features that each can claim a certain segment of the market. For example, a cluster of fast-food outlets at a shopping mall might include different stores featuring hamburgers, pizza, Chinese food, cookies, frozen yogurt, corn dogs, soup and salad, and so on.

Therefore, while keeping in mind the importance of marketing considerations, in this chapter we will consider the aspects of choosing a location that will affect the efficiency of the operations themselves. We will see that there are many of these considerations, that they are sometimes difficult to measure, and that it is quite difficult to put them all together to come to a decision. From a marketing standpoint, our goal is to maximize revenues attributable to our location choice, while from an operations point of view we seek to minimize the various costs of operation.

We also need to keep in mind that choosing a location is a process of several steps. We first need to choose a general region for the facility, then a particular community, and finally, a specific site. Different factors come into play at each step of this process. In light of the increasing internationalization of operations today, the first step might even involve choosing a country for our facility. In that case, in addition to the usual factors involved in choosing a region, we need to consider cultural aspects of the decision. Will there be a language problem? What are the different ways of doing business (financial, legal, traditional)? How are relationships different between workers and managers and within these groups? The attraction of cheaper labor rates, larger supplies of workers with appropriate skills, or easier access to suppliers may be tempered by less obvious and less tangible problems in these cultural areas. Obviously, a great deal of extra information-gathering is necessary in considering foreign locations.

FACTORS TO CONSIDER

Choosing a location is difficult because of the many varied factors that must be considered. Not only is it time-consuming to obtain the information needed in the proper form, but then we also have the problem of putting it all together to reach a decision.

Of course, different firms can place vastly different emphasis on these factors. Labor-intensive manufacturing plants naturally are most concerned with the supply of labor and its cost, while firms dealing mostly with distribution of products are more concerned with transportation costs.

Some of the factors involved in the location decision, such as some of the direct costs of operating mentioned below, can be quantified easily. Other factors have a less direct effect on costs and are more difficult to quantify. Still others are almost completely qualitative; to quantify these factors each firm must subjectively assess how beneficial such factors are to themselves. Even those factors that are highly quantitative will be measured in a snapshot of a single point in time. Any future trends that might cause changes must still be forecast, and thus even these factors become less quantifiable.

In the following list we have included a variety of factors that might be important to different firms, and we have grouped them according to their relative quantifiability. Some sources of information regarding these factors are also mentioned.

Relatively Quantifiable Factors

Transportation Costs

Transportation costs between locations depend on the distance between them as well as on the type of transportation available and the corresponding cost per mile. Thus, the company is concerned with the availability of interstate highways, rail lines, shipping ports, and so on. The location chosen for a facility is but one point of an entire logistics network for the company. Shipping costs are relevant from suppliers to the facility, from the facility to distributors, and between the facility and other facilities of the firm. It is not always necessary to be close to the suppliers or close to the customers, but these distances do become quite relevant in determining the overall transportation cost. Besides the cost involved, distances between facilities may also be important because of the *time* it takes to ship goods. For example, the goods involved may be perishable, or the timing may simply be important for the coordination of operations at different facilities.

The transportation cost factor may not be a large percentage of the cost of doing business for some firms, but it nevertheless may prove crucial in choosing a location. The reason for this is that some of the major cost factors, such as labor cost, may not vary much from one potential location to another (unless the choices include quite disparate locations, such as foreign ones). However, the transportation cost factor is directly affected by the location decision, since the cost is directly related to distance.

Because of the importance of the transportation cost factor and because of its high degree of quantifiability, there have been quite a few successful quantitative models created for logistics problems. These will be discussed in a later section.

Information regarding transportation costs is readily available from carriers, shipping companies, and maps. It should not be difficult, then, to obtain mileages between locations and cost-per-mile figures for different types of carriers.

Labor Supply and Cost

These factors are listed together because of the intricate relationship between them. Like other resources, labor is subject to the laws of supply and demand. Therefore, in locations where labor is more plentiful, the hourly cost of labor should be lower. On the other hand, there are several factors that prevent the

full functioning of these economic laws. These include the degree of unionization of the workers, government laws regarding wages, such as minimum wage
laws, and the lack of mobility of workers to meet labor demands in more distant
locations. Thus, a company choosing a particular location will be pretty much
stuck with the number of workers residing within a short distance, with the
prevailing climate regarding unionization, and with whatever government regulations that location might have.

A firm is interested both in the number of workers available with the required
qualifications and in the hourly wage rate of these workers. Fortunately, government statistics on these factors are published for every metropolitan area in
the United States and are available at most libraries.

Utility Costs

Some of the major costs of operating include the costs of electricity, natural
gas, water, sewage, telephone, and waste disposal. This is another area where a
company might find significant differences between locations. Every community
has its own mix of utility providers, and this structure is likely to persist for a
long time. Some utilities are owned and operated by cities, some by counties,
and some by private companies regulated by the states. Occasionally, a city will
go into or out of the business of operating some utility, but these changes are
infrequent.

If a city or county government is eager to attract a certain company, it might
be willing to provide discounts to the company for those utilities which it operates. Such incentives might be for a specified length of time or forever. In any
case it should be easy to obtain utility rates by contacting utility companies and
through discussions with local government officials.

Climate

Weather bureau statistics can tell us such things as the average annual rainfall
of an area, the average temperature at different times of the year, average wind
speed, the average number of sunny days per year, and so on. For some companies, especially those that work outside, these numbers can be quite important.
While not a cost factor like the others mentioned above, these climate factors
can translate into costs, such as calculating the labor cost of days lost because
of the weather.

Fairly Quantifiable Factors

Land and Construction Costs

It is difficult to pin down land and construction costs until we get down to
the specifics of site selection and facility design. However, we can at least get
reliable average figures of land cost per acre and building cost per square foot
through government reports or perhaps through chamber of commerce statistics.

This is another factor that might show a great deal of variability at different locations around the country or the world. Obviously, these costs can change rather rapidly in some parts of the country, so it is necessary to obtain recent figures and to be aware of possible cost increases over the length of the location-selection process and the actual construction period. Of course, if an existing building is selected, we can get much better cost figures. At the stage of selecting a general region or a community for the facility, though, we can't really determine these costs exactly.

Taxes

It should be fairly easy to obtain tax *rates* for different locations even though it is more difficult to assess the effect of these rates on overall operations costs. There are several state and local taxes to consider, including income taxes, property taxes, utility taxes, and many types of fees and licenses peculiar to a given community. This is another place where a local government eager to attract industry can offer some incentives to a company.

Community Services Provided

Communities differ in the amount they provide of such services as fire protection, police protection, beautification, street maintenance, and hospital and emergency services. To the extent that a company might need services not provided by the community, the company would have to pay for its own services. For example, a company might have its own security force, its own health care system, and so on. While it should not be difficult to discover the range of community services provided through discussions with city officials and the chamber of commerce, it is less obvious how to translate this information into operations costs for the firm.

Legal Restrictions

Every company must comply with local regulations regarding such areas of operation as pollution, noise, traffic, and waste disposal. Also, when getting down to the selection of a particular site, zoning laws come into play. Zoning maps, published ordinances, and discussions with government officials should allow a company to determine very accurately the limitations it will be operating under. However, here again it is very difficult to determine the effect of these limitations upon operating costs.

Site Factors

In choosing a specific site for our facility, we need to consider first of all the size of the site relative to our facility. Is there enough room for the design we would like, including parking areas, loading areas, room for future expansion, and so on? Is there convenient access to streets, highways, or rail lines? Is the topography of the site easy to work with, or will we need to spend a lot of money on grading, beautification, or noise abatement? Each site will have its own idiosyncrasies, so it is difficult to rate it overall or to determine the extra costs attributable to that particular site.

Relatively Nonquantifiable Factors

Living Conditions

Choosing a new location for a facility often implies that a number of present company employees will be relocating to that new facility. Certainly, they will want to choose a place where they will enjoy living. Besides existing employees, potential new employees may be attracted to the area both by the opportunity for employment and the living conditions for their families. These factors, then, can be important considerations even though they are very difficult to quantify. Factors that make a community desirable or undesirable to live in would include the climate, cultural and educational opportunities, shopping, crime, pollution, accessibility, traffic congestion, overall cost of living (housing, food, utilities, taxes, insurance, etc.), recreational opportunities, aesthetic values, and community services. Information regarding these factors can probably be obtained through the local chamber of commerce, although it might tend to paint an overly rosy picture of the area. It would seem that nothing could take the place of extensive personal inspection by the company.

The relative desirability of an area can eventually show up in more tangible ways to the company. Labor supply and cost might easily be affected by the desirability of living in a certain area. Also, many factors that make an area nice to live in are the same factors that the company must consider for itself—taxes, land costs, transportation facilities, and so on.

Community Support and Local Politics

If a community actively seeks to attract a company, we have seen several tangible ways that it can offer incentives. However, the company must also take into account the political volatility or stability of the community. Are there two or more strong rival factions in the community, some in favor of attracting industry and some opposed? If so, the group in power today may not be there tomorrow. The local government can make it very easy or very hard to do business there. When the company desires to expand or to purchase a new site, the community attitude is very important. New and more stringent standards for pollution or noise can cause additional costs. Locally owned utilities might decide to charge industrial users heavily in order to pacify residential users. Reading local newspapers and visiting town council meetings can help provide a feeling for the attitudes of the community and its leaders.

SOLUTION TECHNIQUES

With all (or at least several) of the factors mentioned above to consider, a company is faced with a very complicated decision. Even if it is possible to accumulate some reliable data on these factors, how do we put them all together to reach a solution? While some of the factors can be described quite well quantitatively, others can not. Even those that are relatively quantitative may be expressed in various kinds of units. In other words, how can we combine dollars with numbers of workers, degrees Fahrenheit, particles per million of pollutants, miles, acres, and so on? The problem seems overwhelmingly complex.

Point-Rating System

Because of the great complexity of the problem, only some rather simple quantitative models are generally used. The most common approach is some type of point-rating system. In this system the problem of combining data expressed in different (or no) units is handled by using an arbitrary rating scale.

In the following example a company has narrowed its location choice to three communities: Smog City, Podunk, and Megalopolis. It has also identified six factors that it feels are most important for the company, including transportation cost, labor cost, land and building cost, climate, living conditions, and utility cost. Each potential location has been evaluated on each of the six factors using a scale of 1 to 10, where 10 is considered the best possible rating. The company has decided to keep it simple by using only whole numbers in the ratings. (It is hard enough to boil the data down to a single rating without having to consider fractions of a point!)

In the ratings given we see, for example, that Smog City rates high on the transportation cost and climate factors but fares poorly on living conditions. Podunk has a very low land and building cost, resulting in a rating of 10, and a rather low labor cost. Megalopolis has extremely low transportation costs but high land and building costs and poor living conditions.

POINT RATINGS FOR POTENTIAL LOCATIONS

	Smog City	Podunk	Megalopolis
Transportation cost	8	2	10
Labor cost	4	8	3
Land & building cost	4	10	2
Climate	9	3	4
Living conditions	2	6	2
Utility cost	4	3	7

It is worth noting some of the difficulties involved in arriving at these ratings:

1. *Lack of information*—No matter how much data we have collected on the important factors, we will never be certain about our ratings. However, because of time and cost considerations, we have to stop collecting data at some point and assign ratings.

2. *Interpretation of information*—Data collected from various government reports, personal interviews with officials, and other sources have to be put together to determine a rating. Also, it is likely that the persons doing the data collection are not the same as those doing the analysis, so there is a potential communication problem.

3. *Subjectivity*—For some factors it is not at all clear just what is good or bad on the rating scale. For example, on the living conditions factor some people prefer an urban environment, some prefer suburbs, and some prefer a more rural area.

4. *Evaluating factors separately*—In assigning ratings it may be tempting to allow one's feelings about one factor to color the rating of another factor. For example, in rating locations on the living conditions factor, a rural location might be downgraded because of the fact that it is far from suppliers and customers. However, that fact more properly should affect the rating of the transportation cost factor and should not intrude on rating living conditions. Each factor must be evaluated entirely independently.

5. *Consistency on scales*—It is important to be consistent in assigning ratings from a 10-point scale. For example, if all potential locations are fairly close to average on a certain factor, then they should receive ratings around 5 or 6. It is not necessary to assign a 1 to the worst location and a 10 to the best; rather, it is important to recognize the whole range of possible locations regarding that factor and to rate the locations under consideration in reference to that entire range, not just to each other. In other words, we don't want to build in any artifical differences between locations. If they are close together on a certain factor, we want to know that. It is always the *differences* between ratings that are important. If one rater is more generous than another and always assigns a rating that is 2 points higher to all locations on all factors, the decision will be completely unaffected because the differences between ratings remain the same.

If we were simply to add up the ratings for each of the three potential locations, we would see that Podunk leads with a total of 32, while Smog City follows with 31, and Megalopolis with 28. However, such an approach is too simplistic. Surely the six factors are not equal in importance, so their ratings should not count equally in the total. We want to build in the importance of each factor by assigning it a weight. Then we multiply the ratings by the weights of the different factors to obtain weighted ratings, as shown on the following page.

Weights have been assigned to the six factors according to their importance to the company, with an arbitrary total of 100. A weight of 20 for utility cost means that this factor is twice as important as climate, which has a weight of 10.

As with assigning the ratings, there are several difficulties in assigning these weights:

WEIGHTED RATINGS

	Weight	Smog City	Podunk	Megalopolis
Transportation cost	25	200	50	250
Labor cost	20	80	160	60
Land & building cost	15	60	150	30
Climate	10	90	30	40
Living conditions	10	20	60	20
Utility cost	20	80	60	140
Total:	100	530	510	540

1. *Lack of information*—Here again we can never be completely certain that we have assigned weights correctly. We would need to have perfect knowledge of the company's goals and of how each factor contributes to accomplishing these goals.

2. *Subjectivity*—Because we can never know all of the effects of a factor on the company's goals, our weight assignments necessarily contain some subjectivity. Factors that seem very important to one decision-maker may not seem so important to another.

3. *Factors that are not independent*—Ideally, our list of important factors would be chosen in such a way that the factors don't affect each other. When factors overlap in some way, it is very difficult to assign them weights. Our list avoids this problem largely, but some interrelationships probably remain. If we had included such factors as labor supply and degree of unionization along with the labor cost factor, we can see some more obvious connections. Unions tend to promote higher wages, and labor supply can certainly affect labor cost as well.

4. *Keep weights separate from ratings*—The assigning of weights should be done with no consideration at all for the particular locations considered or their ratings. There might be a temptation, for example, to assign a low weight to a factor where the potential locations have similar ratings on the theory that that factor won't affect the total decision much anyway. However, this artificially increases the weights of other factors and exaggerates the differences between locations. Again, if the different locations are equally desirable, we want to know this.

5. *Consistency on ratios*—While the differences between ratings are important, it is the *ratios* that are important between weights. The reason is that we are using these weights to multiply the ratings. Thus, it is very important that all ratios between factors accurately reflect their relative importance to the company. The total of the weights is arbitrary, so it would generally be easier to assign proper weights if there is no particular total required. On the other hand, we have used a total of 100 in this example in order to make the numbers easy to work with.

After multiplying the ratings by the weights and totalling them, we find that Megalopolis now has the highest total. Podunk has slipped to last place because its high ratings relative to the other two locations tended to fall on the less important factors. However, the totals for all three are very close together. Since our total of the weights was 100, a 530 for Smog City means that the weighted average rating for Smog City was 5.5. Podunk and Megalopolis averaged 5.1 and 5.4, respectively.

The above example shows a two-step type of point-rating system, assigning the ratings and assigning the weights. Some might prefer to combine the two steps in a similar procedure that is exactly the same mathematically. To show how this would work, let's consider the transportation cost factor. In our analysis we assigned transportation cost a weight of 25. Since the maximum rating was 10, the maximum number of points a location might have received would have been 250 for that factor. Therefore, we could just as well have asked the rater to rate each location on a scale of 1 to 250. In this way the weight is already built in ahead of time. Different factors would have different maximum point totals, such as 200 for labor cost and 150 for land and building cost. Since the person doing the rating never has to worry about the weights, all that remains is to assign the point ratings and to add them up. The drawback of this method would seem to be that it should be easier to assign reliable point ratings on a consistent scale of 1 to 10 rather than on varying scales.

Example 2.1—Taj Mahal Car Washes

Taj Mahal Car Washes will soon choose one of three locations for its newest car wash—Pennsylvania Ave., State St., or Broadway. It has collected the following data regarding the three sites:

	Penn. Ave.	State St.	Broadway
Peak traffic	450 cars/hr.	500 cars/hr.	500 cars/hr.
Access to site	Very good	Good	Fair
Site capacity	3 cars	3 cars	4 cars
Land cost	$200,000	$250,000	$300,000
Construction cost	$100,000	$80,000	$70,000

Company analysts have decided that the traffic flow is the most important factor, so they have assigned it a weight of 40. The costs of land and construction are both one-time costs, so they have been combined and assigned a weight of 15. Access has been assigned a weight of 20 and capacity a weight of 25. Since the information of the various factors comes in all different kinds of units, the analysts have assigned a point-rating to each site on each factor. Ratings are on a scale of 1 to 10, with 10 being best. The ratings they have assigned are as follows:

	Penn. Ave.	State St.	Broadway
Peak traffic	5	7	7
Access to site	9	7	5
Site capacity	5	5	8
Costs	6	5	3

After multiplying the ratings by the weights of each factor, the analysts got the following results:

	Penn. Ave.	State St.	Broadway
Peak traffic	200	280	280
Access to site	180	140	100
Site capacity	125	125	200
Costs	90	75	45
Total:	595	620	625

By a slender margin Broadway comes out the winner, with a point total of 625, or an average rating of 6.25. Because of the closeness of the totals of all three potential sites, the analysts should be especially careful that their ratings and weights assigned are accurate and appropriate. For example, if the traffic rating of Pennsylvania Ave. were just 1 point higher, with a weight of 40, it would jump from third-best to best. Note also that in this example of a service operation the factors considered include such marketing-related factors as traffic, access to the site, and customer capacity as well as the more usual factors relating to the cost of the operation.

Transportation Method of Linear Programming

As noted earlier, the transportation cost factor is often a very important determinant in choosing a location because it is affected directly by the location. In transportation networks where several supply points ship to several demand points, such as from factories to warehouses or from warehouses to distributors, and where the only constraints on shipments are the supply and demand limitations, the transportation method of linear programming is a simple and effective tool to minimize transportation cost. It is beyond the scope of this book to examine the various quantitative techniques for solving transportation problems, but we will show how the technique might be applied in choosing a location.

Slipshod Manufacturing Company currently produces toasters at two factories, A and B. Finished units are then shipped to distributors at locations C, D, and E. The company is now trying to decide whether to build a new factory at location L1 or at L2. Each of the current and potential factories has its own cost of production, depending on its various cost factors, and each distributor receives a different revenue per unit, depending on the market in that region. The following table shows these production costs and revenues at the various locations,

SLIPSHOD MANUFACTURING TRANSPORTATION DATA

Factory	Prod. Cost	Capacity	Distrib.	Revenue	Demand
A	$12	120	C	$25	150
B	14	120	D	23	130
L1	11	150	E	24	160
L2	10	140			

as well as the production capacities at the factories per week and the weekly demands at the distributors.

The table below shows the transportation costs per unit of shipping between each factory and each distributor. These figures depend mainly on the distance between the locations.

SHIPPING COSTS PER UNIT

From Location	To Location		
	C	D	E
A	$7	$6	$9
B	8	5	6
L1	9	7	7
L2	7	10	8

We would like to calculate the total weekly profit with L1 in the transportation network and compare it to the profit with L2 in the network. In each case we first need to find the shipping pattern that will maximize the total profit for that set of locations. In Figure 2.1 we have tried putting L1 into the network, and we have calculated the profit-per-unit figure for each factory-to-distributor route. To obtain the profit per unit, we have added the production cost from a given factory and the transportation cost from that factory to a given distributor and then subtracted this total cost from the revenue per unit at that particular distributor. For example, if factory A ships to distributor C, there is a production cost of $12 per unit and a transportation cost of $7 per unit. Subtracting this total cost of $19 from the $25 revenue at distributor C, we have a profit of $6 per unit.

In Figure 2.1 each box represents the quantity shipped from the factory in that row to the distributor in that column. The profit figure for that route appears in the upper right-hand corner of the box. Eventually, we will fill in some of the boxes with the quantities shipped on those routes. Each row's quantities must add up to the total capacity of that factory, and each column's quantities must add up to the total demand for that distributor. It will turn out that only a few of the routes will actually be used (the most profitable ones).

Because the total supply capacity and total demand will rarely be equal, it is necessary to set up a dummy row or column with the appropriate supply or demand quantity to make the totals agree. Since quantities shipped to or from a dummy are not actually shipped at all, the profits for these boxes will always be 0. This process is necessary only to make the solution easier to find. Figure 2.1, then, shows all of the relevant figures in a convenient table.

Transportation problems can be solved fairly easily just by shifting numbers around in the table. A two-step process is involved. First it is necessary to get some initial solution of quantities in the boxes that add up to the appropriate

Figure 2.1
Transportation Method for Location Analysis

Optimal Solution with Location L1

	C	D	E	Total Supply
A	120 [6]	[5]	[3]	120
B	[3]	110 [4]	10 [4]	120
L1	[5]	[5]	150 [6]	150
Dummy	30 [0]	20 [0]	[0]	50
Total Demand	150	130	160	440

Optimal Solution with Location L2

	C	D	E	Total Supply
A	10 [6]	110 [5]	[3]	120
B	[3]	20 [4]	100 [4]	120
L2	140 [5]	[5]	[6]	140
Dummy	[0]	[0]	60 [0]	60
Total Demand	150	130	160	440

row and column totals. Then these quantities are shifted around to utilize the routes with higher profits and thus maximize the total profit. There are several simple techniques available both for getting off to a good initial solution and then moving to an optimal solution. With small problems such as this one, it is not difficult to solve by trial and error. Figure 2.1 shows the optimal shipping pattern with L1 in the network.

According to this solution, factory A should ship 120 units per week to distributor C, factory B should ship 110 units to distributor D and 10 to distributor E, and factory L1 should ship 150 units to distributor E. These are the only routes actually used. The dummy is shown to ship 30 units to distributor C and 20 to distributor D each week. This means that those distributors will not meet all of their demand by those amounts. The total weekly profit of this solution with L1 in the network would be (120)($60) + (110)($4) + (10)($4) + (150)($6) = $2,100 per week.

It should be noted that the same profit could also be obtained if we were to move the 10 units shipped on route B–E to route B–D, making that quantity 120, and shifting 10 of the 20 on route Dummy-D to Dummy-E. This would also spread out the unmet demand among all three distributors.

We now repeat the above procedure with location L2 in place of L1. Since L2 has a capacity of only 140 per week as compared to 150 at L1, the dummy row must now have a capacity of 60 to make up the difference. Note also that the profit figures in rows A and B are unchanged, but L2 has different profits from L1.

Figure 2.1 shows the table with L2 in the network and indicates the optimal solution for that network. It is interesting to note that the routes used in the optimal solution are quite different from those used with L1 in the network. Now factory A ships 10 units to distributor C and 110 to D, factory B ships 20 units to D and 100 to E, and L2 ships all 140 of its units to C. Distributor E has all of the unmet demand, but again there is an alternative optimum solution where 20 units could be shifted from route B–D to route B–E, while Dummy-D would be 20 units and Dummy-E would be reduced to 40 units.

The total weekly profit of the optimal solution with L2 in the network would be (10)($6) + (110)($5) + (20)($4) + (100)($4) + (140)($8) = $2,210. This produces a weekly profit that is $110 more than the solution with L1 in the network, despite the fact that L2 would be producing 10 fewer units per week than L1. The main reason for the increased profit is the highly profitable L2–C route. Thus, if these were the only cost and revenue figures that were relevant in choosing between the two, L2 would be chosen. It would also appear to be advantageous to try to find a way to make L2's capacity a little larger if possible.

Other Mathematical Programming Applications

We have seen that the transportation method of linear programming is a simple and useful technique that allows us to build in production costs and transportation costs, while considering supply and demand constraints. For more complicated problems with other costs and other constraints, however, more sophisticated methods of mathematical programming are needed. If the problem gets even more complicated, we need to resort to simple techniques like the point-rating system.

There have been many useful applications of mathematical programming techniques, though, for fairly well-defined logistical problems. These include locating a set of fire stations or ambulance stations throughout a city so as to minimize the average response time or choosing locations for a number of warehouses to minimize delivery time or cost. With linear and nonlinear programming techniques many different constraints may be built in, many different objectives may be considered, and a large number of variables (such as possible location sites) may be included.

CHAPTER 3

Layout of Facilities

OVERVIEW

The design of the facilities layout is a problem that is interwoven with the facilities location decision and with the design of the production or service process. In Chapter 1 we distinguished different types of operations ranging from an extreme job shop system to an extreme mass production system. This distinction plays an important part in determining the way to arrange the facilities.

There are several performance criteria of an operation that are affected by the layout of the facilities. One measure of an efficient operation is the efficient use of space. Since it costs money to create space for our operations system, a compact layout obviously is desirable. Less obvious savings can also result from reduced handling costs and lower inventory levels when the layout is designed for efficient transportation of materials.

A layout should be designed to conserve time as well as space. Cost savings can result both in the operations process itself and in the customers' time when the layout is designed for quick throughput. Especially in job shops and service operations, saving the customers' time can be a powerful marketing tool.

Job Shop System

In a job shop, each job is basically different from the others, so there is no single path that jobs follow through the system. Therefore, a job shop does not lend itself to an assembly line arrangement. It is more logical and convenient to set up departments according to the function, or process, that each department performs. For example, in a machine shop all the drills would be put together in a drilling department, all lathes in a lathe department, and so on. That way, whenever a job needed drilling of any kind, it would be obvious where to route it. This type of layout, called a *process layout*, is shown in Figure 3.1.

What would be the goal of an operations manager in setting up a process layout? Even though each job follows a different path through the system, the job shop does perform some particular type of work, so there must be some paths that are used more than others. Transporting parts back and forth between departments by means of fork lift trucks, hand trucks, or other methods is expensive, both in equipment cost and in labor cost. Therefore, we would like to minimize this cost by locating departments close together if they tend to have a lot of traffic between them. The goal, in other words, is to minimize the transportation cost of materials. We can express this goal through the following general objective function:

Minimize Σ (loads/wk.) (cost/load/ft.) (ft. between depts.), summed over all possible pairs of departments

In order to minimize this cost function, what information do we need? First, we need to know the number of loads per week (or whatever time period is convenient) between all pairs of departments. Since we don't know in advance what jobs will be coming in, we will probably have to base these figures on historical traffic data. The cost per load per foot of transporting items between departments depends on the method of transportation used. Besides fork lift trucks and hand trucks, more sophisticated methods such as conveyor belts or gravity-feed chutes are sometimes possible. Also, this cost certainly depends on what the "load" consists of. Some materials are much heavier or bulkier than others. Determining the cost of labor and equipment to transport a load one foot may not be too easy to do, but some relative estimates may be made at least.

The final part of the transportation cost function is the distance between departments. This, however, is our decision variable. These distances will be determined by how we arrange the departments.

After we determine a general arrangement of departments, we will need to provide a much more specific layout, including the arrangement of machines within departments. Additional information needed at this stage would include the area requirements of each department, which in turn would depend on the size and number of machines, walkways, storage areas, room for workers, and so on. Also, we need to know about any special requirements for the different departments. For example, it would be nice to have our Shipping and Receiving Department on an outside wall of the building so we could have doors to the loading dock. Other departments might have special requirements for electricity, water, air, ventilation, temperature control, and so on, to accommodate the activities performed there. All of these details are necessary for our final layout. Since these details vary a great deal with the operation, we will be concerned

Figure 3.1
Types of Layouts

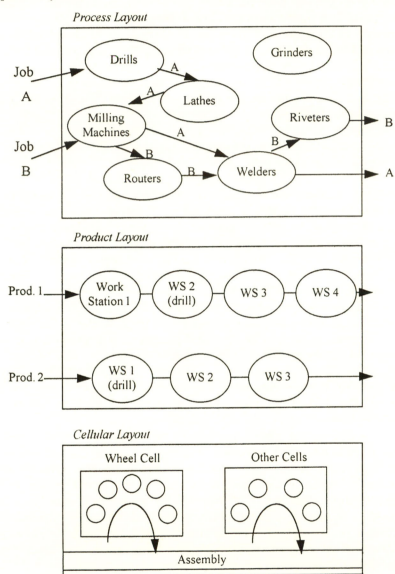

Process Layout

Job A

Drills   A

Grinders

A   Lathes

Milling Machines   A

Riveters → B

Job B

B

Routers   B → Welders   B

B → A

Product Layout

Prod. 1 → Work Station 1 — WS 2 (drill) — WS 3 — WS 4 →

Prod. 2 → WS 1 (drill) — WS 2 — WS 3 →

Cellular Layout

Wheel Cell

Other Cells

Assembly

here with determining the general arrangement of departments, taking into account the different department sizes.

As mentioned in Chapter 1, service operations are very similar to job shops. They also generally have no particular flow through the system, so the process layout is again appropriate. For example, in a hospital we find an intensive care unit, a maternity ward, an x-ray department, a laboratory, and so on, all grouped by their functions. Marketing considerations are very important in service operations, so a layout that minimizes the customers' time and distance traveled, as well as those of the system's workers, will be advantageous.

Mass Production System

With a mass production system we do have very repetitive work that lends itself to an assembly line layout. For each product produced there is a definite sequence of activities necessary to produce it. Of course, we hope that we have designed a process with the appropriate machines and workers to be efficient, as discussed in the following chapter. Because each product of a mass production operation basically has its own layout, we call such an arrangement a *product layout*. Figure 3.1 shows a general product layout.

With a product layout we really don't have much of an arrangement problem. Of course, we need to fit the assembly line into our building, and we can choose whether to have a straight assembly line, a U-shaped line, or whatever, but the arrangement of workers and machines is pretty much determined by the process. If drilling is needed in the first step of the process, then a drill is provided at the start of the assembly line. Machines are no longer grouped according to function, but placed wherever they are needed for that product's production process.

Our goal for a product layout, then, is not to minimize the transportation cost, but to group the required tasks into work stations in such a way that the work flows smoothly down the assembly line. Thus, the problem is more one of timing than arrangement. A work station is a spot on the assembly line where a worker is situated with perhaps several pieces of equipment ready to perform several small tasks. The question is how to assign tasks to workers to maintain a smooth flow. Another way to express our goal is that we would like to minimize the total idle time in our work stations. If each work station required the same amount of time, then each worker would pass the work along to the next station at the same time, and there would be no idle time in the system. Of course, such an ideal is impossible in the real world and maybe even undesirable; some idle time is usually necessary as a buffer for variable task times.

If one work station takes longer than the others, all the others will have to slow down to the speed of that one. Otherwise, work from the previous work station would pile up. A work station that follows a slower station has no choice but to wait for the work to be passed along. Therefore, an optimal system is one where all stations take the same amount of time per unit, and an acceptable system is one where all stations can work at least as fast as the desired production rate and idle times are reduced as much as possible.

This problem of assigning tasks to work stations to smooth out the flow is called the assembly line balancing problem. In order to perform this analysis, we need several pieces of information. First, we need to know the time requirements for all of the tasks or activities that must be performed. These tasks should be broken down into the smallest possible units of work in order to give ourselves the greatest flexibility in assigning them to workers. The determination of these times will be discussed in Chapter 5. For now we will assume that we have access to time standards for all tasks.

Besides the times of the tasks, we need to know the required sequencing of the tasks. Some tasks obviously need to go before others. We can't insert a bolt until we've drilled the hole. These sequencing requirements will serve as constraints on the possible combinations of tasks we may assign to the work stations.

A third piece of information that is necessary is the desired rate of production. Each work station must be designed to take the desired time or less, since the slowest station determines the overall production rate. Without regard to costs, it is theoretically possible to keep adding workers and equipment to reduce our time per unit as far as we might like. We do need to recognize the trade-off, however, between the speed of production and the equipment and labor cost. We may, in fact, determine a desired production rate that is less than our rate of demand simply because we would need a large increment in cost to move up a step in production rate.

With the desired production rate and the required sequencing as constraints, then, we will consider various combinations of tasks at each work station in order to produce a balanced assembly line.

Fixed Layout System

Some operations systems, such as large construction projects, must necessarily be arranged at one particular location. That is, all workers, equipment, energy supplies, and material supplies must be sent to that one site. Since such a system's layout is pretty well determined by necessity, there are really no interesting problems to analyze.

Hybrid Operations Systems

Few operations systems fall neatly into the category of an extreme job shop or extreme mass production. Most are somewhere in the middle and have some aspects of each. Generally, though, it is most efficient to design operations to be as repetitive as possible. Many job shops nevertheless have some small processes that are very repetitive; these can be handled in much the same way as mass production systems for greater efficiency.

Cellular manufacturing (or group technology) systems set up mini–assembly lines called cells to handle those parts of the operations of a job shop or intermittent production system that are fairly repetitive. For example, let's assume that a toy maker makes several toys with wheels. These wheels may be slightly different in size and materials, but they are made with basically the same process on the same types of machines. This company could then set up a wheel-making cell that would supply wheels for all the various toys (see Figure 3.1). Within this cell the work would be quite repetitive, although there would need to be some flexibility for the different wheel requirements.

Cells may be staffed by one or more workers who handle the various machines in the cell much as in an assembly line. Different workers may be responsible for different machines within the cell, or the worker(s) may move around in a circle operating all of the machines in the cell (a rabbit-chase cell). Of course, the more machines a worker has to operate, the more different skills are needed. To the extent that some parts of the cell are automated, the worker's efficiency is enhanced. The machinery must be capable of being set up quickly to handle all of the variations needed for that part being produced.

If we extend this idea of more repetitive yet flexible production as far as possible, we arrive at the concept of a flexible manufacturing system (FMS). At the extreme, all work would be automated using robots, and any variations in manufacturing needed would be handled by the computer controlling the system. By using robots we are able to make production changes through software rather than by continually setting up the machines in different ways. Of course, the robots we are talking about don't much resemble those in science fiction movies. Most consist largely of mechanical arms with many joints to make a wide range of motions. Modern robots are being built with increasingly sophisticated senses of touch and even sight in order to perform more accurately.

Flexible manufacturing systems can provide a great savings in labor cost, and the machines can produce more consistent output than human systems. Because of the programmability of the machines, setup time is greatly reduced, and work is completed more quickly. Also, it is not necessary to have a lot of different machines, with many sitting idle much of the time, when a few machines can be programmed to do a wide variety of tasks. The obvious drawback to these systems is the initial outlay for such high-technology machines, as well as the fact that current technology just hasn't progressed far enough to be suitable for all production systems.

PROCESS LAYOUT ANALYSIS

We begin the process of determining the layout that will minimize transportation costs between departments by collecting data on traffic between departments and the costs of transportation:

LOADS PER WEEK BETWEEN DEPARTMENTS

From Dept.	A	B	C	D	E	F	G	H
A	—	45	25		5	5		
B	12	—	24	6	12		4	
C	5	15	—	5		10		
D	5	5	8	—	2	14	5	8
E	10	10			—	20	25	
F	10	10	20	10	15	—		5
G		20			20		—	10
H				9		8	9	—

To Dept. (column group heading)

COST PER LOAD PER FOOT BETWEEN DEPARTMENTS

From Dept.	A	B	C	D	E	F	G	H
A	—	.04	.04		.04	.04		
B	.05	—	.05	.05	.05		.05	
C	.04	.06	—	.04		.04		
D	.06	.06	.05	—	.05	.05	.06	.05
E	.03	.03			—	.03	.04	
F	.04	.04	.04	.03	.04	—		.04
G		.03			.03		—	.03
H				.10		.10	.10	—

To Dept. (column group heading)

Next we multiply the cost per load per foot by the number of loads per week to give us the cost per week per foot on each route:

COST PER WEEK PER FOOT

From Dept.	A	B	C	D	E	F	G	H
A	—	1.80	1.00		.20	.20		
B	.60	—	1.20	.30	.60		.20	
C	.20	.90	—	.20		.40		
D	.30	.30	.40	—	.10	.70	.30	.40
E	.30	.30			—	.60	1.00	
F	.40	.40	.80	.30	.60	—		.20
G		.60			.60		—	.30
H				.90		.80	.90	—

To Dept. (column group heading)

Finally, we add together the cost per week per foot for the same two departments. That is, we add the cost from A to B and the cost from B to A to get the total cost per week per foot between departments A and B (since the distance is the same in either direction):

COST PER WEEK PER FOOT BETWEEN DEPARTMENTS

To Dept.

From Dept.	A	B	C	D	E	F	G	H
A	—	2.40	1.20	.30	.50	.60		
B		—	2.10	.60	.90	.40	.80	
C			—	.60		1.20		
D				—	.10	1.00	.30	1.30
E					—	1.20	1.60	
F						—		1.00
G							—	1.20
H								—

Schematic Diagram Analysis

Having determined the costs per foot between departments, we now try to minimize the total transportation cost per week. To approximate the distances between departments, we first set up an arrangement of departments on a grid called a schematic diagram (see Figure 3.2). This schematic diagram positions departments in very simple relationships to each other, either directly to the left or right or directly above or below. We will define the distance between adjacent departments as one step. Even departments that only touch diagonally at the corners will be defined as one step apart. We are only approximating the distance, and we don't have any idea where within each department supplies must be shipped from or to, so these step approximations are accurate enough.

We would like to arrange the departments on the schematic diagram in such a way that those departments with larger costs per foot are close together, touching if possible. Remember that the total cost function to be minimized consists of the cost per week per foot multiplied by the distance, which we have approximated here by steps. It makes sense, then, to put those departments on the schematic diagram first which have larger costs in order to ensure that they are adjacent.

Therefore, we would probably start by putting departments A and B on the diagram next to each other. Department C has a large cost with department B and a fairly large cost with department A, so it should be placed next to both A and B. We keep adding departments in this manner, trying to keep departments next to each other if they have large travel costs between them. While there is no single way to produce this schematic diagram, an initial solution might look like the first one in Figure 3.2. Cost figures are shown for each route. Those routes that are more than one step apart are listed.

The initial solution gets us off to a pretty good start, although it is unlikely to be optimal. We see that there are only four pairs of departments that have some traffic between them and that are not next to each other. Since the best we can ever do is to have departments one step away from each other, in order to minimize the total transportation cost, we need only to minimize the cost of

Figure 3.2
Job Shop Layout

Initial Schematic Diagram   Extra Cost

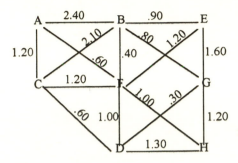

A - D	(1)(.30) =	.30
A - E	(1)(.50) =	.50
B - D	(1)(.60) =	.60
D - E	(1)(.10) =	.10
	Total:	1.50

Optimal Schematic Diagram   Extra Cost

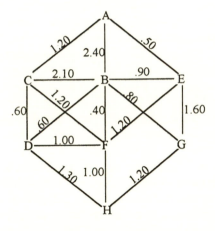

A - D	(1)(.30) =	.30
A - F	(1)(.60) =	.60
D - E	(1)(.10) =	.10
D - G	(1)(.30) =	.30
	Total:	1.30

those trips that are more than one step apart. That is, we will minimize the *extra* cost (that cost above the minimum for one step) and thereby also minimize the total cost. This extra cost is the product of the number of extra steps and the cost per week per foot. The cost calculation in Figure 3.2 shows a total extra cost of $1.50. Since we don't know how many feet are in a step on the schematic, we really don't know what units this cost figure is in—the dollar cost would be some multiple of our figure.

Next we try to improve the solution by trying to get some of those routes listed down to one step apart. At the same time, though, we don't want to disrupt the high-cost routes that are currently next to each other. This process is really a trial-and-error approach, looking for ways to switch departments or slide them around on the schematic diagram to improve the solution. There are several computer programs available to help in this search, but without one of these it is difficult to determine just when the optimal solution has been found. For the above example, the final solution is shown on the bottom of Figure 3.2. It turns out that our initial solution was very close to optimal; the final solution has an extra cost of $1.30.

Final Arrangement

The optimal schematic diagram gives us a general arrangement of the departments, but the actual layout may turn out to look somewhat different. The real layout need not have departments arranged exactly on a grid, and the sizes of the departments may dictate small changes in the arrangement. Assuming that we are designing a new building, we are free to try various shapes for our departments. However, the shapes should be kept fairly simple for construction purposes and for easy utilization of the space. Rectangular, L-shaped, and perhaps even Z-shaped departments may be used, but no terribly exotic shapes. Similarly, the outside shape of the building needs to be kept simple to control construction costs.

PRODUCT LAYOUT ANALYSIS

We turn now to the problem of grouping tasks together into work stations in order to produce a balanced assembly line. Assume, for example, that a company desires to produce 200 units of a certain product per week (in a 40-hour week). As shown below, it has collected data on task times and sequencing requirements. The sequencing requirements are given by specifying what other tasks each task must follow. For example, task B must follow task A according to the list below.

ASSEMBLY LINE DATA

Task	Minutes	Must Follow
A	3	—
B	4	A
C	2	B
D	5	C
E	3	C
F	7	—
G	4	—
H	5	F,G
I	8	E,H
J	5	I
	46	

Sequencing Diagram

In order to visualize the sequencing requirements, we construct a diagram. Each task is represented by a circle, and an arrow from one task to another shows that the second task must follow the first. Thus, there is one arrow for each requirement listed in the "Must Follow" column above. Any tasks not required to follow any other tasks are placed on the left, and the diagram runs from left to right. When tasks D and J are completed, the whole unit is completed. Time requirements have been included along with the tasks in the diagram in Figure 3.3.

Preliminary Calculations

In order to meet our desired production of 200 units in a 40-hour week, we must produce one unit every 12 minutes: (40 hrs./wk.) $\times$ (60 mins./hr.) / (200 units/wk.) = 12 mins./unit. Therefore, each work station must complete its work in 12 minutes or less in order to pass the work along to the next station and to have one unit coming off the line every 12 minutes. Our job, then, is to group tasks into work stations requiring 12 minutes or less, staying within the sequencing requirements given. This 12-minute figure is called the *cycle time*.

Another way of putting it is that we need to do 46 minutes worth of work in 12 minutes. Dividing 46 by 12 shows us that we need 3.83 work stations working simultaneously in order to do this. Since we must have a whole number of work stations, we actually need at least 4 work stations. (Our calculations must always be rounded up to have sufficient capacity to handle our output requirement.) It remains to be seen whether it is indeed possible to obtain a solution with 4 work stations. The sequencing requirements and time figures of the tasks may not lend themselves to 4 convenient groupings of tasks. If we do end up with a solution containing 4 work stations, our total capacity will be $4 \times 12 = 48$ minutes per cycle, slightly more than the 46 minutes required per unit. However, if we need to have 5 work stations, our capacity would be $5 \times 12 = 60$ minutes per cycle, leaving 14 minutes of idle capacity within our system every cycle. Obviously, we hope to have a solution with 4 stations, and if we do find one, we know that we can do no better while still getting all the work done in a 12-minute cycle.

Priority Ranking System

Even in a small problem like ours, which contains only 10 tasks, there are many potential groupings of tasks into work stations. Starting from the left side of the sequencing diagram, we can identify several groupings of tasks for the first station where the tasks are in sequence and add up to 12 minutes or less.

Figure 3.3
Assembly Line Balancing

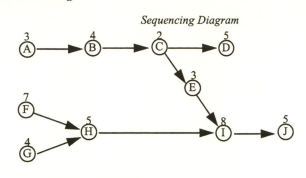

Sequencing Diagram

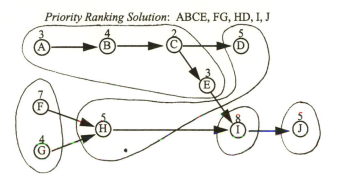

Priority Ranking Solution: ABCE, FG, HD, I, J

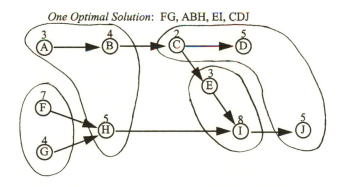

One Optimal Solution: FG, ABH, EI, CDJ

Tasks F and G could be combined for a total of 11 minutes, A and F for a total of 10 minutes, A, B, and G for a total of 11 minutes, or A, B, C, and E, for a total of 12 minutes. Although the last grouping uses the full 12 minutes and includes 4 different activities, it is not necessarily the best. For each of these groupings for the first station, there are several possible groupings for the second station, then several for the third station, and so on. All in all, we find that there are quite a few groupings that must be considered. In larger problems the possibilities increase dramatically. We need some method to weed out alternatives and to zero in on the best possible grouping with the fewest work stations (preferably 4 in this case).

There are several heuristic (rule-of-thumb) techniques that have been used to arrive at a good, though not necessarily optimal, solution. We will apply one such technique called the priority ranking system. In this system each task is assigned a priority. The priority is calculated by adding the time of that task with the times of all tasks that follow (through all arrows) that task. This sum will tell us the total amount of work depending on that task. This figure then gives us a pretty good measure of how desirable it is to perform that task early in order to permit all of the following work to be performed. We see in our example that tasks B, C, D, E, I, and J all depend on task A's completion. The total time for tasks A, B, C, D, E, I, and J is 30 minutes, so this is task A's priority figure. Other priorities are calculated similarly:

TASK PRIORITIES

Task	Priority
A	30
B	27
C	23
D	5
E	16
F	25
G	22
H	18
I	13
J	5

After calculating priorities, we assign the task with the highest priority to the first available work station, so long as all preceding tasks have already been performed and the total time of a work station does not exceed 12 minutes. Therefore, we first assign task A to work station 1 (since it has no task preceding it). Next, task B is also assigned to work station 1 because it has the next highest priority. It is eligible to be assigned since task A preceding it has already been assigned, and the total time now assigned to work station 1 is 7 minutes, still less than 12.

Activity F has the next highest priority (25), and it has no other tasks which it must follow. However, its time of 7 minutes is too large to add to work station 1, as it would then exceed 12 minutes. Therefore, we will put task F on hold for now; it will be the first task assigned when we get to work station 2.

The task with the next highest priority is task C (23). Since its time is only

2 minutes, and since task B has already been assigned, we can go ahead and assign C to work station 1. This brings our total time at work station 1 to 9 minutes. Even though its priority is well down on the list, we can see that the only task that we can add to this station is task E because of its time requirement of 3 minutes. We end up, then, with tasks A, B, C, and E assigned to the first work station, for a total of the full 12 minutes available.

Task F has the highest remaining priority and will be the first activity assigned to work station 2. Next is G with a priority of 22. F and G together require 11 minutes, which is as close as we will get to 12 in this example, so they comprise the second work station.

Work station 3 begins with task H (priority 18). Task I has the next priority (13), but its time of 8 minutes is just barely too big to combine with task H in work station 3. Therefore, we must assign task D to work station 3, for a total of 10 minutes. Note that J is not eligible until I has been assigned.

Only tasks I and J remain. Unfortunately, their combined times are too large for one station, and they must be assigned separately to work stations 4 and 5. Thus, our priority ranking system has given us a solution requiring 5 stations, not as low as we had hoped.

Any heuristic technique such as this one will sometimes fail to provide the optimal solution. Here it turns out that there are indeed two solutions which require only 4 work stations: ABG, FH, EI, CDJ, or FG, ABH, EI, CDJ. The priority ranking system, however, will generally give solutions that are optimal or very close to optimal, and it is among the easiest to apply, especially for problems that are larger than this example.

Utilization Rate

A quick calculation will tell what proportion of the production facility's capacity is being utilized for a given solution. The utilization rate is just the ratio of the time required per unit to the time available per unit. The time available per unit is the number of work stations multiplied by the cycle time. Thus, for our solution with 5 work stations we have:

Utilization rate = $46/(5 \times 12) = 46/60 = .77$

If we use one of the two optimal solutions with 4 work stations, we have:

Utilization rate = $46/(4 \times 12) = 46/48 = .96$

This comparison shows us proportionally how much better utilization we have of our facilities with 4 stations rather than 5. A utilization rate of .96 is quite high; .70 to .85 is more common.

Multiple Cycles

What do we do when a task's time by itself is larger than the cycle time? The tasks as listed have theoretically been broken down already into the smallest possible units, so we can't chop the task into two smaller parts. The answer is to have two (or more) work stations in the assembly line in parallel, each performing the same task. Two stations in parallel would each have tasks assigned up to the time of a double cycle, three stations could handle a triple cycle, and so on. In that way the two stations would put out two units in the time of a double cycle, thus averaging one unit per cycle. In fact, the two stations can have their timing staggered if desired so that one piece comes off one of the stations every cycle.

In our example problem let's change task G's time from 4 minutes to 14 minutes, longer than the 12-minute cycle. This also changes our total time to 56 minutes and our minimum number of stations needed to $56/12 = 4.67$, or 5 stations. A double cycle would be 24 minutes, so we could assign tasks A, F, and G to each of two stations in parallel. The other stations would remain at 12 minutes each, so the remaining 3 stations could be BCH, EI, and DJ.

Multiple cycles are always a possibility, and they can be especially useful to increase utilization if the time and sequencing requirements don't work out nicely otherwise. However, there is a trade-off involved. The more we use multiple cycles with duplicate work stations, the more machines we need of the same type, increasing our equipment cost and our space cost, as well as complicating the flow of materials. After all, if we wanted to, we could just have each worker perform the entire job, but this would be throwing away all the advantages of an assembly line operation.

CHAPTER 4

Process Planning and Job Design

OVERVIEW

Inherent in our analysis of plant location and plant layout has been the design of the production process itself. Naturally, we are talking about an operations system where there *is* some fairly repetitive process—toward the mass production end of the spectrum. This production process may be examined on several levels, from the very macro level (process planning) to the micro level (job design).

At the process planning level our analysis is very much guided by the *product* design. The product should be designed not only to have the features desired by consumers, but also to provide for a simple, efficient production process. The human engineering, or ergonomics, that must be considered in process planning and job design is also an important component of product design. That is, human capabilities, ease of use, and comfort must be considered for consumers as well as for the workers who must produce the product. Therefore, most larger companies have ergonomics specialists who study human attributes, such as muscular, visual, and aural capabilities, and then apply their findings both to product design and to job design.

At the macro level, process planning can be assisted by the use of various process charts to document and visualize both current processes and proposed improvements. Different charts can show different aspects and different levels of detail of the process.

At the micro level, there are several issues that must be dealt with in determining the actual jobs to be assigned to individual workers. Certainly, it is desired to maximize the speed and accuracy of the production process. However, there are several other competing goals to consider. Even if the process is technically efficient, the system also includes human workers, and they must be motivated to perform well if this efficiency is to be achieved.

Since repetitive manufacturing systems can become very boring and unmotivating, several programs have been used to promote interest in the job. Job rotation, for example, allows workers to trade jobs with each other every so often. That way no one gets stuck with the worst jobs forever, and the variety of tasks makes the work more challenging. On the other hand, job rotation requires workers to be skilled and trained in several different areas rather than just one.

Job enlargement programs make workers responsible for several different tasks (all the time, rather than by rotating), again in an effort to add interest to the job. To the extent that workers perform different tasks, though, setup times increase, and we lose the benefits of specialization.

Job enrichment programs go beyond job enlargement to make the jobs intrinsically satisfying and to include some degree of decision-making on the part of the worker. In other words, workers are given some amount of managerial responsibility in addition to their other work. Such programs have indeed been found often to increase workers' satisfaction with their jobs, although the connection between satisfaction and performance has long been debated.

Japanese companies have popularized the idea of the "team concept" in assigning jobs. Small teams of workers are responsible for a certain phase of production. These teams have a rather large amount of latitude in assigning individual jobs and in deciding just how the work will progress. Thus, workers enjoy the benefits of job enrichment, and teams are able to make up for the absence or lower productivity of some of their workers. Some American companies have recently adopted the team concept, with mixed results as yet. Both unions and managers must be convinced of the benefits of the plan and must give it their full support in order for it to succeed.

Besides speed, accuracy, and motivation, jobs must be designed with safety in mind. Aside from the moral and ethical questions of a company's responsibility to its workers, even the coldest-hearted company can appreciate the loss of profitability created by downtime of machines and workers.

Finally, the ergonomics issue, mentioned above, needs to be addressed in job design. How can jobs be designed to take advantage of, rather than work against, human capabilities? How can worker comfort be improved to support the goals of efficiency and motivation? Which jobs should be performed by machine and which by humans? Machines outperform humans when it comes to reliable repetition of simple tasks, while humans generally are better at recognizing complicated stimuli and adapting to different circumstances.

PROCESS CHARTS

Several different types of process charts are available to help visualize the production process, some showing the process at a very macro level and some showing every small motion at the micro level. In a job shop operation the analogous document would be the routing sheet. Since each job in a job shop is different, the routing sheet would show the process required for that particular job, including the sequence of machining, setup specifications, and so on.

The purpose of documenting a process by process charts is to spot ways to improve the process, perhaps by eliminating some of the steps of the process, perhaps by combining tasks, perhaps by rearranging the sequence of tasks, or perhaps by changing the nature of the tasks by changing the tools and equipment used. Inefficiencies and idle times become much more obvious when shown through process charts.

Several different types of process charts use a common set of symbols for different steps in a process:

○ *operation*—something actually done to the piece being worked on

□ *inspection*—examining the piece worked on or possibly reading an instrument

⇨ *transportation*—movement of the worker or the piece being worked on

D *delay*—a pause inherent in the process

∇ *storage*—piece is stored permanently or awaiting further processing (possibly being held)

The following are some examples of commonly used process charts showing various aspects of a production or service process.

Operations Process Chart

An operations process chart is used to give a moderately macro view of a process. Only the operations and inspection steps of the process are shown, and these are not broken down into the very smallest motions, only the major steps. Figure 4.1 gives an example of an operations process chart for the process of framing a picture. We see the four main components that go together to form the frame—the mouldings, the glass, the mat, and the backing paper. Time estimates are shown for each step of the process. We can see the sequencing requirements by following the lines from top to bottom; where the lines join is where the components of the product are joined.

A slightly simpler version of the operations process chart, called the assembly chart, would omit such details as the times of the activities and the machines used, showing only which parts went together.

Flow Process Chart

A process consisting of a single chain of events can be shown by a flow process chart. This chart again gives a rather macro view of the process. While an operations process chart can show a fairly complicated process consisting of

Figure 4.1
Operations Process Chart for Framing a Picture

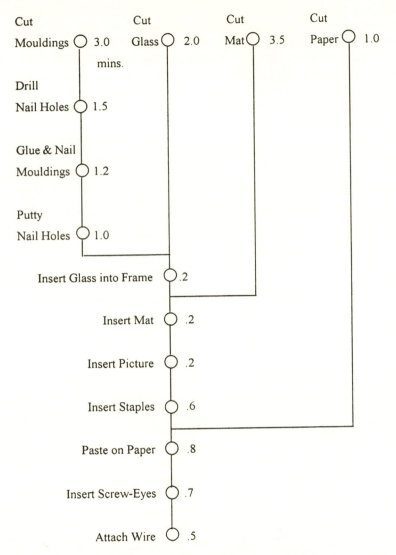

several chains of activities occurring simultaneously, the flow process chart shows the activities of a single person or perhaps the activities of several people who perform one after the other in sequence. In this respect the flow process chart is similar to a computer flow chart.

All five types of activities may be included in the chart. Time figures are given for all activities, as well as distance figures for transportation steps. A flow process chart may also be superimposed over a diagram of the layout of

Figure 4.2
Flow Process Chart for Changing a Tire

Symbol	Task	Time	Distance
O	Open trunk	.1 min.	
O	Remove spare tire	.5	
O	Remove jack	.4	
⇨	Carry tire and jack to flat tire	.2	10 ft.
O	Remove hubcap	.4	
O	Assemble jack	.4	
O	Jack up car slightly	.3	
O	Loosen nuts	1.5	
O	Jack up car the rest of the way	.5	
O	Remove nuts and wheel	.7	
O	Place spare tire on bolts	.2	
O	Put nuts on loosely	1.0	
O	Lower car partially	.5	
O	Tighten nuts	1.2	
O	Lower car	.3	
O	Replace hubcap	.6	
O	Disassemble jack	.3	
⇨	Carry jack and tire to trunk	.3	10 ft.
O	Place jack in trunk and secure	.7	
O	Place tire in trunk	.1	
O	Close trunk	.1	
		10.2	

the facilities to give what is called a flow diagram. For simple processes we can then see where each step takes place.

Figure 4.2 shows a flow process chart for the process of changing a tire on a car. As with any process chart, our purpose in creating it is to analyze the efficiency of the process and then to propose improvements. For example, we could speed up the process somewhat if we had more than one person working on the tire. Two people could perhaps carry the equipment to the flat tire more quickly. Also, they could work simultaneously on two different activities, such as removing the hubcap and assembling the jack. Unfortunately, there are not too many such opportunities for two to work at once, so the time savings would probably not be worth carrying an extra passenger around with you in case you had a flat tire! In a production setting, though, similar possibilities would be considered.

Similarly, in the flat tire example we might consider improving our technology, just as a business might. Here we might invest in a better jack, such as a hydraulic jack we could carry in our trunk. There are also spray cans of sealants for flat tires that would be helpful in some cases. Of course, any technology improvements would require capital investments that must be weighed against improvements in the process. Processes that occur much more regularly than changing a flat tire both in manufacturing and in service operations would lend themselves to a similar analysis.

Activity Chart

This chart, also called the multiactivity chart or the man-machine chart, gives a very macro look at the activities being performed simultaneously by all the components of an operations system, whether workers or machines. This time, though, the point of view is that of the components rather than that of the process. That is, we see what each component will be doing over a cycle rather than looking at the process from start to finish. The chart consists of a time scale and a column to show the activities of each component of the system. The starting point of the chart is arbitrary, some point in time when all the components of the system are already in action (as opposed to showing the start-up of the system). The chart concludes at the end of a cycle, so that the activities following the end of the chart would be exactly the same as those back at the top of the chart for each component. Thus, it is possible to project the activities of any component at any time in the future so long as the system stays on schedule.

In Figure 4.3 we see an activity chart for a laundry system consisting of 1 worker, 2 washers, 1 extractor (a machine that wrings out much of the water from heavy laundry), and 1 dryer. The chart starts arbitrarily with the unloading of the washer, followed by the loading of the new load. The worker then proceeds to the extractor, removes the old load, and puts in the new load from the washer. Then the worker takes that load to the dryer, removes the old load, and puts in the new load. At the end of two loads of laundry (one for each of the two washers) the process repeats itself exactly.

Besides showing the activities of all of the system's components, the activity chart gives us a good view of the idle time of each component in the system. We will see more examples of activity charts in the section on man–machine systems.

Figure 4.3
Activity Chart for a Laundry Operation

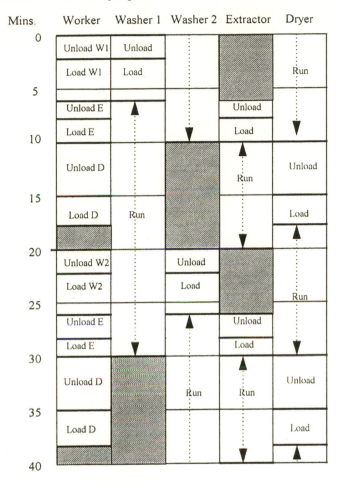

Left Hand–Right Hand Chart

The left hand–right hand (LH–RH) chart is similar to an activity chart but gives a much more micro view of a process. It shows the very small motions performed by the two hands of a worker. Although the LH–RH chart has no time scale, the activities of the two hands are positioned so that simultaneous activities are shown opposite each other on the chart. The five symbols used for operations process charts and flow process charts may also be used for the LH–RH chart (where the "storage" symbol is used for the "hold" activity of the hands). The LH–RH chart also traditionally provides a diagram of the work

Figure 4.4
LH–RH Chart for Assembling Caramel Apples

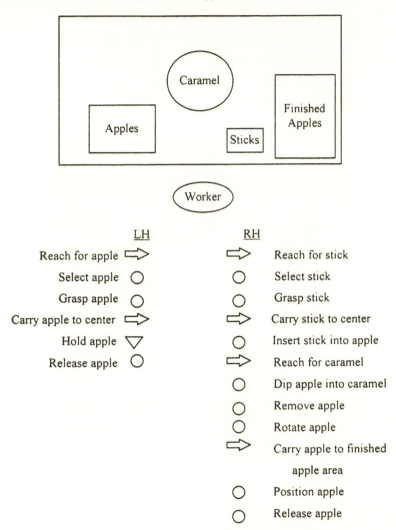

station so that we may see where materials, tools, and fixtures are situated. A "simo" chart is a LH–RH chart that also includes a time scale.

The LH–RH chart can be very useful in micromotion analysis, as discussed in a later section. The chart can show inefficient physical arrangements as well as inefficient uses of the two hands. Figure 4.4 gives an example of a LH–RH chart for the process of assembling caramel apples. We can see that the left hand is not very productive in this process, and we could then explore ways to improve the process.

MAN–MACHINE SYSTEMS

We have seen the use of the activity chart to illustrate the activities of man–machine systems. One of the major issues to decide with such systems is how many of each type of component to have in the system. We would like enough of each component to have a smooth and efficient system that meets our demand rate and avoids costly idle time in the components.

Consider the operation of excavating and hauling off dirt at a construction site. Let's assume that a company has one shovel for the operation and is trying to decide how many dump trucks to have. The table below shows the times required for the activities of the shovel and trucks.

ACTIVITY TIMES FOR SHOVEL AND TRUCKS

Shovel		Trucks	
Load truck	12 min.	Load truck	12 min.
		Go to dump	20
		Dump dirt	2
		Return	18
Total cycle:	12 min.	Total cycle:	52 min.

For the system to work perfectly smoothly there would have to be $52/12 = 4.33$ trucks in the system, the ratio of the truck cycle time to the shovel cycle time. That way, the shovel would load 4.33 trucks in 52 minutes and would finish just when the first truck completed its cycle. Obviously, however, we can't have .33 of a truck in our system. The constraint of having just one shovel prevents us from reaching this optimum ratio of trucks to shovels exactly. If we allowed ourselves to consider a larger number of shovels, we could come much closer to this ratio, such as with 13 trucks and 3 shovels. However, this larger system might well work faster than we need, and we would have to pay for all the unnecessary equipment.

In the current situation, then, we would consider having either 4 or 5 trucks in the system to come fairly close to the optimal ratio. The fact that a ratio of 4 to 1 is closer to 4.33 than a ratio of 5 to 1 does not necessarily mean that 4 trucks would be better than 5, however. It all depends on what criterion we use to choose our system. We will consider several possible criteria and see which number of trucks we would choose in each case.

Speed

4 Trucks

For ease of calculation let's see how long it would take each type of component of the system (shovel and truck) to complete 4 loads (one for each truck).

Shovel: (12 min./load) (4 loads)/(1 shovel) = 48 min./shovel
Trucks: (52 min./load) (4 loads)/(4 trucks) = 52 min./truck

In this case we can see that the trucks will take longer than the shovel. Just as in the assembly line balancing case, whichever part of the system takes the longest determines the overall cycle time. Therefore, a 4-load cycle will take 52 minutes, which works out to 13 minutes per load overall.

5 Trucks

Here we will first calculate the time to complete 5 loads.

Shovel: (12 min./load)(5 loads)/(1 shovel) = 60 min./shovel
Trucks: (52 min./load) (5 loads)/(5 trucks) = 52 min./truck

This time the shovel takes longer than the trucks, so the overall cycle for 5 loads is 60 minutes. This gives us a speed of 12 minutes per load.

If we think about it, the above results are obvious. When we have fewer trucks than the 4.33 break-even ratio, the trucks are always busy, and the shovel has some idle time. With 5 trucks (above the ratio) the shovel is kept busy, and the trucks have some idle time. Also, we would intuitively know that the system would work faster overall with 5 trucks than with 4 trucks. However, what is important is *how much* faster the system works. In our system the difference is from 13 minutes per load to 12 minutes per load. If we knew how many loads we had to haul in all, we could calculate the completion time of the system in either case. Then if we had any deadlines to meet or other jobs to start on, we could make a reasonable decision on how much speed we actually needed.

Except as insurance against a breakdown, it would obviously be silly to have any more trucks than 5 in the system. With 5 trucks the shovel is already kept constantly busy, and the overall system's speed is equal to that of the shovel, 12 minutes per load. Also, if we used fewer than 4 trucks, we would just have much more idle time on the shovel and a proportional loss of speed in the system overall.

Meeting Some Specified Speed

Let's relax for a moment our assumption of having just 1 shovel and either 4 or 5 trucks. In general, we can calculate the number of each component needed to meet a desired production rate. This calculation is exactly the same as the one used to calculate the number of work stations needed in an assembly line balancing situation (Chapter 3). That is, we divide the work to be done (this time separated by components of the system) by the desired cycle time.

If we assume a desired production rate of 6 loads per hour, for example, we would need to have a cycle time of 10 minutes per load ((60 min./hr.)/(6 loads/

hr.)). The shovels would then have to perform 12 minutes of work in 10 minutes, so we would need to have $12/10 = 1.2$ shovels. Just as in the line balancing situation, we always have to round up, so we actually would need 2 shovels. For the trucks to do 52 minutes of work in 10 minutes, we would need $52/10 = 5.2$ trucks, rounded up to 6 trucks. Thus, our system would need to consist of 2 shovels and 6 trucks to produce 6 loads per hour. Actually, since both of our calculations had to be rounded up, our system's speed would be faster than necessary. However, no smaller number of shovels or trucks would do.

Cost of Idle Time

Returning to our example of 1 shovel and either 4 or 5 trucks, we can see that speed of the system is not the only consideration. We have not taken into account the cost of operating the system. The 5-truck system would obviously cost more than the 4-truck system. The criterion of the cost of the idle time in the system can indicate how efficient or wasteful our system is. This idle time cost would be similar to an opportunity cost. If we had other uses for our equipment, we can calculate how much we're wasting by using it here. Let's assume that the shovel costs us $100 per hour to operate, including the cost of the operator, fuel, and depreciation. Assume that each truck costs $60 per hour.

4 Trucks

When we looked at the speed of the system, we found that in the 4-truck system the shovel took 48 minutes and the trucks took 52 minutes to handle 4 loads. Thus, the shovel is idle 4 minutes out of every 52 minutes, or 1/13 of the time. We can get this same result by comparing the shovel's 12 minutes per load and the trucks' 13 minutes per load. No matter how many loads we look at, the ratio stays the same. Therefore, the shovel's idle time costs us $(1/13)$ $(100/hr.) = \$7.69/hr.$

5 Trucks

In the 5-truck system it was the trucks that had some idle time. In our calculations for producing 5 loads we found that the shovel required 60 minutes and the trucks 52 minutes each. Therefore, each truck is idle $8/60 = 2/15$ of the time. At a cost of $60/hr. each, we have an idle time cost of $(2/15)$ ($60/ hr./truck) (5 trucks) = \$40.00/hr.$ While a little faster, then, the 5-truck system is much more wasteful than the 4-truck system.

Overall Cost per Load

Probably the most direct cost comparison between the two alternatives can be made by computing cost per load. This cost incorporates both the speed of the system and the wastefulness caused by idle time.

4 Trucks

Our earlier calculations have shown that this system takes 13 minutes per load. In an hour, then, we produce

(60 min./hr.)/(13 min./load) = 4.62 loads/hr.

The cost of the system is:

(1 shovel) ($100/hr.) = $100/hr.
(4 trucks) ($60/hr.) =   240/hr.
                         $340/hr.

The cost per load, then, is:

($340/hr.)/(4.62 loads/hr.) = $73.67/load

5 Trucks

The 5-truck system produces at a rate of 12 minutes/load, so we produce:

(60 min./hr.)/(12 min./load) = 5 loads/hr.

The cost of the system is:

(1 shovel) ($100/hr.) = $100/hr.
(5 trucks) ($60/hr.) =   300/hr.
                         $400/hr.

The cost per load in this system is:

($400/hr.)/(5 loads/hr.) = $80/load

Through these calculations we find that the 4-truck system is slightly cheaper per load. Unless our criterion is speed, then, it seems that the 4-truck system would be the best.

MICROMOTION ANALYSIS

Much work has been devoted to the level of the very smallest hand motions of a worker in order to design jobs efficiently. Frank and Lillian Gilbreth were pioneers in breaking the job down into these micromotions in order to make it more efficient. They developed 17 categories of these micromotions, which were called "therbligs" from a backwards spelling of "Gilbreth." Their original 17 therbligs included: search, select, grasp, transport empty, transport loaded, hold, release, position, pre-position, inspect, assemble, disassemble, use, unavoidable delay, avoidable delay, plan, and rest. While others have used slightly different names and have pared the list down a bit, the idea is to look at hand motions of a very small duration. These micromotions can be observed and timed by taking moving pictures of an operation and playing them back in slow motion.

The goal of micromotion analysis is to eliminate wasteful idle time, as well as any unnecessary motions or waste of energy. To this end several theorists have developed lists of "principles of motion economy," or ways to make jobs more efficient. For the most part, these principles are just common sense. For example, it is obviously inefficient for hands to be idle. If both hands are idle at the same time, something is really wrong! The easiest way to keep both hands busy is to have them do the same thing as much as possible, with their movements in opposite, symmetrical directions. To save energy, arm motions should be smooth rather than jerky, and small motions of the muscles save more energy than large motions.

The arrangement of equipment can also be crucial in designing an efficient job. Obviously, the motions of the arms (and the eyes!) are directly affected by where the materials and tools are located. Also, the design of the equipment can make quite a difference in efficiency. Simple, cost-effective tools and fixtures can save the arms from a lot of wasted motions, as well as promote greater accuracy in the process. The whole question of how automated to make the system comes in at this point, including the possibility of using robots. Costs and capabilities of machines versus human workers need to be analyzed in each particular situation.

Our caramel apple assembly process shown in a LH–RH chart in Figure 4.4 was a rather inefficient operation. To avoid so much idle time in the left hand, we could perhaps assemble two apples at once, with each hand performing exactly the same motions. This necessitates a small expenditure for fixtures to hold the apples while we stab them with sticks. (If we had really wanted to automate, we could have bought a stick-stabbing machine!) While a couple of extra steps are now needed, the fact that we are producing two apples rather than one at a time will surely speed up the process. In order to stab two apples at once, it is important that our fixtures be very close together so that we can see both apples easily. Other than these changes, the layout of our work station would stay pretty much the same.

Obviously, we could continue to automate the caramel apple system by adding more and more sophisticated machinery until we got to the point where our LH–RH chart might consist of just pushing a button. However, such automation would be realistic only for a very high-volume, very repetitive operation.

CHAPTER 5

Time Studies

OVERVIEW

We have already used time figures for activities (whether micro or macro) in our process planning and job design analyses and in our assembly line balancing. These figures are necessary in order to choose among various alternatives in setting up our production process. Later we will need time figures in our medium-run and short-run planning as well.

Again there is no clear time sequence of these different topics of analysis. We need time figures of small motions and individual activities before we can determine our exact process. Then, when we have determined this process, we can calculate time standards for larger activities and for whole jobs. These completed time standards may be used in fine-tuning capacity requirements, in scheduling production, in assigning jobs to workers and then monitoring their work, and possibly in administering compensation plans for the workers. Much of the analysis in these areas depends on accurate time studies. A great analysis based on erroneous data will only result in a costly, inefficient system.

Types of Time Studies

When most people think of time studies in industry, they probably think of an efficiency expert with a clipboard and a stopwatch walking around observing and timing workers on the job. This, however, is just one approach to time studies. Besides the stopwatch study there are two commonly used approaches to time studies.

Some jobs that consist of very standard motions can make use of predetermined times for those motions. Reliable published standards based on previous studies are widely available, and the company may have some time standards of its own from previous studies that can be adapted to new jobs.

The third type of time study is the statistical method of work sampling. Here no actual timing is done; rather, the worker is observed a large number of times at random to determine what *proportion* of the time is spent doing different things. These proportions can then be converted into time figures.

Each of these methods has its advantages and disadvantages, and each may be the preferred method in certain circumstances.

Compensation Plans

Paying a worker according to output was popularized by the scientific management theorists early in the twentieth century. While the idea still has definite appeal, it is fair to say that the number of incentive-based compensation systems has declined in recent years. The main obstacle in administering such a program is the perceived fairness of the system. It is extremely difficult, even with very accurate time studies, to set up standards for a wide range of jobs in such a way that each worker has the same opportunity to earn incentive bonuses. Jobs change fairly quickly over time, either by the workers learning new methods or by improved technology. Thus, a worker who somehow learns to "beat the system" may achieve large bonuses without much effort while another struggles just to meet the standard. Add to this problem the fact that no time study can be completely accurate and the fact that humans are skeptical by nature, and you have a real problem of *perceived* fairness, regardless of the actual fairness of the system. No wonder then that many companies have given up on the ability of such incentive systems to satisfy their own needs for productivity and to satisfy the perceptions of unions and individual workers.

If a company does decide to institute an incentive pay system, there are infinite ways to set it up. Some systems focus on individual workers. A production standard is determined, and the worker receives some amount of additional compensation for beating this standard. However, the standard may be set at various levels, and the percentage of increased pay above the standard may also be set at many different rates. Some plans may have more than one standard, with corresponding pay increases above each level. Some may also have step increases at certain levels of production. Obviously, the production standards used in incentive systems are not necessarily equal to those we determine from our time studies. Time studies tell us only what to *expect* from the workers, not where to set our incentive standards to motivate workers the most.

Some companies have chosen to institute group incentive systems where each individual in a work group is compensated according to the performance of the whole group. The Scanlon plan and the Lincoln Electric plan are well-known early examples of group incentive systems. Again, the possible structures of such a plan are innumerable.

Learning Curves

In most activities the more a person performs the activity, the less time it takes. In other words, people develop skills through practice that allow them to work more quickly than they did at first. Therefore, we can expect (and plan for) a new worker's speed to increase over time. Similarly, in a system that is always producing new projects, such as an aerospace company, we can expect the *aggregate* labor time to decrease with each new unit produced.

The learning curve is a concept that describes mathematically the systematic decrease in labor time of a person or group as they produce more and more units. The mathematical function that is generally assumed (because it seems to fit well in many real-life applications) is of the following form:

$$Y = aX^b,$$

where Y = time required to produce the xth unit
$\quad\quad\quad a$ = time required to produce the first unit
$\quad\quad\quad X$ = the number of the unit produced
$\quad\quad\quad b$ = a negative exponent corresponding to the decrease in time required for each unit

Learning curves are generally described in terms of the percentage of the xth unit's time that will be required by the 2xth unit. In other words, how far will the time drop after the worker has completed twice as many units as currently? Thus, an 80% learning curve (probably the most common) represents the situation where the 2xth unit takes only 80% of the time of the xth unit (see Figure 5.1).

For example, if a worker has an 80% learning curve and takes 100 seconds to produce the first unit, the second unit should only take 80 seconds. Then the fourth unit (twice as many as the second unit) should take 64 seconds, the eighth unit 51.2 seconds, the sixteenth unit 40.96 seconds, and so on. The curve drops off rather quickly at first and then almost levels out after a large number of units have been completed.

In comparison, a 90% learning curve would not fall as quickly. If the first unit took 100 seconds, the second would take 90 seconds, the fourth 81 seconds, the eighth 72.9 seconds, the sixteenth 65.61 seconds, and so on.

If past experience shows that workers or groups of workers tend to follow certain learning curves, then time studies should certainly take account of just where the worker is on the learning curve, and the company should adjust time study figures to project future improvements for new workers or new projects.

Automation

As companies increasingly try to make jobs more repetitive, enabling them to be more automated, they also can expect a reduction in the variability of the

Figure 5.1
80% and 90% Learning Curves

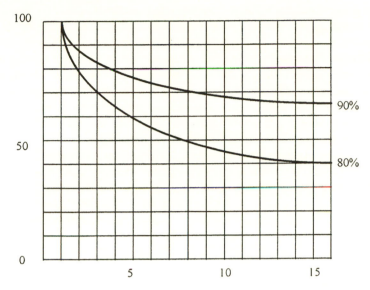

time required for those tasks automated. In fact, compared to human variability, machine variability may turn out to be negligible. In that case machine-controlled activities can be separated from those controlled by humans when performing a time study. The machine's activities can be timed accurately with a much smaller sample.

A machine's performance, however, can decline over time (almost a reverse learning curve!), so that the machine may take longer to complete a task or may break down more frequently, with the same result. Careful monitoring of machine performance can help in predicting future machine times just as a learning curve can help predict future human times.

STOPWATCH STUDY

While a stopwatch study of a job is the most directly applicable type of time study, it is also the most expensive. The person doing the time study needs to be highly trained, and a chunk of direct observation time is required for each job.

The job to be studied must first be broken down into identifiable *elements*. An element of a job is generally not as small as a therblig, but rather some larger but distinct step of the process. The observer may time each element separately (snap-back stopwatch) or simply let the watch run and record the completion time of each element (continuous stopwatch), later subtracting to obtain the times of the elements.

There are several reasons for breaking the job down into elements rather than simply timing the job as a whole. First, some elements do not occur each cycle; by timing them separately we can multiply the elements' times by the appropriate frequencies to obtain the overall job time. Also, some elements may be controlled by a machine and not subject to the worker's efforts. These machine times may then be added to the other elements' times. Workers may be more skillful in performing some of their job's elements than others. By timing them separately and giving them separate performance ratings, we can obtain a more accurate total than by simply assigning a single average performance rating for the whole job. Finally, by timing elements separately, we can use the resulting time figures for other jobs that include the same elements.

The worker is observed through several cycles, or repetitions, of the process. The number of cycles observed depends on the degree of accuracy desired in the time standard. Since we will be taking the mean time of several cycles, we can construct a confidence interval for the mean. The following equation will tell us the sample size required for a certain level of confidence and a certain interval width:

$$n = \frac{Z^2 \sigma^2}{e^2}$$

where n = number of cycles required
         Z = standard normal variate corresponding to desired confidence level
         σ = estimate (perhaps from previous studies) of the standard deviation of the individual element times
         e = allowable error on either side of the estimated mean time

For example, if we desire to be 95% confident that our mean time estimate for an element is within 2 seconds of the real mean time, and the estimated standard deviation of element times is 5 seconds, our calculation would be:

$$n = \frac{(1.96)^2 \, (5)^2}{(2)^2} = 24.01 \text{ cycles}$$

(since $Z = 1.96$ for a 95% confidence interval).

Select Time

The mean time of an element in the study is called the *select time*. In the example below we have a job broken down into three elements. The worker has been observed for 5 cycles (a very small sample for illustration purposes), and the select time has been calculated for each element.

STOPWATCH TIME STUDY
Cycle

Element	1	2	3	4	5	Select Time
1	4	2	6	5	3	20/5 = 4.0 secs.
2	9	7	10	10	11	47/5 = 9.4
3	12	16	11	12	13	64/5 = 12.8
						26.2 secs.

The total of the select times for one cycle is 26.2 seconds. However, this figure really only applies to the worker who was studied. This worker may have been exceptionally fast or slow at this job. Also, regardless of the worker's skill, there may have been some motivation to work either quickly or slowly during the time study. Perhaps the worker wanted to look good in the eyes of the time studier. More likely, though, the worker would rather see a slow time standard result from the study, making it easier to meet the standard in the future and, if an incentive system is used, making it possible to earn more money. At any rate, the time of this one worker will surely not be applicable to all the workers who might perform this job.

Normal Time

What we would like to have, then, is a time standard that can be applied to the whole population of workers who might perform this job. That is, we want to know the time that a "normal" worker would take to perform the job. It is generally assumed that the distribution of times that all capable workers would take to perform a particular job would follow a normal curve. The hypothetical "normal" person is defined to be the one whose time is at the slowest 5% point of the population. That is, 95% of the workers could perform the job faster than the normal worker. If the normal worker is defined as the average worker, as would seem more natural, then 50% of the population would be unable to work as fast as this normal worker. Defining the normal person as we do provides us with a very conservative time standard which 95% of the population can meet or beat.

In order to determine the *normal time* for a job element, we need to relate the time of the observed worker to the time of the hypothetical normal worker. This is done by giving the observed worker a performance rating. A worker who is judged to be performing at the same rate as the normal person is given a rating of 100%. Faster workers are rated above 100% and slower workers below 100%. The actual rating assigned is the percentage of the normal worker's speed at which the observed worker is judged to be working.

Obviously, assigning performance ratings is very difficult and requires extensive training. The job has never been seen by the time studier before (or there would already be a time standard!), and yet a number must be assigned from out of the air based only on the time studier's experience in watching people move. This performance rating is not only difficult to make, but it is also the number to which the final time standard is most sensitive. The timing itself can be made with very little error, but errors in the performance rating will drastically affect the result.

If it were possible to observe a large number of workers performing the same job, the entire distribution of times could be determined without the necessity of resorting to performance ratings. However, usually only one or two workers are studied because of the costliness of the study, as well as the fact that often there simply are not more than one or two workers performing the same job in a company.

In our example problem, we have assigned performance ratings for the three elements. This worker apparently is quite variable in speed in performing the different elements. This is precisely the situation where it is most valuable to have the elements timed separately. Normal times are then determined by multiplying the select times by the performance ratings. That is, if a worker is judged to be working at 90% of the normal person's speed, then the normal time should be 90% of the observed worker's time. Normal time calculations are shown below:

CALCULATION OF NORMAL TIMES

Element	Select Time	Performance Rating	Normal Time
1	4.0 sec.	85%	3.40 sec.
2	9.4	110	10.34
3	12.8	120	15.36
			29.10 sec.

Because the observed worker was substantially faster than normal on two of the three elements, the overall normal time comes out a little longer than this worker's time of 26.2 seconds. We now have a time figure of 29.10 seconds which we expect can be met or bettered by 95% of the population.

Standard Time

This normal time figure may apply to the general population, but it still applies only while the worker is actually working. There are many times during a typical work day when a worker is not actually performing this job. These downtimes during the day are known as *allowances*. Typical categories of allowances would include personal time (when a worker gets a drink of water, uses the restroom, talks to a co-worker, etc.), unavoidable delay (a supervisor interrupts, a machine breaks down, etc.), start-up and clean-up time (at the start and end of the day, before and after breaks and lunch), scheduled breaks, and fatigue. The amount of unproductive time due to these allowances varies quite a bit from job to job and from company to company. While such allowances as scheduled breaks are probably determined mainly by law and by company policy, other allowances may themselves be determined through time studies.

The list below shows the amounts of time allocated to the various allowances in our example problem. The total of 120 minutes per day (assumed to be 8 hours) seems like quite a bit of wasted time, but it is not too far out of line with many operations.

ALLOWANCE TIMES PER 8-HOUR DAY

Personal time	20 min.
Start-up & clean-up	30
Unavoidable delay	25
Scheduled breaks	30
Fatigue	15
	120 min.

In this example, then, 25% (120 min./480 min.) of the work day is nonproductive, and only 75% is productive. The normal time that we calculated really only applies during the productive time. Therefore, we would like to expand our normal time per unit to include these allowances, giving us a more realistic time per unit that will apply to any extended period of time that includes these downtimes. This more realistic time figure is called the *standard time*. The standard time can be calculated by the following formula:

Standard Time = Normal Time / (1 − allowances/total time)

In our example the ratio of allowances to total time is 1/4. Therefore, 1 − 1/4 = 3/4, the ratio of working time to total time. When we divide by this ratio, we are actually expanding our normal time by a ratio of 4/3, which is the ratio of total time to working time. Thus, our time standard is expanded from the time it takes while actually working to the time it takes with allowances included proportionally. The standard time for this job, then, is (29.10 sec./unit)(4/3) = 38.8 sec./unit.

The standard time is the one that is ordinarily used whenever time standards are needed in analysis. From the standard time we are able to calculate output figures (units per time), which are just the inverse of our time figures (time per unit). For example, the standard output for our problem above would be 1/38.8 units/sec. Converting this figure to a more useful time period such as a week (assumed to be 40 hours), we have:

$$\text{Standard Weekly Output} = \frac{(40 \text{ hr./wk.}) \ (60 \text{ min./hr.}) \ (60 \text{ sec./min.})}{38.8 \text{ sec./unit}}$$
$$= 3711.3 \text{ units/wk.}$$

Thus, the normal worker could be expected to produce 3711 units per week, and 95% of the population could produce even more. Note that we could have obtained this same output figure by taking the productive part of the week (3/4 × 40 hr./wk. = 30 hr./wk.) and dividing by the normal time (29.10 sec./unit), as follows:

$$\text{Standard Weekly Output} = \frac{(30 \text{ hr./wk.}) (60 \text{ min./hr.}) (60 \text{ sec./min.})}{29.10 \text{ sec./unit}}$$
$$= 3711.3 \text{ units/wk.}$$

In the above calculation both the numerator and denominator are 3/4 of those in the previous calculation, so the result is the same. However, it is usually more convenient to refer to standard times and total time available rather than to normal times and working time available.

PREDETERMINED TIMES

When a job can be broken down into standard small motions, or therbligs, the use of published times for these small motions can save time and money. Since these studies have been based on large samples of workers, they give accurate normal times without the need to use performance ratings. Predetermined times may also be used to study processes or jobs that do not yet exist, simply by combining the motions of interest. Some training is still required, however, to use predetermined times accurately. While looking up times is no problem, there still is the need to break the job down accurately into small motions. The only other potential drawback to predetermined times is that they may not be easy to apply to all situations. Some jobs, especially those that are less repetitive, may not lend themselves to micromotion analysis.

The MTM (Methods-Time Measurement) Corporation publishes probably the most widely used predetermined time standards. Figure 5.2 shows some of the standards for common motions. Note that the times are given in TMU's (time measurement units), each of which is equal to .00001 hour, or .036 seconds. Each TMU, then, represents a very small time interval, less than 1/30 of a second.

Let's examine a very simple job using MTM data. The job consists of picking up a sheet of paper from a desk in front of us, carrying it to a desk to our right and setting it down in an approximate location about two feet from its original position. Assume that we start with our hand right next to the paper.

Our first micromotion, then, is to grasp the paper, an object which is lying against a flat surface. The relevant micromotion from the Grasp table would be a pickup of type 1B, which requires 3.5 TMU. Next we move the paper 24 inches to the right to an approximate location. The Move table shows this to be Case B, which for 24 inches requires 20.6 TMU. A normal release (Case 1) takes 2.0 TMU. Finally, bringing our hand back to the original position is a reach of 24 inches. Assuming that there are more papers to be picked up, this

Figure 5.2
Predetermined Times from MTM Association

METHODS-TIME MEASUREMENT
MTM-I APPLICATION DATA

1 TMU	= .00001	hour		1 hour	= 100,000.0 TMU
	= .0006	minute		1 minute	= 1,666.7 TMU
	= .036	seconds		1 second	= 27.8 TMU

TABLE I – REACH – R

Distance Moved Inches	Time TMU				Hand In Motion		CASE AND DESCRIPTION
	A	B	C or D	E	A	B	
3/4 or less	2.0	2.0	2.0	2.0	1.6	1.6	A Reach to object in fixed location, or to object in other hand or on which other hand rests.
1	2.5	2.5	3.6	2.4	2.3	2.3	
2	4.0	4.0	5.9	3.8	3.5	2.7	
3	5.3	5.3	7.3	5.3	4.5	3.6	B Reach to single object in location which may vary slightly from cycle to cycle.
4	6.1	6.4	8.4	6.8	4.9	4.3	
5	6.5	7.8	9.4	7.4	5.3	5.0	
6	7.0	8.6	10.1	8.0	5.7	5.7	
7	7.4	9.3	10.8	8.7	6.1	6.5	C Reach to object jumbled with other objects in a group so that search and select occur.
8	7.9	10.1	11.5	9.3	6.5	7.2	
9	8.3	10.8	12.2	9.9	6.9	7.9	
10	8.7	11.5	12.9	10.5	7.3	8.6	
12	9.6	12.9	14.2	11.8	8.1	10.1	
14	10.5	14.4	15.6	13.0	8.9	11.5	D Reach to a very small object or where accurate grasp is required.
16	11.4	15.8	17.0	14.2	9.7	12.9	
18	12.3	17.2	18.4	15.5	10.5	14.4	
20	13.1	18.6	19.8	16.7	11.3	15.8	
22	14.0	20.1	21.2	18.0	12.1	17.3	E Reach to indefinite location to get hand in position for body balance or next motion or out of way.
24	14.9	21.5	22.5	19.2	12.9	18.8	
26	15.8	22.9	23.9	20.4	13.7	20.2	
28	16.7	24.4	25.3	21.7	14.5	21.7	
30	17.5	25.8	26.7	22.9	15.3	23.2	
Additional	0.4	0.7	0.7	0.6			TMU per inch over 30 inches

TABLE V – POSITION* – P

CLASS OF FIT		Symmetry	Easy To Handle	Difficult To Handle
1—Loose	No pressure required	S	5.6	11.2
		SS	9.1	14.7
		NS	10.4	16.0
2—Close	Light pressure required	S	16.2	21.8
		SS	19.7	25.3
		NS	21.0	26.6
3—Exact	Heavy pressure required.	S	43.0	48.6
		SS	46.5	52.1
		NS	47.8	53.4
SUPPLEMENTARY RULE FOR SURFACE ALIGNMENT				
P1SE per alignment: > 1/16 ≤ 1/4"		P2SE per alignment: ≤ 1/16"		

*Distance moved to engage—1" or less.

Figure 5.2 (Continued)

TABLE II – MOVE – M

Distance Moved Inches	Time TMU			Hand In Motion B	Wt. Allowance			CASE AND DESCRIPTION
	A	B	C		Wt. (lb.) Up to	Dynamic Factor	Static Constant TMU	
3/4 or less	2.0	2.0	2.0	1.7				
1	2.5	2.9	3.4	2.3	2.5	1.00	0	A Move object to other hand or against stop.
2	3.6	4.6	5.2	2.9				
3	4.9	5.7	6.7	3.6	7.5	1.06	2.2	
4	6.1	6.9	8.0	4.3				
5	7.3	8.0	9.2	5.0	12.5	1.11	3.9	
6	8.1	8.9	10.3	5.7				
7	8.9	9.7	11.1	6.5	17.5	1.17	5.6	B Move object to approximate or indefinite location.
8	9.7	10.6	11.8	7.2				
9	10.5	11.5	12.7	7.9	22.5	1.22	7.4	
10	11.3	12.2	13.5	8.6				
12	12.9	13.4	15.2	10.0	27.5	1.28	9.1	
14	14.4	14.6	16.9	11.4				
16	16.0	15.8	18.7	12.8	32.5	1.33	10.8	
18	17.6	17.0	20.4	14.2				
20	19.2	18.2	22.1	15.6	37.5	1.39	12.5	C Move object to exact location.
22	20.8	19.4	23.8	17.0				
24	22.4	20.6	25.5	18.4	42.5	1.44	14.3	
26	24.0	21.8	27.3	19.8				
28	25.5	23.1	29.0	21.2	47.5	1.50	16.0	
30	27.1	24.3	30.7	22.7				
Additional	0.8	0.6	0.85		TMU per inch over 30 inches			

TABLE IV – GRASP – G

TYPE OF GRASP	Case	Time TMU	DESCRIPTION	
PICK-UP	1A	2.0	Any size object by itself, easily grasped	
	1B	3.5	Object very small or lying close against a flat surface	
	1C1	7.3	Diameter larger than 1/2"	Interference with Grasp on bottom and one side of nearly cylindrical object.
	1C2	8.7	Diameter 1/4" to 1/2"	
	1C3	10.8	Diameter less than 1/4"	
REGRASP	2	5.6	Change grasp without relinquishing control	
TRANSFER	3	5.6	Control transferred from one hand to the other.	
SELECT	4A	7.3	Larger than 1" x 1" x 1"	Object jumbled with other objects so that search and select occur.
	4B	9.1	1/4" x 1/4" x 1/8" to 1" x 1" x 1"	
	4C	12.9	Smaller than 1/4" x 1/4" x 1/8"	
CONTACT	5	0	Contact, Sliding, or Hook Grasp.	

TABLE VI – RELEASE – RL

Case	Time TMU	DESCRIPTION
1	2.0	Normal release performed by opening fingers as independent motion.
2	0	Contact Release

would seem to be Case D, where accurate grasp is required, so the time required would be 22.5 TMU. These micromotions are summarized below.

**MTM TIME STANDARDS FOR MOVING
A PAPER**

Micromotion	Symbol	TMU
Grasp paper	G1B	3.5
Move paper	M24B	20.6
Release paper	RL1	2.0
Return hand	R24D	22.5
		48.6

The entire job requires a total of 48.6 TMU, or 1.75 seconds. This would seem to be a reasonable estimate for this activity. You can verify its accuracy by moving a pile of 10 sheets, one at a time, two feet to the right and seeing whether the total time is 17.5 seconds. It is obvious from this small example, though, that breaking a job down into micromotions and then matching them with those in the table is not quite as easy as it sounds and definitely requires some training.

WORK SAMPLING

The work sampling method of time study has the advantage of being cheaper than the stopwatch method and requiring less training. An observer simply keeps a tally of the number of times a worker is observed doing different things in a large number of random observations. It is important that observations be truly random so that each activity of the worker is fairly represented. Thus, some observations need to be made right after work starts, near the end of the day, and so on. The observer makes a list of times predetermined through the use of a random number table and then just looks at the worker when those times arrive. A properly situated observer can thereby perform time studies on a number of workers simultaneously, saving time and money.

The steps of a worker's job that are tallied are generally broader than in other types of time studies. Micromotions would certainly not be used. For instance, a time study made to determine allowances would include work categories such as working, on break, personal time, unavoidable delay, and so on. At the extreme the study could just distinguish between working time and idle time. Because of this use of broad categories of work, work sampling especially lends itself to studying jobs that are less repetitive or jobs that have very long cycle times.

Besides keeping a tally of the various work categories, the time studier does have to make performance ratings of the worker for any categories that involve work. However, no timing is done at all. The times for the various work categories are determined from the *proportions* of time spent out of the total. Our calculations progress from the select time to the normal time to the standard time, just as in the stopwatch study. However, the calculations required for the select time are a bit simpler, and there are usually fewer categories (elements) than in a stopwatch study.

Before conducting a work sampling study, we again need to determine the required sample size for a certain level of accuracy. Since we are dealing with confidence intervals for proportions this time, the relevant standard error is the standard error of the proportion. With p defined as the proportion we are estimating, and with n, Z, and e defined as before, the formula for the required sample size is

$$n = \frac{Z^2 p\,(1 - p)}{e^2}$$

Note that this formula includes p, the number we are trying to estimate! If we have any estimate of what p might turn out to be, we can insert that number in the equation. However, the most conservative approach would be simply to insert p = .5. This figure gives the largest product of p(1 − p) in the numerator, thus resulting in the largest required sample size. Our conservative formula, then, would be

$$n = \frac{.25Z^2}{e^2}$$

Suppose that a worker has the job of cutting and stacking lumber. We would like to estimate the proportion of time spent on each of those jobs within .06 with 99% confidence. According to the normal table, the Z value for a 99% confidence level is 2.58. Therefore, our required sample size would be

$$n = \frac{(.25)\,(2.58)^2}{(.06)^2} = 462$$

Now let's assume that we have taken 500 observations (a nice round number that is greater than the required 462). The observations have been tallied in three categories—cutting, stacking, and idle. The worker has also been given performance ratings while cutting or stacking, and the total number of boards produced by the worker in a week have been counted. Finally, let's assume that the company uses a standard 15% for allowances for all jobs. The data for the work sampling study appear on the following page:

WORK SAMPLING DATA FOR LUMBER WORKER

Work Category	Observations	Proportion	Performance Rating
Cutting	170	.34	110%
Stacking	220	.44	120%
Idle	110	.22	
	500	1.00	

Total boards produced per 40-hour week: 1260

The select times for the worker are simply the total times spent on each activity over the course of the week divided by the number of boards produced for the week. Since 34% of the worker's time was spent on cutting, the total amount of time spent on cutting during the week was:

$$(.34)(40 \text{ hr./wk.})(60 \text{ min./hr.}) = 816 \text{ min./wk.}$$

Therefore, the select time for cutting is:

$$(816 \text{ min./wk.})/(1260 \text{ units/wk.}) = .65 \text{ min./unit}$$

Similarly, the worker spent 44% of the week stacking, so the total stacking time that week was:

$$(.44)(40 \text{ hr./wk.})(60 \text{ min./hr.}) = 1056 \text{ min./wk.}$$

The select time for stacking is:

$$(1056 \text{ min./wk.})/(1260 \text{ units/wk.}) = .84 \text{ min./unit}$$

To obtain the normal times for the two activities, we multiply as usual by the performance ratings:

$$\text{Cutting: } (.65 \text{ min./unit}) (1.10) = .715 \text{ min./unit}$$
$$\text{Stacking: } (.84 \text{ min./unit}) (1.20) = \underline{1.008 \text{ min./unit}}$$
$$1.723 \text{ min./unit}$$

Overall, the normal time is 1.723 min./board. We can now build in the 15% allowance factor (either to the two individual times or to the total time, depending on which we need). The total standard time per unit would be:

$$(1.723 \text{ min./unit})/(1-.15) = 2.027 \text{ min./unit}$$

With this standard time the standard weekly output of boards would be:

$$(40 \text{ hr./wk.})(60 \text{ min./hr.})/(2.027 \text{ min./unit})$$
$$= (2400 \text{ min./wk.})/(2.027 \text{ min./unit})$$
$$= 1184 \text{ units/wk.}$$

We can see that the worker we studied produced more than the standard number of boards (1260 compared to 1184). This worker also took more idle time (22% of the time as compared to the standard 15% allowance factor) by working faster than normal during working times (110% and 120% for the two job categories).

PART II

Medium-Run Decisions

In this section we examine decisions that will last for about one year (although these decisions may still be updated within that time). Some medium-run decisions may be for as little as a half year or as long as two or three years, but on the average we will focus on about one year.

Our long-range decisions have given us a facility with a certain capacity and a certain layout based on the process chosen. However, there still remains some flexibility in the system. Capacity can be changed somewhat by squeezing in more machines and more workers (especially if our long-run plans have been made with some foresight!) or by reducing the work force. The product mix can be changed to some extent, and the layout can be rearranged as well. Therefore, we are able to respond to changing conditions and to plan our production for the next year accordingly.

In order to make our medium-run plans, though, we need an accurate forecast of our demand for the next year. While our long-run plans have presumably been made using a long-range forecast of demand, it is for our medium-run decisions that we need a more exact and detailed forecast. For that reason our consideration of forecasting techniques is presented in this section.

In general, long-range forecasting is undertaken by the top levels of management with the objective of predicting long-range trends and important turning points in the life cycle of our products. These demand forecasts are necessarily rather inexact and look only at very general, highly aggregated demands.

Medium-range forecasting is undertaken by middle-level managers in the marketing and/or operations areas. In many cases it is actually the marketing managers who put together the forecast, but, as we noted in Chapter 1, this information becomes the basis of many operations management decisions. Therefore, the operations managers must work closely with the marketing managers and must be able to interpret the work of marketing managers. In other situations, of course, the operations managers may be directly involved in the forecasting. In any case, the forecasts made must be more detailed and more accurate than the long-range forecasts. However, the demand is still somewhat aggregated rather than broken down into every small item or model produced.

Of course, when we get to short-run decisions, we will need even more accurate and detailed forecasts of demand in order to implement production scheduling on a daily basis. Here lower-level operations managers are involved, and their forecasts are often based on actual orders already received. These managers must be able to revise their forecasts quickly and cheaply in order to act quickly in scheduling production, ordering materials, and so on.

In Chapter 6, then, we will look at several different forecasting techniques that are useful for medium-range demand forecasts for medium-run decision-making. However, many of these same mathematical techniques are also useful in making long-range and short-range forecasts and for forecasting other variables besides demand.

Having determined a medium-range demand forecast, we can then proceed to plan the aggregate production for the next year or so. We need to determine the needed capacity for machines, labor, and materials throughout the next year. It takes time to hire and train new workers, and it also takes a certain amount of notice to lay off workers. Materials also need to be ordered ahead of time, and any new machines need to be ordered and put into operation over a period of time. For these reasons it is necessary to have an overall production plan extending for at least a year into the future.

CHAPTER 6

Forecasting

OVERVIEW

As mentioned, a firm has a need for long-range, medium-range, and short-range forecasts. There are also several different types of information that a firm would like to forecast. For example, changes in technology will affect not only the market for the company's product, but also the production processes used by competitors in the industry. Therefore, it would be very useful to have a good long-range forecast of technological improvements. Obviously, though, such forecasts are very difficult.

The company would also like to forecast other costs of doing business, such as the cost of energy and raw materials. The supply of these resources available in the future will have a great effect on their prices. Forecasts of general business conditions will also help to predict demand for the company's products. Both demand and resource costs may also depend on political conditions around the world in the future, so we would also like to be able to forecast these conditions. We can see, then, that both the demand for a company's products and its costs of doing business depend on several diverse variables that we would like to be able to forecast. In this discussion, though, we will focus on forecasting demand.

In choosing a forecasting model a prime consideration is, of course, the accuracy of the model. However, other very important considerations are the cost of preparing the forecast and the ease of using the forecasting model. Only for long-range forecasts that are made infrequently is a very costly forecasting justified. A general principle of using any quantitative technique is that the cost of using the technique must be less than the savings that can be expected to result from the presumably better decision made using that technique. Thus, as our time frame gets shorter and expected cost savings get smaller, only cheaper forecasting techniques make sense. Also, the frequent updating of shorter-range forecasts increases the necessity for quick, cost-efficient forecasting.

The implementation issue is also important. Who will be collecting the data to feed into the forecasting model? Who will actually perform the analysis? How much special knowledge or training will be required of these people? Again the objective is to provide a forecasting model that is easy to use without extensive training.

Types of Demand Forecasting Models

One approach to demand forecasting is simply to ignore the many underlying variables affecting demand and just try to establish the pattern of demand over time. This approach is the *time series model*. If we find that our demand follows a fairly consistent pattern, we can determine what this pattern is and extend it into the future. Simply analyzing a demand pattern over time is a cheap, simple approach that can be implemented easily. The problem with this approach, though, is that we have to hope that whatever factors have caused our demand to behave as it has will continue into the future, or at least that any changes in these factors will tend to balance each other out. If we keep a close watch on our demand pattern over time, we can revise our estimates of the pattern when significant changes occur. We can also measure the amount of deviations from our actual demands in the past to the underlying pattern we have determined in order to have an idea of the deviations we can expect in our future demands. We will then at least have an idea of how far off our forecasts might be.

Another type of forecasting model does try to examine the relationship between demand and various other factors. This is the *correlational model*. Such other variables as economic conditions, pricing of our product and competing products, and demographic changes in the market for our product might provide some insight into the future pattern of our demand. Correlational models seek to discover just what mathematical relationships exist between our demand and other variables (without ever seeking to prove that one variable *causes* another variable to change). Such an approach is more costly and time-consuming than just using a time series model, but it can provide much greater insight into an organization's demand. Thus, changes in a demand pattern may be predicted ahead of time as other variables change.

The difficulty of constructing a correlational forecasting model is in finding other variables that do help predict our demand and then in obtaining accurate data for those other variables. It does little good to find variables that are highly correlated with our demand if those variables must themselves be forecast and are thus subject to significant error.

Besides these very quantitative forecasting techniques, there are also several more subjective techniques of forecasting. These would include estimates of the sales force and sales managers, opinion surveys, and the Delphi technique, where opinions are elicited systematically from a group of experts. These more subjective techniques are most useful in forecasting broad, long-range trends in the economy, the market, technology, and politics.

TIME SERIES MODEL

In a time series model the independent variable is always the time, while the dependent variable is the variable being forecast, demand in this case. The nice part about working with a time series is that the independent variable, since it is time, can be measured in evenly spaced intervals. On the other hand, a model using some other variable as the independent variable has to deal with whatever values happen to occur in that other variable. For example, if demand seems to be connected with daily temperature, we have to use whatever temperatures we obtain in our observation period, along with the corresponding demand figures. Thus, the calculations in working with a time series model are somewhat simpler than other models.

Our main problem in constructing a time series forecasting model is to determine just what the demand pattern is over time so that we can extend it into the future. Some rather complicated-appearing demand patterns can be decomposed into several simpler patterns. These simple patterns can then be extended into the future and put back together to make a forecast.

As shown in Figure 6.1, there are four standard types of patterns that appear frequently in time series data: random fluctuations, trend (often linear), seasonal fluctuations, and cyclic variations. Graph A shows a pattern consisting only of random fluctuations. These fluctuations by definition are unpredictable; the best we can do is to measure the fluctuations so that we know what size errors to expect in future forecasts.

In graph B we add an upward linear trend. Of course, demand patterns can also go downward, and trends are not always linear. However, linear trends are very common, and even those that are not linear can often be approximated fairly well by a straight line.

Graph C shows seasonal fluctuations along with the random and trend components. These are fluctuations that repeat exactly once a year. Many products do have identifiable seasonal patterns which remain consistent from year to year. For example, toys sell much better before Christmas, swim suits sell best in late spring, and so on. The pattern need not be as smooth and regular as that shown on the graph; any pattern that repeats once a year is seasonal. Actually, there are many demand patterns that repeat weekly or monthly as well as yearly, such as those of supermarket or bank customers, and these may also be classified loosely as "seasonal" patterns. The techniques used to handle these shorter periods are the same as those used for yearly patterns.

Some recurring patterns may exist which span some time period longer than a year. Economists speak of the "business cycle," in which the overall economy goes through cycles of expansion and contraction. Of course, government sees it as its job to flatten out such cycles. However, there may still exist certain

Figure 6.1
Common Time Series Components

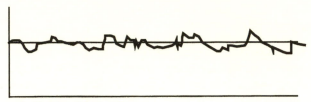

A. Random Fluctuations

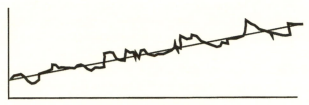

B. Linear trend and random fluctuations

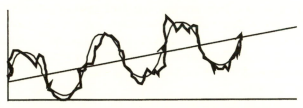

C. Linear trend, seasonal, and random fluctuations

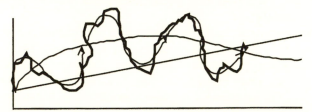

D. Linear trend, cyclical, seasonal, and random fluctuations

long-range cyclic variations in certain industries for various reasons. In graph D we see an example of a five-year cycle underlying the other three components. The end result is a rather complicated demand pattern. However, if we can break it down into its various components, it then becomes rather easy to extend these patterns and make a forecast.

Moving Average

The moving average is a simple and popular method for forecasting demand patterns that consist mainly of random fluctuations (graph A). In that case all we can do is try to use our latest data to update our estimate of the base line (i.e., the average demand). This average "moves" in the sense that as new data come in, they replace the oldest data in our calculation of the average. Our calculation of the average is always based on some fixed number of the most recent demand observations.

Consider, for example, the number of calls per month received by Rancho Ambulance Company in the table below. We can see that there doesn't appear to be any particular trend in the data. Also, one year of data is not enough to see if there is any recurring seasonal or cyclical pattern. It appears, though, that the fluctuations are just random.

Month	Calls (Demand)
Jan.	120
Feb.	90
Mar.	110
Apr.	130
May	100
June	90
July	110
Aug.	80
Sept.	100
Oct.	90
Nov.	120
Dec.	110

The demands listed above, of course, are not known until the end of each month. As we go through the year, then, we want to calculate an average based on the most recent data. In our first try we have arbitrarily chosen a 4-month moving average, starting by averaging the first four months of the year we are given. Using our data we have $(120 + 90 + 110 + 130)/4 = 550/4 = 112.5$. This average then becomes our forecast for month five (May). After May is over, we again calculate the average of the four most recent months. This time May's demand (100) is included, while January's (120) is dropped. The average of months 2–5 (February to May), then, becomes our forecast for month 6 (June). This process is continued for the rest of the year, with the results as shown.

Error Calculations

We have also calculated the values of our errors each month. These errors can then be used to compare different forecasting techniques to see which results in the smallest errors. The simplest calculation is the Mean Absolute Deviation (MAD), which is the average of the absolute values of the errors. This criterion is concerned only with the size of the errors, not whether they are positive or negative. The formula is:

$$MAD = \Sigma |A-F|/n,$$

where   A = actual demand in a time period
        F = forecast demand in a time period
        n = number of time periods

Another criterion is the mean squared error (MSE). By squaring the errors, we again get a positive number, and the larger errors are penalized more severely by the squaring process. The formula is:

$$MSE = \Sigma(A-F)^2/n$$

To see whether our forecasting process is unbiased, we can also calculate the mean forecast error (MFE) without the absolute values:

$$MFE = \Sigma(A-F)/n$$

An unbiased forecast should produce errors that average approximately 0. While some errors are positive and some are negative, there should be no consistent pattern of errors in either direction. Overall, they should cancel each other out and result in an average of 0. Of course, a small sample of errors cannot be expected to average exactly 0. A calculation called a "tracking signal" can be made at the end of each time period to see whether the errors are averaging close enough to 0 statistically. The tracking signal is the ratio of the sum of the forecast errors to the MAD at each point in time. If we have n time periods in our data set, then

$$\text{Tracking signal} = \frac{\text{Sum of forecasting errors}}{\text{MAD}} = \frac{n(\text{MFE})}{\text{MAD}}$$

If this tracking signal is between −4 and +4, then it is within approximately three standard deviations of the expected 0. If outside this range, there is almost certainly some kind of bias in our forecasting, and we will be consistently either too high or too low. In our table we have calculated the tracking signal only at the end of December although it could actually be calculated at the end of each month using the MFE and MAD up to that point.

4-MONTH MOVING AVERAGE

Month	A Actual Demand	F Forecast	(A−F)	|A−F|	(A−F)²
Jan.	120				
Feb.	90				
Mar.	110				
Apr.	130				
May	100	112.5	−12.5	12.5	156.25
June	90	107.5	−17.5	17.5	306.25
July	110	107.5	2.5	2.5	6.25
Aug.	80	107.5	27.5	27.5	756.25
Sept.	100	95.0	5.0	5.0	25.00
Oct.	90	95.0	−5.0	5.0	25.00
Nov.	120	95.0	25.0	25.0	625.00
Dec.	110	97.5	12.5	12.5	156.25
			−17.5	107.5	2056.25

$$\text{MAD} = \Sigma|A-F|/n = 107.5/8 = 13.44$$
$$\text{MSE} = \Sigma(A-F)^2/n = 2056.25/8 = 257.03$$
$$\text{MFE} = \Sigma(A-F)/n = -17.5/8 = -2.19$$
$$\text{Tracking Signal (Dec.)} = \Sigma(A-F)/\text{MAD} = -17.5/13.44 = -1.30$$

Our 4-month moving average results in an MAD of 13.44 and an MSE of 257.03 for the eight months where we made a forecast. Until we try some other forecasting techniques, we have no way of knowing whether these are good or bad. The MFE is −2.19, which seems fairly close to 0, and indeed the tracking signal at the end of December is −1.30, well within the acceptable range.

Changing the Number of Time Periods

We can try a moving average of as many time periods into the past as we would like. The more time periods are included, the more stable our forecast will be and the slower to change in response to new data. In other words, if we are averaging eight time periods, and each time we replace the oldest demand with a new demand, we still have seven of the same numbers out of eight, so the average won't change too much. If we prefer a forecasting model which responds quickly to changes, we should use a moving average with just a few time periods. We can't really know which moving average will work best unless we try out several and compare their errors on our past data. Therefore, we have tried a moving average of only two time periods in the past. This model will change very quickly in response to fluctuations in our demand. Of course, we could just use this month's demand as next month's forecast (in effect, a one-period moving average) at the extreme. Although we can start making forecasts from our data for March, we have only calculated errors starting in May to compare with our 4-month moving average.

2-MONTH MOVING AVERAGE

Month	A Actual Demand	F Forecast	(A−F)	|A−F|	(A−F)²
Jan.	120				
Feb.	90				
Mar.	110	105.0			
Apr.	130	100.0			
May	100	120.0	−20.0	20.0	400.00
June	90	115.0	−25.0	25.0	625.00
July	110	95.0	15.0	15.0	225.00
Aug.	80	100.0	−20.0	20.0	400.00
Sept.	100	95.0	5.0	5.0	25.00
Oct.	90	90.0	0.0	0.0	0.00
Nov.	120	95.0	25.0	25.0	625.00
Dec.	110	105.0	5.0	5.0	25.00
			−15.0	115.0	2325.00

$$\text{MAD} = \Sigma|A-F|/n = 115.0/8 = 14.38$$
$$\text{MSE} = \Sigma(A-F)^2/n = 2325.00/8 = 290.63$$
$$\text{MFE} = \Sigma(A-F)/n = -15.0/8 = -1.88$$
$$\text{Tracking Signal (Dec.)} = \Sigma(A-F)/\text{MAD} = -15.0/14.38 = -1.04$$

We can see that our forecasts using a 2-month moving average are much more volatile than those using a 4-month moving average. Overall, the MAD and MSE calculations turn out to be slightly worse than before. The MFE is slightly closer to 0, and the December tracking signal is a bit smaller than before. It appears that the 4-month moving average with its more stable forecast does a better job with this particular data set. We could continue to try other numbers of time periods to determine which gives us the best forecasts.

Exponential Smoothing

If we want a slightly more sophisticated method for forecasting a demand pattern that is basically flat, we can use exponential smoothing. We can view this method in several different ways. First, exponential smoothing can be seen as a method which continually updates the demand forecast by adding to the previous forecast some fraction of the most recent observed error. Viewed this way, the forecast formula can be expressed as:

$$F_{t+1} = F_t + \alpha(A_t - F_t)$$
where F_t = forecast for time period t

A_t = actual demand in time period t
α = smoothing constant (a fraction between 0 and 1)

Thus, our forecast for the next time period (t+1) is equal to our forecast for our current time period (which was made last time period), plus some fraction of the current error (which can be either positive or negative). If we set α at a fairly low number, such as .1, then our forecast will change very little from period to period. A high α, on the other hand, will cause our forecast to react quickly to the most recent data. In fact, if we set α at 1, then our next forecast is the same as this time period's actual demand, the same as a one-period moving average. Again we need to experiment with different values of α in order to find the one that minimizes our errors.

If we rearrange the terms of our exponential smoothing formula, we can see the exponential smoothing process in a different light:

$$F_{t+1} = F_t + \alpha A_t - \alpha F_t$$
$$= \alpha A_t + (1 - \alpha)F_t$$

This version of the formula shows the calculation as a balance between the latest actual demand and the previous forecast. The weights on these two terms, α and $(1 - \alpha)$, always add up to 1. Again we see that a larger α puts more weight on the most recent data and less weight on the previous forecast, which represents the past data.

Looking at the formula a third way, we realize that exponential smoothing forecasting is a recursive process. That is, next time period's forecast is based on this time period's forecast, which was based on last time period's forecast, and so on infinitely into the past. Below we have repeated the formula (second version) for the next time period's forecast and also the formula for the current time period's forecast, where the subscripts have just gone back one time period:

$$F_{t+1} = \alpha A_t + (1 - \alpha) F_t$$
$$F_t = \alpha A_{t-1} + (1 - \alpha)F_{t-1}$$

Substituting this second formula for F in the first formula, we have:

$$F_{t+1} = \alpha A_t + (1 - \alpha) (\alpha A_{t-1} + (1 - \alpha)F_{t-1})$$

If we keep repeating this process of substituting the formula for the previous forecast, we get this result:

$$F_{t+1} = \alpha A_t + \alpha(1-\alpha)A_{t-1} + \alpha(1-\alpha)^2 A_{t-2} + \alpha(1-\alpha)^3 A_{t-3} + \ldots$$
$$= \alpha(A_t + (1-\alpha)A_{t-1} + (1-\alpha)^2 A_{t-2} + (1-\alpha)^3 A_{t-3} + \ldots)$$

Now we can see that the exponential smoothing forecast is in fact an infinite series of weighted data points. The weights fall off exponentially as we go back into the past, each weighted a constant fraction $(1 - \alpha)$ of the next more recent weight. Here again we can see that a large α results in a forecast that heavily weights the more recent data. If $\alpha = .9$, the weights going back into the past are 1, .1, .01, and so on, before multiplying by α, or .9, .09, .009, and so on, after multiplying by α. Only the very recent data points have any significant weight at all. Similarly, if $\alpha = .1$, then $(1 - \alpha) = .9$, and the weights are 1, .9, .81, .729, and so on, before multiplying by α, or .1, .09, .081, .0729, and so on, after multiplying by α. In this case many past data points have significant weight. Generally, fairly low smoothing constants, in the range of .1 to .3, for example, are most common in order to provide some stability to the forecast.

Because of the fact that exponential smoothing theoretically requires an infinitely long list of past data, it is necessary to start with some arbitrary forecast. Then the succeeding forecast is based on the starting forecast, and so on. This arbitrary forecast can be an estimate of the overall average from past data, or it can just be set equal to the first time period's demand (so that there is no error in the first time period, and that forecast remains as the next forecast). Whatever initial forecast is used, its effects will be wiped out after a few time periods (depending on α), and further forecasts will be identical. Thus, error calculations should not include the first few time periods when the effects of the initial forecast are still felt.

Below we have tried an exponential smoothing model with a smoothing constant of .1 with our ambulance demand data. For our initial forecast for January we have arbitrarily chosen 100, a convenient number close to the overall average demand.

We can see that because of our small smoothing constant our resulting forecasts change very slowly. This stability has provided us a much better forecast than any other we have tried, as shown by its MAD of 11.2 and MSE of 176.47. Note that we have only included errors from May on in our error calculations. This procedure makes the error calculations comparable to those of the other models we have tried, and it also helps eliminate any effects of our arbitrary starting forecast of 100 in January. The errors of January through April are still shown in the table, though, to help illustrate the calculation of our forecasts. For example, if we use the first form of our exponential smoothing formula to calculate February's forecast, we have:

$$
\begin{aligned}
F_{t+1} &= F_t + \alpha \, (A_t - F_t) \\
&= 100.0 + (.1) \, (120 - 100) \\
&= 102.0
\end{aligned}
$$

EXPONENTIAL SMOOTHING, $\alpha = .1$

Month	A Actual Demand	F Forecast	$(A-F)$	$|A-F|$	$(A-F)^2$
Jan.	120	100.0	20.0		
Feb.	90	102.0	−12.0		
Mar.	110	100.8	9.2		
Apr.	130	101.7	28.3		
May	100	104.5	−4.5	4.5	20.25
June	90	104.1	−14.1	14.1	198.81
July	110	102.7	7.3	7.3	53.29
Aug.	80	103.4	−23.4	23.4	547.56
Sept.	100	101.1	−1.1	1.1	1.21
Oct.	90	101.0	−11.0	11.0	121.00
Nov.	120	99.9	20.1	20.1	404.01
Dec.	110	101.9	8.1	8.1	65.61
			−18.6	89.6	1411.74

MAD $= \Sigma|A-F|/n = 89.6/8 = 11.20$
MSE $= \Sigma(A-F)^2/n = 1411.74/8 = 176.47$
MFE $= \Sigma(A-F)/n = -18.6/8 = -2.33$
Tracking Signal (Dec.) $= \Sigma(A-F)/MAD = -18.6/11.20 = -1.66$

Our MFE and December tracking signal show a little more tendency toward negative errors, but they are still well within the acceptable range.

Changing the Smoothing Constant

To illustrate the effects of a large smoothing constant, we have recalculated our forecasts with $\alpha = .9$. Again we have used 100.0 as our initial forecast and have started our error calculations in May. The result for this particular data set is disastrous. Our forecasts swing violently back and forth in response to changes in the demands. Since our data sometimes seem to alternate between high and low demands, our forecasts are usually moving in the wrong direction. Thus, our MAD and MSE are much worse than any other forecasting model tried. At least the forecasts remain unbiased, as shown by the MFE and December tracking signal.

The Rancho Ambulance Company could continue trying different values of until they found one that minimized their errors. However, there is no guarantee that this, or any, time series technique will continue to provide the best forecasts without continually checking the errors over time.

EXPONENTIAL SMOOTHING, $\alpha = .9$

Month	A Actual Demand	F Forecast	(A−F)	|A−F|	(A−F)²
Jan.	120	100.0	20.0		
Feb.	90	118.0	−28.0		
Mar.	110	92.8	17.2		
Apr.	130	108.3	21.7		
May	100	127.8	−27.8	27.8	772.84
June	90	102.8	−12.8	12.8	163.84
July	110	91.3	18.7	18.7	349.69
Aug.	80	108.1	−28.1	28.1	789.61
Sept.	100	82.8	17.2	17.2	295.84
Oct.	90	98.3	−8.3	8.3	68.89
Nov.	120	90.8	29.2	29.2	852.64
Dec.	110	117.1	−7.1	7.1	50.41
			−19.0	149.2	3343.76

$$\text{MAD} = \Sigma \ |A-F|/n = 149.2/8 = 18.65$$
$$\text{MSE} = \Sigma \ (A-F)^2/n = 3343.76/8 = 417.97$$
$$\text{MFE} = \Sigma \ (A-F)/n = -19.0/8 = -2.38$$
$$\text{Tracking Signal (Dec.)} = \Sigma(A-F)/\text{MAD} = -19.0/18.65 = -1.02$$

Trend and Seasonal Components

Robo-Rover, Inc., is a company that produces mechanical pets. Naturally, the bulk of their business occurs near Christmas, with much less demand in the summer months. Besides this seasonal pattern, the company's demand has experienced steady upward growth over the past few years. The table below lists quarterly demands for Robo-Rover over the last three years. Several years of data are needed in order to determine whether there is any regular seasonal pattern each year. In order to sort out the upward trend component of the demand pattern from the seasonal fluctuations, we first need to deseasonalize our data. This is done by taking one year's worth of demands (4 quarters, 12 months, 52 weeks, or however the data are broken down) and calculating the average demand per period for that year. We then move ahead one time period and take the average of that one year's worth of data. This moving average must always extend exactly one year so that we include all the different seasonal effects, thus deseasonalizing our data. For example, our first average is quarters 1, 2, 3, and 4, and our next average is quarters 2, 3, 4, and 5 (which is quarter 1 of the second year). The average of the first four quarters is $(4.1 + 2.8 + 3.5 + 6.3)/4 = 16.7/4 = 4.175$, as shown in the table. We will not use this moving average as a forecast for the next time period as we did before; we simply calculate it to give a deseasonalized average for that one-year interval.

The deseasonalized averages do tend to fall very close to a straight line. Therefore, we can perform a linear regression of these deseasonalized averages versus the time periods around which they center. For example, quarters 1, 2, 3, and 4 are centered around 2.5, the average of the four numbers. The demand for that one-year interval, then, should be matched against the center of that interval, time 2.5.

ROBO-ROVER DEMAND DATA AND REGRESSION CALCULATIONS

		Deseasonalized			
X	Y				
Quarter	Demand (thous.)	X	Y	X^2	XY
1	4.1				
2	2.8				
3	3.5	2.5	4.175	6.25	10.4375
4	6.3	3.5	4.400	12.25	15.4000
5	5.0	4.5	4.525	20.25	20.3625
6	3.3	5.5	4.700	30.25	25.8500
7	4.2	6.5	4.825	42.25	31.3625
8	6.8	7.5	4.975	56.25	37.3125
9	5.6	8.5	5.100	72.25	43.3500
10	3.8	9.5	5.300	90.25	50.3500
11	5.0	10.5	5.500	110.25	57.7500
12	7.6	58.5	43.500	440.25	292.1750

A linear regression line has the following form:

$$\hat{Y} = a + bX$$
where   a = intercept on the Y-axis
          b = slope

Using the least-squares technique, we have the following formulas for the intercept and slope of the line that best fits our data points:

$$b = \frac{n\Sigma XY - \Sigma X\Sigma Y}{n\Sigma X^2 - (\Sigma X)^2}$$

$$a = \overline{Y} - b\overline{X} = \Sigma Y/n - b\Sigma X/n$$

From our calculations in the table we can determine the regression line:

$$b = \frac{(9)(292.175) - (58.5)(43.5)}{(9)(440.25) - (58.5)^2}$$

$$= \frac{2629.575 - 2544.75}{3962.25 - 3422.25}$$

$$= \frac{84.825}{540}$$

$$= .157$$

$$a = 43.5/9 - (.157)(58.5/9)$$

$$= 4.833 - 1.021$$

$$= 3.812$$

Our baseline, then, is $\hat{Y} = 3.812 + .157X$. This slope of .157 (thousands) per quarter does show a significant upward trend in our demand.

Next we would like to see just how much the 4 quarters vary from the baseline each year. This variation will be expressed by a *seasonal index*. There are two types of seasonal indexes which we might use, a multiplicative index and an additive index. A multiplicative index expresses the *ratio* of a given quarter's demand to the baseline, while an additive index expresses the *difference* from that quarter's demand to the baseline. If our pattern seems to indicate that, regardless of the overall level of demand, our seasonal variations maintain approximately the same distance from the baseline, we should use an additive index. However, in many cases when demand gets larger because of the trend in our data, the fluctuations increase proportionally. In that case a multiplicative index will work better. Most applications of seasonal indices, such as government reports, use a multiplicative index, so we will use that approach in our example.

INDEX CALCULATIONS

X Quarter	Y Demand (thous.)	$\hat{Y} = 3.812 + .157X$ Baseline	$Y/\hat{Y}$
1	4.1	3.969	1.033
2	2.8	4.126	.679
3	3.5	4.283	.817
4	6.3	4.440	1.419
5	5.0	4.597	1.088
6	3.3	4.754	.694
7	4.2	4.911	.855
8	6.8	5.068	1.342
9	5.6	5.225	1.072
10	3.8	5.382	.706
11	5.0	5.539	.902
12	7.6	5.696	1.334

Multiplicative Indices
Quarter 1: (1.033 + 1.088 + 1.072)/3 = 3.193/3 = 1.06
Quarter 2: (.679 + .694 + .706)/3 = 2.079/3 = .69
Quarter 3: (.817 + .855 + .902)/3 = 2.574/3 = .86
Quarter 4: (1.419 + 1.342 + 1.334)/3 = 4.095/3 = 1.37

In order to compare our actual demands each quarter to the baseline, we first calculate the baseline values for each quarter by plugging the quarter number into the regression line formula. Then for each quarter we have calculated the ratio of the actual demand to the baseline ($Y/\hat{Y}$). Our seasonal indices are calculated by averaging these ratios for the quarters appearing in the same position of each year (quarters 1, 5, and 9 are the first quarters of each year, quarters 2, 6, and 10 the second quarters, etc.). The four multiplicative indices should average approximately 1, since the average demand is on the baseline (a ratio of 1 to the baseline). Here we have an average index of 3.98/4 = .995.

Below we have used our regression line and multiplicative indices to calculate what the forecasts would have been for each of the 12 quarters. Then we have calculated the forecasting errors using MAD and MSE. While the resulting error calculations appear quite low, we must keep in mind the fact that these demand data were the ones we used to calculate the regression line and indices in the first place. Thus, it is no big surprise that the resulting forecasts fit the data rather well. To the extent that our trend and seasonal components are consistent from year to year, we will have quite small errors. The real test, of course, is to use this forecasting model on future data and then to calculate the errors.

ERRORS USING MULTIPLICATIVE INDICES

X Quarter	Y Demand	$\hat{Y}$ Baseline	I Index	F = ($\hat{Y}$)(I) Forecast	|Y−F|	(Y−F)²
1	4.1	3.969	1.06	4.21	.11	.0121
2	2.8	4.126	.69	2.85	.05	.0025
3	3.5	4.283	.86	3.68	.18	.0324
4	6.3	4.440	1.37	6.08	.22	.0484
5	5.0	4.597	1.06	4.87	.13	.0169
6	3.3	4.754	.69	3.28	.02	.0004
7	4.2	4.911	.86	4.22	.02	.0004
8	6.8	5.068	1.37	6.94	.14	.0196
9	5.6	5.225	1.06	5.54	.06	.0036
10	3.8	5.382	.69	3.71	.09	.0081
11	5.0	5.539	.86	4.76	.24	.0576
12	7.6	5.696	1.37	7.80	.20	.0400
					1.46	.2420

MAD = Σ\|Y−F\|/n = 1.46/12 = .12
MSE = Σ(Y−F)²/n = .2420/12 = .02

To make a forecast for the next year, we first extend our baseline four more quarters into the future (quarters 13–16), and then we apply the appropriate seasonal index to the baseline figure:

NEXT YEAR'S FORECASTS

Quarter	$\hat{Y} = 3.812 + .157X$ Baseline	I Index	$F = (\hat{Y})(I)$ Forecast
13	5.853	1.06	6.204
14	6.010	.69	4.147
15	6.167	.86	5.304
16	6.324	1.37	8.664

CORRELATIONAL MODEL

Regression with Variables Other Than Time

Meanwhile, back at the Rancho Ambulance Company, the owners were unhappy with the rather high errors remaining, even with the best of the time series models that they tried. The best MAD's obtained still represented about 10% of the typical monthly demand. Therefore, they hired a consultant, Amanda B. Reckonedwith, to study the situation. She felt that perhaps there was some other variable besides time that would have a closer relationship to the company's demands. She theorized that while many factors related to ambulance calls would remain fairly constant throughout the year, one factor that would vary would be the weather. After collecting data on such factors as temperature,

CORRELATIONAL MODEL

Month	X Rainfall (in.)	Y Demand	X^2	XY	Y^2
Jan.	4.3	120	18.49	516	14400
Feb.	2.0	90	4.00	180	8100
Mar.	4.0	110	16.00	440	12100
Apr.	4.8	130	23.04	624	16900
May	3.0	100	9.00	300	10000
June	1.7	90	2.89	153	8100
July	3.6	110	12.96	396	12100
Aug.	0.5	80	.25	40	6400
Sept.	2.8	100	7.84	280	10000
Oct.	2.4	90	5.76	216	8100
Nov.	4.0	120	16.00	480	14400
Dec.	3.5	110	12.25	385	12100
	36.6	1250	128.48	4010	132700

rainfall, and wind speed, she compared these figures to demand. She was pleasantly surprised when she examined the relationship between monthly rainfall and ambulance calls.

Because of the apparent strong linear relationship between the monthly rainfall in inches and the number of ambulance calls, Amanda used a linear regression model. From these figures the regression line parameters are:

$$b = \frac{n \, \Sigma XY - \Sigma X \, \Sigma Y}{n \, \Sigma X^2 - (\Sigma X)^2}$$

$$= \frac{(12)(4010) - (36.6)(1250)}{(12)(128.48) - (36.6)^2}$$

$$= \frac{48,120 - 45,750}{1541.76 - 1339.56}$$

$$= \frac{2370}{202.2}$$

$$= 11.72$$

$$a = \overline{Y} - b\overline{X}$$

$$= 1250/12 - (11.72)(36.6/12)$$

$$= 104.17 - (11.72)(3.05)$$

$$= 104.17 - 35.75$$

$$= 68.42$$

Our regression line is then $\hat{Y} = 68.42 + 11.72X$. While our data show what looks like a very strong linear relationship between the two variables, we would like a quantitative measure of this relationship. One useful measure would be the coefficient of correlation (r). For our model using rainfall we have the following calculation:

$$r = \frac{n \, \Sigma XY - \Sigma X \, \Sigma Y}{\sqrt{(n \, \Sigma X^2 - (\Sigma X)^2)(n\Sigma Y^2 - (\Sigma Y)^2)}}$$

$$= \frac{2370}{\sqrt{(202.2)((12)(132,700) - (1250)^2)}}$$

$$= \frac{2370}{\sqrt{(202.2)(1,592,400 - 1,562,500)}}$$

$$= \frac{2370}{\sqrt{(202.2)(29,900)}}$$

$$= \frac{2370}{2458.8}$$

$$= .964$$

Note that the numerator and first half of the denominator of r are the same as the numerator and denominator of b which we calculated earlier.

Correlation coefficients range from -1 to $+1$, with -1 and $+1$ being perfect correlations with negative and positive slopes, respectively. Our correlation here is close to a perfect positive correlation between rainfall and ambulance calls. We can also calculate r^2, the coefficient of determination. This coefficient tells us what proportion of the variability in our dependent variable, demand, can be explained by our independent variable, rainfall. Here our coefficient of determination is $r^2 = (.964)^2 = .93$. Therefore, 93% of the variability in ambulance calls can be explained by the rainfall that month, leaving only 7% of our variability unexplained. By comparison, if we calculate our coefficient of determination for our time series regression model, we obtain a value of r^2 of only .02, showing virtually no correlation between our demand and time.

For this reason it appears that our correlational model using rainfall will do a very good job in forecasting our demand. The only problem is in obtaining an accurate forecast of the coming month's rainfall to plug into our forecasting model. If we knew, for example, that next month's rainfall would be 3.0 inches, we would forecast our demand as follows:

$$\hat{Y} = 68.42 + 11.72X$$
$$= 68.42 + (11.72)\,(3.0)$$
$$= 68.42 + 35.16$$
$$= 103.58$$

Multiple Regression

If we can't find a single variable with a high correlation to our demand, perhaps we can find a group of variables that together can explain most of the variability in our demand. Multiple regression models are of the form $\hat{Y} = a + b_1X_1 + b_2X_2 + \ldots + b_nX_n$. In constructing such a model the object is to find a fairly small group of variables that have a high multiple coefficient of determination (R^2) and that are not highly correlated among themselves. The process of stepwise multiple regression, commonly available on statistical software packages, first forms a model with one independent variable with the greatest correlation to the dependent variable, then adds another variable that increases R^2 the most, and so on, until adding further variables no longer results in significant increases in R^2. In implementing such a multiple regression model our main concern is in obtaining accurate data for the independent variables to put into our forecast equation. Therefore, the number and exact nature of these variables is important.

CHAPTER 7

Aggregate Planning

OVERVIEW

Having obtained a medium-range forecast of demand, a manufacturing company would like to determine a plan for its total production for the next year or so. This plan will have definite effects on the firm's personnel policies, including hiring, layoffs, and overtime work, as well as on the space and equipment required to produce the desired level of output throughout the year. To some extent, service-oriented firms face a similar problem even though they are not producing a physical product. They do not have to worry about having the proper amount of production equipment, but they do need to plan for inventory and staffing levels throughout the year, depending on their demand. Therefore, many of the same techniques are appropriate to attack the problem for both types of firms.

A firm's aggregate demand consists of the total demand for its goods and/or services throughout the planning horizon (usually one year). Some firms that produce a variety of products will find it necessary to convert the various products into a standard kind of unit, sometimes called a "pseudoproduct," in order to determine their total production requirements. One way to handle this problem is simply to determine the number of labor hours required to produce each product and then to express demands in terms of labor hours rather than units of products.

After expressing the various demands in a common type of unit, the firm will need to put them together to form an aggregate demand. A "bottom-up" approach may be used, where demands are forecast separately for all products and then combined. The total requirements for labor and equipment may then be compared to the available capacity. If the aggregate demand exceeds the firm's total capacity, some adjustments will then need to be sent back "down" re-garding the individual products' production quantities. A "top-down" approach to aggregate planning would start with the firm's total capacity and then deter-mine the appropriate mix of individual products that would best meet the firm's goals within that limitation.

The Problem

The trouble in aggregate planning is that a firm's aggregate demand is gen-erally not constant throughout the year. That is, the forecast for the coming year may very well have a significant seasonal component. Almost any consumer product that one can think of is at least somewhat seasonal. Some industries have a traditional yearly calendar, such as the automobile industry with its new models introduced each September, or the fabric industry with its annual "white sales." Many products are seasonal by their very nature, such as clothing and sporting goods. Even producers of raw materials and parts often experience significant seasonality in their demands. Therefore, a firm is unable to plan a constant production level in many cases and must find some way to meet the changing demands throughout the year. The ways that a firm might attempt to do this may be classified broadly as either "smoothing strategies" or "adaptive strategies."

Smoothing Strategies

Smoothing strategies are those that seek to change the firm's total demand in order to make it smoother, less seasonal. Thus, the firm will be able to plan a more constant production level throughout the year. One strategy might be to change the company's mix of products in such a way that different products have peak demands at different times of the year. For example, a manufacturer of snow skis might very well produce water skis as well. While such a strategy of "countercyclical" products has obvious appeal, the company is limited by its total capacity, its financial resources, and its technical expertise. Many com-panies have carefully defined "what business we're in" and are justifiably re-luctant to stray very far from that definition.

A firm might prefer to attempt to influence the demands for its existing prod-ucts. Special promotions and price reductions can help to raise demand during slack periods, while raising prices might even be considered during heavy de-mand periods.

Such strategies can help a great deal in smoothing out aggregate demand, but these strategies are not really the responsibility of operations managers. Top managers of the firm must make the decision regarding the product mix; mar-keting managers are largely responsible for promotion and pricing decisions.

Adaptive Strategies

Therefore, of most interest to operations managers are the adaptive strategies of reacting *to* the seasonal fluctuations of demand. The operations manager must try to accommodate whatever seasonality remains as cheaply as possible. Each type of adaptive strategy will incur costs beyond what the company could achieve if demand were smooth. Thus, it is up to the operations manager to find the strategy or mix of strategies that will minimize this extra cost.

One strategy for accommodating the seasonal demands is simply to ignore them and to produce at a constant rate throughout the year. By maintaining a steady labor force, the company will help to maintain good relations with organized labor and will also ease the burdens of the personnel department. At the same time, short-term production planning and supervisory loads will be reduced as compared to a constantly changing schedule. These effects will show up as real cost savings. On the other hand, maintaining a constant production in the face of fluctuating demands means that these fluctuations must be absorbed by inventory. That is, when demands are low, inventory stock will build up. When demands increase, inventories will be used up and may even run into a stockout or back order situation. Large buildups of inventory can strain building capacities and can cause significant extra costs. These costs of holding inventory will be described in more detail in Chapter 8, but it is obvious that there are costs associated with physically storing and handling inventory, as well as the more subtle opportunity costs of holding inventory. At the same time, there are costs associated with running out of inventory. While difficult to measure, the costs associated with dissatisfied customers, extra paperwork on back orders, and the disruption of schedules for catch-up work are quite real.

The opposite approach would be to try to match the fluctuating demand by varying production. There are several ways a company might do this. Probably the least disruptive would be for the workers to work overtime during heavy demand periods. In some situations workers may be eager to earn extra money; in others they may prefer not to work any overtime. If the company is unionized, the union may have the power to help determine the amount of overtime allowable. In any case, if a company uses an overtime strategy, it will have to pay an overtime bonus, and productivity may not be as good as usual because of such factors as fatigue. Similarly, in some operations systems it may be possible to work undertime (shorter work weeks or forced unpaid vacations) when demand is lower. However, most workers would oppose having to work less and receive less pay. Some might quit in order to find steadier work.

Another method of varying production would be hiring and laying off workers as needed. Here again, though, there are extra costs involved. The process of selecting and training workers is costly, and their productivity may not be as good as experienced workers for a while. Also, when a worker is laid off, there are generally benefits that must be paid, as well as the less tangible chilling effect on labor relations.

A method of varying total production without affecting the workers very much would be the use of subcontracting. When demand is too heavy for the system's capacity, some of it could be sent to a subcontractor. When sending work out, though, the firm must pay for the subcontractor's profit, and the subcontractor may not be as cost-efficient in producing that product as is the firm itself. The subcontractor also may not adhere to the same quality standards as the firm. Another drawback is the real possibility that similar firms are experiencing peak demands at the same time and are thus unable to help out by taking in subcontracting. For example, a large defense contractor may find it difficult to send out work during a period when the government is spending more on defense in general.

When demand is low, work could be accepted from a company with heavy demand. However, when taking in work, the firm may well be doing work for which it is not quite as efficient.

Therefore, no matter which strategy a company might use, it will incur costs beyond its usual costs of production. It is the job of operations management, then, to find the strategy or combination of strategies that will minimize these extra costs.

Service Operations

It may seem strange to think of service operations using aggregate planning techniques, but they also often have the problem of seasonal demands for their services. While not all of the strategies mentioned will necessarily be applicable, some of them can still be used to meet these seasonal demands.

For example, consider a small accounting firm. With tax season and quarterly statements to produce, the work is quite seasonal. A firm may decide to hire temporary workers for tax season, or it may prefer to use overtime. It may subcontract out some of its tax work to less established accountants. It may elect to have a "stockout" by filing for extensions on tax returns. While it is difficult to stockpile services, it may even produce "inventory" of a sort by working early on returns for its regular clients or by preparing standardized forms on its computer system to help cut down the work later. Certainly, an accounting firm could pursue some of the smoothing strategies mentioned also, such as diversifying the services it provides or raising its fees for tax clients.

Solution Techniques

Because of the complexity of the aggregate planning problem and because of the different conditions in different firms, no single quantitative model will always be applicable. Linear programming can be used to determine an optimal solution in cases where all the costs are linear functions. Other theorists have developed specialized mathematical models that work well under certain conditions.

Where the situation is complex enough or unusual enough that the standard quantitative models do not fit well, or when these models are simply not available, the operations manager can still use an iterative approach to zero in on a good, though not necessarily optimal, solution. In the following sections, an example problem will be attacked with the iterative approach, and the resulting solution will be compared to the linear programming solution.

ITERATIVE APPROACH

In the following example problem, it is assumed that the relevant cost, demand, and productivity figures are available and reasonably accurate. However, in a real situation these numbers may not be so easy to determine with any confidence. The cost figures will all necessarily involve some assumptions, as will the productivity figures. The demands must either be forecast approximately a year in advance or be based to some extent on an existing backlog of orders. In either case it is unlikely that they will be completely accurate. Nevertheless, we must use all of these figures as if they were certain; further analysis can show the sensitivity of our final solution to any changes in numbers that we might want to explore.

Demands are forecast for six 2-month periods, as shown in the table below. It is evident that the company has a very seasonal demand pattern, ranging from a low of 850 units per period to a high of 1850. Each worker is assumed to produce 36 units per period during regular working hours and up to 9 more units per period in overtime. (In this example the 2-month time periods are assumed to contain an equal number of working days. A more detailed analysis might consider the actual calendar of the coming year.)

The holding cost of inventory is $1.50 per unit per period based on ending inventory (as a good approximation of average inventory). If the company desires a certain amount of safety stock at the end of each period, we will not include those units in our inventory figures—the holding cost of this safety stock is fixed. Any desired *changes* in safety stock from period to period are assumed to be included in the projected demand figures. A negative ending inventory will incur a stockout cost of $5.00 per unit due to dissatisfied customers and extra paperwork. Any negative inventory will be carried into the next time period as a back order; that is, the sales will not be lost. It is possible to subcontract work at an additional cost of $3.00 beyond the normal production cost, while overtime work costs an extra $10.00 per unit. The costs of selecting and training a new worker total $200 per person, and the costs of laying off a worker are $250 per person.

Our objective will be to minimize the total of the above extra costs for the coming year. It is not necessary to include the regular cost of production; this is a fixed amount as long as our total annual production is always equal to our total demand. The costs given are all expressed as the increases above the normal cost of production. Our procedure will be to examine first several extreme, or "pure," strategies where we just try one policy at a time. From these pure strategies we hope to learn enough to enable us to combine strategies and further decrease our cost. We can steer our analysis in promising directions simply by comparing the various per-unit costs, but we will almost surely need to try out some alternatives to see how many units these costs will apply to.

PROJECTED DEMANDS

Time Period	Demand
1	1850
2	1425
3	1000
4	850
5	1150
6	1850

Constant Production

We assume that the year will begin with 0 inventory (exclusive of any safety stock) and also end with 0 inventory. All alternatives must follow these constraints to be comparable. Otherwise one alternative would produce a different total number of units than another, contrary to our assumption that the basic production cost for the year is constant. Also, if we assume that the same cycle of demands repeats each year, any positive or negative ending inventory at the end of the year would cause a built-in increase or decrease each year into the future. Thus, we will always produce a yearly total equal to the total projected demand, 8125 units in this case. The average demand per period, 1354.17, will be our constant production amount. For ease of calculation we will use a whole number of 1354 units per period, correcting with 1355 in period 6 to account for the accumulated rounding error. The difference in cost that this causes will be minuscule.

CONSTANT PRODUCTION STRATEGY

Period	Beg. Inv.	Production	Available	Demand	End. Inv.
1	0	1354	1354	1850	(496)
2	(496)	1354	858	1425	(567)
3	(567)	1354	787	1000	(213)
4	(213)	1354	1141	850	291
5	291	1354	1645	1150	495
6	495	1355	1850	1850	0

Extra Costs:

Holding costs—(786 units)($1.50/unit) = $1179
Stockout costs—(1276 units) ($5.00/unit) = $6380
Total = $7559

The costs associated with positive or negative inventories are the only costs incurred in this alternative. Note that if we had started this policy of constant production in some time period other than period 1, we would have experienced a completely different set of inventory figures. For example, if we start in period 3 from a beginning inventory of 0 and end the year in period 2 (next year), we would see a fairly large buildup of inventory early in the year, with no stockouts at all. Since holding cost is much cheaper than stockout cost per unit, this alternative turns out to be much cheaper overall, with a total extra cost of only $4365. However, the best time period to start with turns out to be period 2— with a small stockout in the first period and relatively small positive inventories the rest of the year, the total extra cost comes out to only $4189. Thus, if a company has a demand pattern that repeats with no change from year to year, it should consider starting such a constant production strategy in each possible time period to determine which would be the cheapest. This same analysis could also be applied to other strategies; to avoid a large increase in the complexity of our example, though, we will restrict our alternatives to those beginning with period 1. In many situations there may not be a choice as to when to start the cycle, anyway.

Hire and Fire to Meet Demand

This strategy is the opposite extreme from alternative 1. This time there will be no extra inventories at all, only changes in production through hiring and firing.

HIRE AND FIRE TO MEET DEMAND

Period	Beg. Inv.	Production	Available	Demand	End. Inv.	Chg. in Prod.
1	0	1850	1850	1850	0	0
2	0	1425	1425	1425	0	(425)
3	0	1000	1000	1000	0	(425)
4	0	850	850	850	0	(150)
5	0	1150	1150	1150	0	300
6	0	1850	1850	1850	0	700

Extra Costs:

> Hiring cost—(1000 units increase)/(36 units per person) = 27.77 workers hired
> (27.77 workers)($200/worker) = $5556
> Firing cost—(1000 units decrease)/(36 units per person) = 27.77 workers fired
> (27.77 workers) ($250/worker) = 6944
> Total = $12,500

There are several points worth noting in the above calculations. First, it should be obvious that the number of people hired must equal the number fired throughout the year in order to return to the same level of production at which we started (assuming that the cycle repeats). In this problem the production in period 6 is the same as that in period 1. However, this is merely a coincidence. If period 6 demand (from the previous year) had been some other number, we would have incurred a production change in period 1, rather than 0 as here. Second, we are assuming that fractions of a worker hired or fired represent part-time workers and are therefore acceptable in our calculations; the hiring and firing costs are assumed to be proportional. We are also assuming that we are able to increase or decrease our work force without limitations of space or union objections. In some situations a worker who is laid off may return during the next hiring cycle. In these cases the hiring cost may be reduced; however, this effect should be included in our average hiring cost figure. Finally, we notice that the total extra cost of this alternative is quite a bit worse than that of Alternative 1. Hiring and firing does not appear to be a very effective strategy compared to constant production.

Constant Low Production with Subcontracting

We can avoid the costs of hiring and firing as well as the costs of inventory by producing at a constant low level and making up the difference in demand through either subcontracting or overtime work. In this problem the cost of overtime is much higher than that of subcontracting, so we can eliminate an overtime alternative immediately. The least we would ever consider producing each period would be 850, our lowest demand. If we were to produce at any lower level, we would just have to pay an extra subcontracting cost each time period. We are assuming that our subcontractor can absorb quite a bit of work from us when needed and will be willing to go along with our quite variable demands for subcontracting.

CONSTANT LOW PRODUCTION WITH SUBCONTRACTING

Period	Beg. Inv.	Units Produced	Units Subcon.	Available	Demand	End. Inv.
1	0	850	1000	1850	1850	0
2	0	850	575	1425	1425	0
3	0	850	150	1000	1000	0
4	0	850	0	850	850	0
5	0	850	300	1150	1150	0
6	0	850	1000	1850	1850	0
			3025			

Extra Costs:

Subcontracting cost—(3025 units)($3/unit) = $9075

This alternative shows some improvement over the cost of hiring and firing, but it is still more costly than simply producing a constant amount equal to the average demand. Also, it would be an unusual situation to be subcontracting more than the company produces itself during some time periods.

Alternatives 1, 2, and 3 are the only reasonable extreme strategies available to the company, since overtime is clearly too expensive. At this point, then, we should stop to see what we have learned from these extreme strategies. In this cost structure, constant production has some definite advantages. The $1.50 per unit cost of holding inventory for one period and the $5.00 per unit stockout cost turn out to be cheap compared to the costs of hiring and firing. The $3.00 per unit extra cost of subcontracting is also fairly small but larger than the holding cost for one time period. However, the constant production strategy sometimes builds up inventory over several periods so that the holding cost is incurred several times. In other words, a little subcontracting might be able to prevent several periods of holding inventory. In this situation, then, it might be a beneficial trade-off to allow a little subcontracting during the early time periods in order to save on holding costs. This leads us to our first mixed strategy.

Constant Production of 1000 with Subcontracting

If we increase our constant production amount to 1000, our second-lowest demand, we will reduce our subcontracting by 150 units per time period while experiencing a holding cost in only one time period (period 4). This would appear to be an excellent trade-off.

CONSTANT PRODUCTION OF 1000 WITH SUBCONTRACTING

Period	Beg. Inv.	Units Produced	Units Subcon.	Available	Demand	End. Inv.
1	0	1000	850	1850	1850	0
2	0	1000	425	1425	1425	0
3	0	1000	0	1000	1000	0
4	0	1000	0	1000	850	150
5	150	1000	0	1150	1150	0
6	0	1000	850	1850	1850	0
			2125			150

Extra Costs:

Subcontracting cost—(2125 units)($3/unit) = $6375
Holding cost—(150 units) ($1.50/unit) = $225
Total = $6600

This mixed strategy gives us our lowest cost yet. We reduced our subcontracting by 900 units (150/period for 6 periods), saving ourselves $2700 in subcontracting costs. Holding cost was incurred on only 150 units for one time period, an increase of only $225.

Given the success of strategy 4, we would next consider increasing our constant production amount again in order to further decrease our subcontracting costs. For example, if we increased our production to 1150 units, our third smallest demand, we would be overproducing in only two time periods (3 and 4). However, we have to wonder just how far we can keep increasing our production without again incurring large holding costs through inventories being carried throughout several time periods. Certainly, if we raise our production to 1354, we are back to producing all we need ourselves with no subcontracting at all, as in strategy 1. Therefore, it seems reasonable to assume that some constant production amount between 1000 (strategy 4) and 1354 (strategy 1) will be best.

From our table above we see that any increase in production in periods 1 and 2 will result in offsetting reductions in subcontracting, and the ending inventory will remain at 0. However, for the next few periods inventory will build up. Whatever inventory has been built up through period 5 will be met by a decrease in subcontracting in period 6 in order to end the year at 0 inventory. Therefore, we will be trading reductions in subcontracting costs in periods 1, 2, and 6 for increases in holding costs the other periods.

In determining how far we can increase our production in this way, the key constraint is that our buildup of inventory through period 5, plus our increase in production in period 6, can be no more than the 850 we are currently subcontracting in period 6. Otherwise, we would come out with an inventory above 0. In the table below we have shown the effects of increasing our production by a quantity X above our previous alternative.

EFFECTS OF INCREASED PRODUCTION WITH SUBCONTRACTING

Period	Beg. Inv.	Units Produced	Units Subcon.	Available	Demand	End. Inv.
1	0	1000+X	850−X	1850	1850	0
2	0	1000+X	425−X	1425	1425	0
3	0	1000+X	0	1000+X	1000	X
4	X	1000+X	0	1000+2X	850	150+2X
5	150+2X	1000+X	0	1150+3X	1150	3X
6	3X	1000+X	0	1000+4X	1850	0

Constant Production of 1212 with Subcontracting

We can see that if we increase our production enough to reduce our subcontracting in period 6 to 0, we must have 1000+4X equal to 1850 to make our final inventory 0. Thus, 4X = 850. This result seems intuitively correct because after offsetting our increased production in the first two periods with reduced subcontracting, we experienced a buildup of X units per period for the next four periods. This buildup will be offset by eliminating the 850 units currently being subcontracted in period 6. We determine X, then, to be 212.5 units of increase in production. We will use a whole number of 1212 units per period, with an adjustment to 1214 in period 6 to make up for accumulated rounding errors.

CONSTANT PRODUCTION OF 1212 WITH SUBCONTRACTING

Period	Beg. Inv.	Units Produced	Units Subcon.	Available	Demand	End. Inv.
1	0	1212	638	1850	1850	0
2	0	1212	213	1425	1425	0
3	0	1212	0	1212	1000	212
4	212	1212	0	1424	850	574
5	574	1212	0	1786	1150	636
6	636	1214	0	1850	1850	0
			851			1422

Extra Costs:

Holding costs—(1422 units) ($1.50/unit) = $2133
Subcontracting costs—(851 units) ($3/unit) = $2553
Total = $4686

This alternative is the cheapest of all that we have tried. While we are not sure that it is optimal, we do know that it is a very good solution, much better than any of the "pure" strategies. We have not tried every possible set of numbers, but we have found a promising mixed strategy after studying the extreme strategies, and we carried that mixed strategy to its logical conclusion with the aid of a little algebra.

Every aggregate planning problem will have its own unique cost structure and its own pattern of demands. However, this iterative method of analysis should generally lead to a very good solution with a little thought.

LINEAR PROGRAMMING APPROACH

The preceding example problem lends itself to solution by a linear programming model because of the fact that all costs and all constraints are linear functions of the variables of the problem. This will be seen in the following formulation of the problem as a linear programming problem.

Formulation

Variables

With the subscript i representing the time period, let

W_i = number of workers in period i

PW_i = positve change in workers in period i (hirings)

NW_i = negative change in workers in period i (firings)

SC_i = units subcontracted in period i

OT_i = units produced in overtime in period i

PBI_i = positive beginning inventory in period i

NBI_i = negative beginning inventory in period i

D_i = demand in period i

The demands are not really variables but rather constants identified here by D_i as a general notation. Note that it is not necessary to list variables for ending inventories because the ending inventory of one time period is the beginning inventory of the next. Also, it is necessary to split the beginning inventories into two variables, since linear programming variables are assumed to be nonnegative. Therefore, a negative inventory must be represented by a positive variable which appears with a negative sign in front of it in a constraint. That is, the beginning inventory of a time period is represented by the expression (PBI_i $-NBI_i$). For any given time period at least one of the two variables must be 0, as there cannot be both a positive and a negative inventory simultaneously.

Note also that we have expressed our production here in terms of the number of workers rather than the number of units produced. The production in a given time period is equal to $36W_i$ since each worker can produce 36 units per period. Defining production in terms of workers will make it easier to count the number of workers hired and fired between periods.

Objective Function

The objective in this problem is simply to minimize the extra costs given. The objective function, then, will just calculate costs in the same way that we have done for our earlier alternatives:

$$\text{Min } Z = 200 \ \Sigma PW_i + 250 \ \Sigma NW_i + 3 \ \Sigma SC_i + 10 \ \Sigma OT_i + 1.50 \ \Sigma PBI_i + 5 \ \Sigma NBI_i$$

Note that the number of workers does not appear in the objective function because we are just minimizing *extra* costs, and the total cost of wages to workers for regular production of 8125 units is a constant.

Constraints

We need to tie the variables together so that they agree with each other through constraints. Thus, one type of constraint simply expresses the arithmetic that we performed within each row of our inventory tables:

$$PBI_i - NBI_i + 36W_i + SC_i + OT_i - D_i = PBI_{i+1} - NBI_{i+1}$$

This constraint starts with the beginning inventory, adds the three possible types of production (regular, subcontracting, and overtime) to give the number of units available, and then subtracts the demand to give the ending inventory, or next period's beginning inventory. There will be one such constraint for each time period, or six in this problem. Note that in a traditional linear programming formulation the demand, which is a constant, would be put on the right-hand side of the constraint, and next period's beginning inventory, a variable, would be moved to the left-hand side.

A second type of constraint (which we never had to worry about in our trial-and-error analysis) is the limitation of overtime in each period. Each worker could produce no more than nine units per period in overtime. The following constraints express this limitation:

$$OT_i \leq 9W_i$$

Again there would be six such constraints, one for each time period, and again the worker variable could be moved to the left-hand side for a more traditional linear programming formulation.

A final type of constraint is more subtle. We need to tie together the number of workers each period with the number of hirings and firings. Otherwise the model would change the number of workers without ever charging us for the hirings and firings. Thus, for each time period we need the following constraint:

$$W_i + PW_{i+1} - NW_{i+1} = W_{i+1}$$

These six constraints could also move the worker variable to the left-hand side in order to have all variables on the left.

Solution

Considering all six time periods, then, we have a linear programming model with 42 variables and 18 constraints. While not a huge problem, it is certainly much too large to solve by hand. The table on the following page shows the computer solution of this problem.

Extra Costs:

Holding costs—(1170 units)($1.50/unit) = $1,755
Stockout costs—(170 units)($5.00/unit) = $850
Subcontracting costs—(595 units)($3.00/unit) = $1,785
Total = $4,390

The optimal solution is only $296 cheaper than our best trial-and-error so-

OPTIMAL LINEAR PROGRAMMING SOLUTION

Period	Beg. Inv.	Units Produced	Units Subcon.	Available	Demand	End. Inv.
1	0	1255	595	1850	1850	0
2	0	1255	0	1255	1425	(170)
3	(170)	1255	0	1085	1000	85
4	85	1255	0	1340	850	490
5	490	1255	0	1745	1150	595
6	595	1255	0	1850	1850	0

lution. This solution, like ours, uses a constant production strategy. However, by allowing a stockout in period 2, several periods' holding costs are reduced. This is a trade-off that we never considered, and indeed it would have been very difficult for us ever to see this possibility.

The linear programming approach, then, can be very useful if the problem lends itself to that model. In some more complicated problems with stepwise or quadratic cost functions, a more sophisticated model incorporating integer or quadratic programming is needed.

PART III

Short-Run Decisions

Assuming that we have designed an efficient operating system and have done some accurate and careful planning, we turn now to the problems of keeping things under control. The one thing we can be sure of is that things will not go as we have planned them. Workers will be absent, machines will break down, supplies will not arrive on time, demands will vary, defective products will be produced, and so on. Therefore, most organizations of any size will have several staff groups to help the line managers with short-run planning and control decisions.

Probably the area that receives the most attention in books, in professional organizations, and in businesses themselves is inventory planning and control. The reason for this concern is that the costs of inventory can be substantial, especially in large companies, and they can make a big difference in a company's profitability. Here is one area where an operations manager can really make a difference for the company. Different types of operations systems require different approaches in inventory management. Also, the fact that several new advances in inventory control have been made recently gives the operations manager a wide variety of tools and techniques to choose from in attempting to control inventory costs.

Besides inventory management, the hottest topic in controlling operations is probably quality control. While the theory has not changed all that much over the years, there have been major shifts in emphasis and implementation. Since quality has recently become a major marketing tool, as well as an operations problem, it has been receiving much more attention. Here again it has come to the point where firms in some industries (such as electronics) simply cannot exist any longer without strict attention to quality control.

Besides these two glamor areas of short-run decision-making, we have the equally necessary area of production scheduling and control. The main concern of most line managers is the day-to-day managing of people, materials, and equipment. As demands come in which are different from those forecast, a constant rejuggling of the schedule is necessary. Again, different types of systems experience this problem to different extents. The more repetitive, process-oriented systems will change their schedules only very slowly, while job shops need to adapt constantly to new orders. For this reason we will focus primarily on scheduling in a job shop system.

A special case in the area of production scheduling and control is the planning and control of large, one-time projects. For such projects as large construction projects or aerospace projects, accurate planning and tight control of materials, labor, and overhead are necessary to prevent the cost overruns we read so much about. We will look at some basic models to help in this project planning and control.

CHAPTER 8

Inventory Models for Independent Demand

OVERVIEW

A manufacturing operation (and even some service operations) may have thousands of inventory items—raw materials, work in process, and finished goods. The decisions to be made regarding each of these items are how much to order or to produce and when to order or start producing the items. The quantities ordered or produced and the timing of these orders or production runs will determine the average amount of that item held in inventory, the frequency of orders or production runs, and the probability of running out of the item. As we shall see, each of these occurrences has a cost attached to it. The object of inventory control is to minimize these costs.

Why, then, do we have inventories in the first place? Wouldn't it be better just to order or to produce exactly what we need when we need it? Even in the impossible situation where our demands are perfectly known and our production system runs without a hitch, there may be some advantages to holding inventory. Ordering in large quantities often allows us to receive a quantity discount, which may more than offset the cost of the extra inventory. Also, in the real world where demands fluctuate and lead times (the times it takes to receive an order from a supplier) are uncertain, inventories can help absorb these fluctuations and avoid a stockout (running out of stock). We have seen in our aggregate planning problems that inventories can help overcome seasonal fluctuations, and the same principle applies to short-range fluctuations in demand and lead time. Finally, inventories can help to ''decouple'' different steps of a production process. One step is not so dependent on the previous step if there is a stock of inventory to draw from. Thus, the demands and lead times we refer to here are not necessarily external; internal demands and lead times also apply between steps of a production process.

All of this is not to suggest, however, that large inventories are normally preferred. In fact, just the opposite is the typical case—the situations mentioned above show that *sometimes* we want *some* inventory. The Japanese have popularized the concept of Just-in-Time (JIT) inventory management. The goal of such programs is to reduce inventory as far as possible in order to save on inventory holding costs. This idea makes sense in operations systems that are highly repetitive and where the costs of setting up a new production run or placing another order are very small. We will discuss this concept in more detail in Chapter 10.

Costs Associated with Inventory Control

There are several types of costs that go into our overall inventory cost which we would like to minimize. We have seen some of these costs in our aggregate planning models. First, and most obvious, is the *holding cost*, or *carrying cost*, of inventory. This is the cost of having inventory items on hand. Actually, there are several costs associated with holding inventories. Physical storage and handling costs would include the warehouse space or other space required for storage, the costs of heating and lighting such space, the labor costs of the workers involved in receiving, placing, moving, and retrieving inventory from storage, and the costs of any machinery involved in handling inventory, such as forklift trucks and conveyors.

There are also several less obvious types of holding costs, such as the costs of taxes and insurance for items held in inventory. Sometimes items held in inventory over a period of time become obsolete because of new technology or changes in product design. Also, some items such as food are subject to spoilage while sitting in inventory. Damage and even theft of inventory items add to holding costs. Probably the major holding cost in most cases, though, is not even an out-of-pocket cost, but rather the opportunity cost of holding inventory. Any items held in inventory had to be either purchased or produced, and that required an expenditure of money, which is now unavailable to the company. If that money were available, it could be used to pay off debts, invest in new profit-making projects, or simply to earn interest in the bank. Thus, especially when the cost of capital is high, this opportunity cost can be a large chunk of the overall holding cost.

With all of these holding costs to consider, it is apparent that it is very difficult to determine a single overall holding cost in a real company. Some parts of the holding cost depend on the size of the item, some on the cost of the item, and some simply on the number of items in stock. Nevertheless, in order to apply the common inventory models, it is necessary to determine a single holding cost per unit of inventory per some time period.

If we try to keep our inventories low, we run into another kind of cost called the *ordering cost*. This cost consists of any costs associated with placing and receiving an order. When inventory is kept low by ordering smaller quantities, the trade-off comes in the form of more frequent orders, and therefore higher ordering costs. For example, the labor cost involved with the paperwork of preparing an order varies not with the number of units ordered, but rather with the number of orders prepared. Any cost that is incurred once per order, then, is considered an ordering cost. Thus, if there is a fixed shipping or handling charge per order, then that would be included in the ordering cost. Also, parts of the labor involved in the receiving process may be incurred once per order and thus should be treated as ordering costs. Of course, any receiving costs that vary with the number of units received, such as the labor involved in actually placing them on a shelf, would be considered holding costs.

When items are produced by the company (work-in-process or finished goods items), there is no ordering cost, but there is a very similar cost called the *setup cost*. This is the cost of setting up the production equipment to produce a different item than the one previously produced on that equipment. Every time a different item is produced, the company incurs the cost of the labor involved in actually resetting the equipment, as well as any lost production time. Thus, the setup cost acts just like the ordering cost, occurring once per production run just as the ordering cost occurs once per order. Again there are several costs involved in determining the ordering or setup cost, and it may not be easy to determine a single cost figure per order or per setup.

Another cost that the company must worry about, especially if inventories are kept low, is the *stockout cost*. Whenever a needed item is unavailable, there will be a cost incurred. If the item is a finished goods item, the customer will be dissatisfied with a postponed delivery. That order and even future orders may be canceled, resulting in lost profits. Even if the customer agrees to accept a delayed shipment, there will be extra labor and paperwork costs involved in expediting and tracking the delayed shipment.

Similarly, stockouts of raw materials and work-in-process items can cause costly internal disruptions of the production system. If an entire assembly line must shut down because of the lack of one item, for example, a great deal of idle-time expense will result. Again, extra expediting and revamping of production schedules will add to the cost.

The kinds of costs associated with stockouts are even more nebulous than holding costs or ordering costs. How can the company determine the cost of dissatisfied customers in terms of lost future profits? Just how can the cost of internal disruptions in production be measured? Despite these difficulties, at least some estimate of stockout cost (or, equivalently, an estimate of the desired probability of avoiding a stockout) is needed to include these costs in inventory models.

Purchase costs or *production costs*, depending on whether the item is ordered or produced, are normally not a factor in inventory decisions. After all, a certain number of each item must be either ordered or produced over the course of a year, so that cost will be incurred sometime during the year, regardless of what size batches the company orders or produces. The time value of money over the course of a year or less is generally not considered important enough that we would need to consider the differences in when the money is actually spent. However, the exception occurs when the purchase price of an item actually depends on the quantity ordered at a time. Often a supplier will offer quantity discounts for larger orders. Therefore, ordering in larger batches can result in purchase cost savings, as well as affecting the holding, ordering, and stockout costs.

With all of these different costs to consider, some of which are very hard to determine, it is no wonder that inventory theory has been a fruitful area of research for many years.

Inventory Models

Figure 8.1 gives an overview of the common inventory models available to handle different situations. The first distinction made in the diagram is between pipeline inventories and cycle inventories. Pipeline inventories consist of those items that are actually being worked on somewhere in the system or are in transit between parts of the system. In an assembly line system, for example, there would be certain items being worked on at each work station. The assembly line could be thought of as a pipeline of items flowing from one end to the other. We can see that pipeline inventories result from the design of the system rather than from any short-run decision-making. The number of work stations and the transit times throughout the system determine the required amounts of pipeline inventories. Therefore, any reduction in these inventories must come from a redesign of the basic operations system. These are not the inventories that we are normally concerned with controlling on a short-run basis; rather, they are a necessary result of the system as it is designed.

The inventories we do try to control are the cycle inventories. These are items which are continually being built up and then depleted in cycles. These are the items for which we need to determine the quantities and the timing of orders or production runs. Therefore, the rest of the diagram is concerned with these cycle inventories.

We next distinguish between those items for which we need to forecast demand and those whose demands are in turn dependent on other items of inventory. Demands for finished goods, for example, often must be forecast (unless we have a large backlog of orders). However, the demands of most raw materials and work-in-process components may be determined pretty exactly once we have decided our production schedule for our finished goods. It makes little sense to forecast our demands for these items based on their past usage when we know how many we will need (and when) to produce the finished goods we have scheduled. This realization has led to the fairly recent development of Material Requirements Planning (MRP), a system which makes use of this

Figure 8.1
Types of Inventory Models

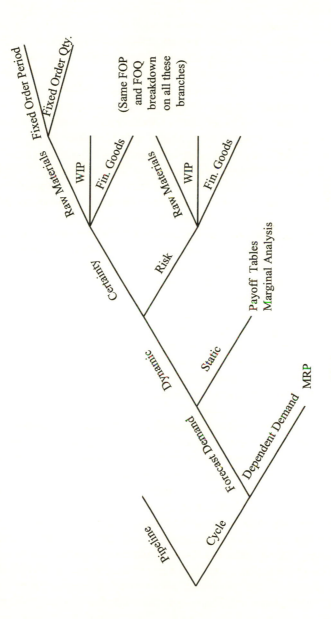

knowledge about demands for raw materials and components. MRP will be discussed in some detail in Chapter 9. The remaining branches of our tree are concerned with the more traditional inventory models utilizing forecast, or independent, demand.

Our next breakdown is between models that are dynamic, or occurring over a period of time, and those that are static, or single-period models. Dynamic models include time as a variable; inventories build up and are depleted, build up and are depleted, over and over again through time. These models determine the quantity and timing of orders over a period of time. Static models are concerned with determining the optimal quantity for a one-time ordering or production decision. Simple quantitative models such as payoff tables or marginal cost and revenue analysis are typically used for these cases. These models are discussed in basic economics and quantitative analysis books.

Continuing with dynamic inventory models, we distinguish between models that assume certainty regarding the states of nature involved and those that assume risk. First, a state of nature is some factor that affects the outcome of the model but which is outside the decision-maker's control. In inventory models the two relevant states of nature are the demand for the inventory item and the lead time from the supplier. Both will definitely affect the inventory pattern and are typically outside of the company's control. Models that assume certainty regarding these factors simply use single numbers, usually a forecast or average figure, for demand and lead time in the analysis. Even though we know that demand and lead time are not certain, we use a single number for each as if they were certain and then determine the best inventory policy. Thus, these models are simplifications of reality.

Models that assume risk, on the other hand, try to come a little closer to reality by incorporating probability distributions rather than single numbers for demand and lead time. These models, then, are more complicated but do a better job of modeling the real world.

Both the certainty and risk branches are next broken down into the three types of inventory items mentioned previously. The reason for this distinction is that the different types of items behave differently. Raw materials are items that are ordered from outside suppliers, and they generally arrive in batches. Therefore, the inventory level takes a large jump when the order is received. Work-in-process and finished goods items, on the other hand, are items that are produced by the company itself. They are produced one at a time, and a production run occurs over a period of time rather than all at once. The inventory level then builds up gradually over time until production stops for that item.

The final distinction in our tree (for all remaining branches) is between models based on a fixed order period and those based on a fixed order quantity. Models using a fixed order period have a predetermined time interval for placing orders, such as once per week or once per month. While the inventory cycle is fixed, however, the quantity ordered varies each cycle. When it comes time to place an order, the items on hand are counted and enough is ordered (or produced) to bring the inventory up to a desired level. Of course, while waiting for the new items, demand is continuing, and the desired peak level of inventory may not be hit exactly when the new items arrive. With a fixed-order-period type of model, it is not necessary to keep track of inventories until it comes time to place an order; at that time the items on hand are counted, and the appropriate order is made. Obviously, this kind of system is a rather loose one; a stockout could easily occur between orders without anyone being aware of it. This system is generally used with items that are not terribly important to control exactly or where there are significant cost savings in ordering regularly. For example, in a supermarket many items are ordered from the same supplier, and combining their orders is the logical procedure.

A fixed-order-quantity model always orders or produces the same quantity each cycle, but the length of the cycle may vary depending on the demand. When the inventory level reaches a predetermined reorder level, we know it is time to place an order. However, we never know just how long it will take to reach the reorder level if our demand is variable. The reorder level is determined to be enough to last during the lead time for our new order. In order to use a fixed-order-quantity model, we obviously need to keep a perpetual count of the items in inventory so that we will know when we have reached the reorder level. For this reason this type of model is appropriate for those inventory items which require very close control.

In situations where our demand for a certain item is assumed to be constant, a fixed-order-period model will end up ordering the same quantity each cycle. Likewise, a fixed-order-quantity model will end up ordering at regular intervals. In such a case, then, the two models end up with identical inventory patterns and ordering decisions.

ABC METHOD OF CLASSIFICATION

Given the multitude of inventory items to keep track of in most companies, it is logical that some items would be more important to control than others. Today many companies, such as supermarkets, have sophisticated computerized inventory systems which automatically record changes in inventory level whenever a transaction is made. However, other organizations, especially smaller ones, must still keep track of their inventory largely by hand. Even when inventory record-keeping is automated, someone must still use this information to determine and to carry out the optimal ordering policy. Thus, it is useful to know which inventory items require the most careful attention.

A popular measure of an inventory item's importance is its *dollar volume*. This figure represents the total amount of money spent on that item over the course of a year. The calculation of dollar volume is simply the product of the item's annual demand (D) and its cost per unit (C). An item can have a high dollar volume because of its high cost, its high usage, or a combination of the two. These items tend to have a higher holding cost because of their high unit

Figure 8.2
ABC Classification of Items

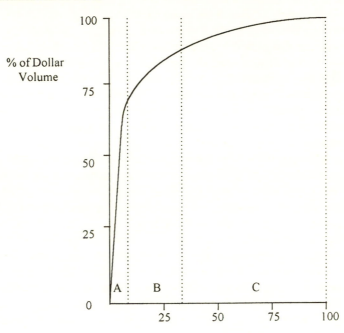

% of Inventory Items

cost, so it is especially wasteful to have unnecessary inventories of these items in storage. Also, finished goods with high dollar volume tend to have higher stockout costs because of their higher profits lost, so we also want to avoid having too few of these items available. Careful record-keeping and thorough analysis of ordering policy are warranted for these items.

It has been noted that generally a rather small number of inventory items represents a rather large proportion of the firm's total dollar volume. In other words, there are usually only a few really important items to keep track of. In fact, a plot of the cumulative dollar volume versus the cumulative number of inventory items usually follows a Pareto curve, as shown in Figure 8.2. This shape of curve is named for the Italian economist Pareto, who observed similar relationships in many aspects of life. For example, in attending a class or in reading this textbook, a relatively small proportion of the material is the most important, a larger portion is moderately important, and the largest proportion is moderately important, and the largest proportion is less important (not to say *un*important!).

In inventory theory the relatively few items (perhaps 10–20%) which represent the largest proportion of dollar volume (perhaps 60–80%) are called the A items. As noted, these items require a perpetual count of inventory so that we always know how many are on hand, and they should be analyzed thoroughly to determine order quantities and timing. The type of analysis which we will explore in our inventory models is really necessary only for the A items. An example of an A item in a large retail store such as Sears might be a large appliance or home electronic equipment. These items are relatively expensive and still have a high volume of sales.

The B category represents the moderate dollar volume items. B items may account for perhaps 20–40% of the items and perhaps 20–30% of the total dollar volume. These items may not require a perpetual count, but rather a periodic count, such as once per week or once per month. Simple ordering rules such as the two-bin system would be appropriate for ordering these items. In this system an item's stock is kept in two bins, usually one large one and a smaller one. Items are used from the larger bin, and when it is empty, it is time to order a new batch. During the lead time for the new order, parts are taken from the smaller bin, and both are refilled when the new order arrives. At Sears examples of B items might be small power tools and clothing.

Most inventory items fall in the C category of low dollar volume items. This group may represent 40–60% of the items but only 10–20% of the dollar volume. At Sears small items such as screws, nails, and candy may be C items. Again a periodic count of these items is sufficient, and it could probably be performed less frequently than for the B items. Little analysis is necessary for these items. If some items sit on a shelf for a while, the holding cost will not be too high. Likewise, if a customer is unable to find one of these items, he is unlikely to storm off and refuse to do business with the company again. In fact, the inventory costs associated with C items are so insignificant that it would be wise to seek out quantity discounts for purchasing larger quantities of these items. The savings in the cost of the item will generally far outweigh the extra inventory cost.

Although the ABC method of classification traditionally uses three categories for inventory items, there is nothing sacred about this number. If a company's items seem to fall nicely into 4 or 5 distinct categories, then these should be used. Nor is it necessary to classify inventory items only by their dollar volume. Some items which are small and cheap may nevertheless be vital to the operation of a large piece of equipment. These could be put into a "cheap but crucial" category. Also, items coming from the same supplier could be grouped to facilitate and save money on ordering and shipping. The point of classifying inventory items at all is to force the company to examine the importance of the various items and to determine the appropriate level of attention that should be given to each of them.

BASIC EOQ MODEL

The classical inventory model that has been used for most of the twentieth century is called the Economic Order Quantity (EOQ) model. This model represents that branch in Figure 8.1 pertaining to cycle inventories, for forecast demand, using a dynamic model, assuming conditions of certainty regarding demand and lead time, for raw material inventories, and using a fixed-order-quantity approach. Several of the other branches are simply variations of this basic inventory model. Besides assuming that demand and lead time are certain (although based on a forecast), the model further assumes that demand is constant over time rather than seasonal or variable. Therefore, the inventory level declines smoothly over time at a constant rate. While these assumptions may seem unrealistic and oversimplified, they do provide a reasonable approximation of many inventory systems. The object of the model is to determine the EOQ, the optimal quantity to order each cycle, as well as the reorder level (R), the level of inventory that signals that it is time to place an order.

Figure 8.3 shows the inventory pattern assumed in the EOQ model. Because of the fact that demand is perfectly known, it is possible to let our inventory level decline all the way to 0, at which point a new order is received. Because lead time is also assumed to be known, in order to receive the new order just when inventory reaches 0, we simply back up from that point in time by the amount of the lead time to place the order. Equivalently, though, we can simply keep track of the inventory level; when we have just enough left to last us during the lead time, we have reached our reorder level. In other words, the reorder level is set equal to the demand during lead time, which is known.

Calculating the Optimal Order Quantity

Since the calculation of R is trivial in this model, the only real question is how large should the order quantity be. In Figure 8.3 we see that we can order large quantities which will last for long cycles or order smaller quantities with shorter cycles. We want to choose the order quantity that minimizes the sum of the inventory costs we have discussed, namely, holding costs, ordering costs, and stockout costs. Because of our assumptions regarding demand and lead time, it is clear that this model will have no stockout costs, however. Nor will we consider the possible savings due to quantity discounts until later. Therefore, our total annual inventory cost (TC) can be expressed as:

TC = annual holding costs + annual ordering costs

Despite the real-life difficulties in determining these costs, let's assume that we can obtain a figure H representing the cost of holding one unit of inventory for one year. We will also define S as the cost of placing one order. Both H and S are *marginal* costs—H consists of all costs that vary with the number of units held, and S consists of all costs that vary with the number of orders. Now we have:

TC = H(average inventory level) + S(no. of orders per year)

Figure 8.3
Inventory Patterns in EOQ and EPQ Models

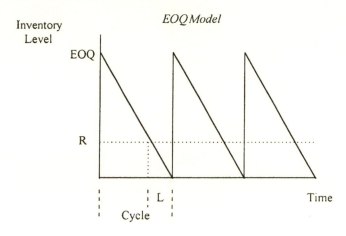

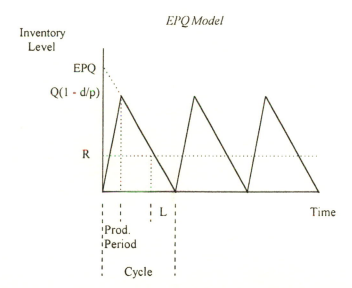

If we order a quantity Q at each order, our inventory pattern will decline smoothly from Q to 0, over and over. The average level of this pattern will then be Q/2. If we order a total annual quantity equal to our annual demand (D) throughout the year by ordering Q units at a time, we will need to place D/Q orders during the year. Therefore, our cost equation becomes:

$$TC = HQ/2 + SD/Q$$

Figure 8.4
Inventory Costs in the EOQ Model

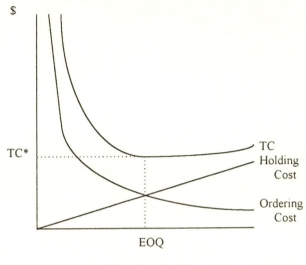

We have assumed that all quantities in this expression are known except for Q. We would like to choose that Q that minimizes TC. We can see in Figure 8.4 that the holding cost (HQ/2) is just a linear function of Q. The ordering cost (SD/Q) varies inversely with Q and is a hyperbolic function. As Q increases, then, the holding cost increases proportionally, but the ordering cost decreases because of the smaller number of orders needed. The TC function is the sum of these two functions, and it has a minimum point, which we are trying to find.

To find the minimum of the TC function with respect to Q, we take the derivative and set it equal to 0, with the following result:

$$EOQ = \sqrt{2SD/H}$$

It should be noted here that the holding cost H is often expressed as a percentage of the item's cost per unit (C). This is convenient because of the fact that a large part of the holding cost is the opportunity cost, which can be expressed as the interest rate foregone by holding inventory. If we express this percentage holding cost as i, then, we have H = iC. A summary of the notation used in our inventory models follows:

Notation Used in Inventory Models
TC = total annual inventory cost
TC* = optimal total annual inventory cost
D = annual demand

Q = quantity ordered per order or produced per production run
EOQ = economic order quantity (optimal quantity ordered per order)
EPQ = economic production quantity (optimal quantity produced per production run)
S = ordering cost per order or setup cost per setup
H = holding cost per unit per year
i = holding cost rate (per $ of inventory value)
C = cost of inventory item per unit
R = reorder level of inventory
L = lead time
d = demand rate (per some time period)
p = production rate (per some time period)
$\bar{d}$ = average demand for some time period
$\bar{L}$ = average lead time
SS = safety stock
σ_{DL} = standard deviation for demand during lead time

Calculating the Optimal Inventory Cost

Having determined the optimal quantity to order each time we place an order, we would probably be interested in calculating just what is the total annual inventory cost that we have just minimized. In other words, what cost is at the bottom of our TC curve on the graph? We can calculate this optimal cost (which we will call TC*) by inserting our optimal order quantity (EOQ) into our TC equation in place of the general quantity Q. After some algebra, we have:

$$TC^* = EOQ(H)$$

It is interesting to note that the TC curve is relatively flat near the EOQ (see Figure 8.4). Therefore, the total inventory cost is relatively insensitive to small changes in the order quantity around the EOQ. If our EOQ calculation needs to be rounded off, then, or if our supplier will only ship certain round quantities, we can choose a convenient quantity near the EOQ without incurring much extra cost.

Other Calculations for the EOQ Model

To implement the EOQ model, we simply order the EOQ whenever our inventory level reaches R, the reorder level—that is our decision rule. R is just equal to the demand during lead time, which we assume is known. Using our notation,

$$R = Ld,$$

where our demand rate, d, is expressed in the same time units as our lead time, L.

In determining our annual ordering cost, we have already used the expression for the number of cycles per year, D/Q. The length of each cycle is just the time it takes to use up our order quantity, Q. Thus, we have

Cycle = Q/d,

with a result in the same time units as d is expressed in. Note that in both of these expressions we have used the general order quantity term, Q, because the equation is true no matter what order quantity we choose. In practice, though, we will be using the EOQ that we have calculated. With formulas for EOQ, TC*, R, the number of cycles per year, and the length of each cycle, we have completely described our inventory system under the EOQ model.

Example 8.1—Axolotl Imbedding Corp. (A)

In applying inventory models in real life the major problem is in determining reasonable estimates for the demand and costs necessary for the models. Here we assume that we have obtained reliable estimates and simply plug them into our formulas.

Axolotl Imbedding Corp. is a company specializing in imbedding stuffed axolotls in plastic. Every day they imbed 10 stuffed axolotls, which they buy for $50 a piece. Ordering costs total $9 per order, and the holding cost rate is 24% of the item's cost. The company works 240 days per year, and the lead time is 4 days.

Probably the first calculation we should make is the EOQ. Here we have:

$$\text{EOQ} = \sqrt{2SD/H} = \sqrt{\frac{2(9)(240)(10)}{(.24)(50)}}$$

$$= \sqrt{\frac{43,200}{12}} = \sqrt{3,600} = 60 \text{ units}$$

Since the lead time is 4 days, and the daily demand is 10 units, we have a reorder level of R = Ld = (4)(10) = 40 units. Therefore, our decision rule is to order 60 stuffed axolotls whenever our inventory level falls to 40 units. If we follow this practice, we will incur an annual inventory cost of TC* = (EOQ)(H) = (60)(12) = $720 per year. Keep in mind that half of this cost is ordering cost, and half is holding cost. Also, of the ordering cost portion, a large part may be opportunity cost rather than out-of-pocket cost.

The number of orders we will send in per year will be equal to D/Q = 2400/60 = 40. Therefore, our cycle will be Q/d = 60/10 = 6 days. We can get this same result by dividing our year of 240 working days by the 40 cycles per year to get a cycle of 6 working days.

What if the company had not done this analysis and had been ordering stuffed axolotls once a month instead? In that case their order quantity would have to be 2400/12 = 200 units per order. We can calculate their inventory costs from our original TC equation:

$$\begin{aligned} TC &= SD/Q + HQ/2 \\ &= (9)(2400)/200 + (12)(200)/2 \\ &= (9)(12) + (12)(100) \\ &= 108 + 1200 = 1308 \end{aligned}$$

We can see that the company is ordering 12 times per year rather than the 40 under the EOQ model. Their inventory level averages 100 units as compared to 60/2 = 30 using the EOQ. The result is a smaller ordering cost but a much larger holding cost. By ordering 200 rather than 60 stuffed axolotls at a time, then, the company is spending $1,308 rather than $720 per year in inventory costs (both out-of-pocket and opportunity costs). In this case the lack of analysis is hurting the company a great deal ($588 just for this one inventory item each year).

QUANTITY DISCOUNTS

So far, we have been concerned only with ordering costs and holding costs. There was no stockout cost to worry about given the assumptions of the basic EOQ model, and the cost of the item itself has been assumed to be constant regardless of our order quantity. Now let's relax this latter assumption and examine the fairly common case where a supplier offers a reduced price for an item if purchased in large quantities. In that case we will want to minimize the total of the ordering cost, the holding cost, and the purchase cost.

Quantity discounts may be offered in different ways. One method would be to charge a certain amount per unit for the first x number of units, then to charge a lesser amount for the next y number of units, and so on. Another method would be to lower the price on *all* units purchased if the purchase quantity exceeds a certain level. In the following analysis we will assume the latter type of quantity discounts, with the price of all units being affected. The former case can be analyzed similarly with a simple adjustment in the calculation of the total purchase cost and perhaps a more complicated adjustment in the calculation of the holding cost.

Example 8.2—Axolotl Imbedding Corp. (B)

In our Axolotl Imbedding Corp. example let's now see what happens if our supplier of stuffed axolotls offers us quantity discounts. If we purchase at least 300 axolotls at a time, they will reduce the price by $ .50 per axolotl (on *all* axolotls ordered). If we order at least 600 at a time, they will reduce the price by another $ .50, for a total discount of $1.00 per axolotl. We need to determine whether to accept either of these discounts or to continue ordering the EOQ.

The EOQ is certainly always one of our alternatives, since we know that it minimizes the total of the ordering and holding costs. However, it may or may not be large enough to take advantage of the discounts. In this example, our EOQ of 60 is far too small to bring us any discount. Still, it could be the best alternative depending on the amount of the discounts offered compared to the increase necessary in our inventory costs.

Besides the EOQ, we will consider any higher order quantities that will give us a discount on the purchase price. In this case we will consider ordering either 300 or 600 units at a time. It would be silly to order any quantity between 300 and 600 because the purchase cost would remain at $49.50 while the inventory costs would just get higher (as we get farther from the EOQ). Similarly, any quantity above 600 would not be considered. For our three alternatives of 60, 300, and 600 units, then, we will calculate both the inventory cost and the purchase cost for the year:

$$TC = SD/Q + HQ/2 = SD/Q + iCQ/2$$
$$TC_{300} = \frac{(9)(2400)}{300} + \frac{(.24)(49.50)(300)}{2}$$
$$= 72 + 1782 = 1854$$
$$TC_{600} = \frac{(9)(2400)}{600} + \frac{(.24)(49)(600)}{2}$$
$$= 36 + 3528 = 3564$$

In the table below we see the total annual inventory costs and the total annual purchase costs of the three alternatives. The alternative with the lowest total cost is 300 units per order at an annual cost of $120,654. Therefore, we will accept the first price break at 300 units but not the second one at 600 units— the inventory cost increase is just too much.

QUANTITY DISCOUNT ALTERNATIVES

Order Quantity	Annual Inventory Cost	Annual Purchase Cost	Total Annual Cost
60	$ 720	(2400)(50.00) = $120,000	$120,720
300	1854	(2400)(49.50) = 118,800	120,654
600	3564	(2400)(49.00) = 117,600	121,164

WORK-IN-PROCESS AND FINISHED GOODS ITEMS

Items that we produce ourselves have a somewhat different inventory pattern than those we order. As shown in Figure 8.3, the inventory level builds up gradually during our production period rather than arriving all at once from a supplier. In order for any buildup to occur at all, it is obviously necessary for our production rate, p, to be larger than our demand rate, d. The rate of buildup is just $p - d$. Then at some point we must stop producing that item, or else our inventory would continue to build up. From that peak inventory level our inventory declines at a rate equal to d until it reaches 0. During the time that we are not producing this item our production facilities are generally not just sitting idle but rather are used for producing a different item. The problem we are faced with is how large our production quantity should be before we stop producing, as well as when we should start setting up for the next production run.

Calculating the Optimal Production Quantity and Cost

Because of the change in our inventory pattern, our formula for the total annual inventory cost has changed. First of all, there no longer is any ordering cost. However, there is a very similar kind of cost that also occurs once per cycle—the setup cost. Whenever a new production run is scheduled, the equipment must be set up to produce that item. The cost of the employees' time required to set up the equipment, plus any extra scrap cost, would constitute the setup cost. Because the setup cost is like the ordering cost in that it occurs once per cycle, the setup cost part of the TC equation appears just the same as the ordering cost did if we redefine S to represent a setup cost per setup.

The holding cost term of the TC equation, though, consists of the average inventory level multiplied by H. With the new inventory pattern shown in Figure 8.3 the average inventory is no longer Q/2 because the peak of the inventory pattern is not Q. If we produce a total quantity of Q over the production period, what we end up with is less than what we produced because of the demand we have already experienced during the production period. In fact, if we extend our downward-sloping segment of the inventory pattern backwards from the peak to the beginning of the cycle, we arrive at Q, as shown on the graph.

The rate at which we use up our production through our demand can be represented by the ratio d/p. Therefore, the fraction of production left over would be $1 - d/p$. Applying that fraction left over to our production quantity, we have a peak inventory level of:

$$\text{Peak} = Q(1 - d/p)$$

The average inventory level would be half of this peak level, or $Q(1 - d/p)/2$, and the annual holding cost would be $HQ(1 - d/p)/2$. All together, then, our new formula for total annual inventory cost would be:

$$TC = SD/Q + HQ(1 - d/p)/2$$

Note that the only change in the formula mathematically is the extra term of $(1 - d/p)$ in the holding cost. Since this term is a constant and appears in the same place as the constant H, when we take the derivative of TC with respect to Q, set it equal to 0, and solve, we get the same result as before except for this added term along with the H. The optimal production quantity is called EPQ for "economic production quantity." Another commonly used name is ELS, or "economic lot size."

$$EPQ = \sqrt{\frac{2SD}{H(1 - d/p)}}$$

When we insert the EPQ formula into the TC formula to determine the optimal inventory cost, we again get a result just like the EOQ model with the addition of the $(1 - d/p)$ term along with H:

$$TC^* = EPQ(H)(1 - d/p)$$

Other Calculations for the EPQ Model

Although we don't have an order period in the EPQ model, the setup period is analogous. The reorder level, R, is the level of inventory at which we start setting up for the next production run, and it is still equal to the demand during the lead time (setup time):

$$R = Ld$$

There are still D/Q cycles per year, and the overall cycle is still the time it takes to use up Q items:

$$Cycle = Q/d$$

There are two new calculations that describe our inventory pattern in the EPQ model that we didn't have in the EOQ model. The peak inventory level has already been identified as $Q(1 - d/p)$. The production period is the time it takes to produce Q items at a production rate of p:

$$Production\ period = Q/p$$

Example 8.3—Axolotl Imbedding Corp. (C)

Suppose that there is a machine on the market that would allow Axolotl Imbedding Corp. to stuff its own axolotls. The machine is able to stuff 15 axolotls per day at a total cost of $30 apiece. It costs $75 and takes half a day to set up the machine for a production run. We start by calculating the EPQ:

$$EPQ = \sqrt{\frac{2SD}{H(1 - d/p)}}$$

$$= \sqrt{\frac{(2)(75)(2400)}{(.24)(30)(1 - 10/15)}}$$

$$= \sqrt{\frac{360,000}{(7.2)(1/3)}}$$

$$= \sqrt{150,000} = 387$$

The peak of the inventory pattern would be $Q(1 - d/p) = (387)(1/3) = 129$ units. The production period would be $Q/p = 387/15 = 25.8$ days, and the whole cycle would be $Q/d = 387/10 = 38.7$ days. Notice that the production period is $2/3$ of the overall cycle, the same as the ratio of d/p. The peak is $1/3$ of the production quantity, $2/3$ of it having been used up during the production period. Since the setup time is half a day, the reorder level would be $R = Ld = (.5)(10) = 5$ units. Therefore, our decision rule would be to set up for a production run of 387 units every time our inventory level dropped to 5 units.

The optimal inventory cost of producing in quantities of 387 at a time would be:

$$TC^* = EPQ(H)(1 - d/p)$$
$$= (387)(7.2)(1/3) = \$929$$

It is interesting to compare the costs under the EPQ model with those under the EOQ model for Axolotl Imbedding Corp. The inventory cost per year has increased from \$720 under the EOQ model to \$929 under the EPQ model (because the setup cost is much greater than the ordering cost was). On the other hand, the company is able to produce its own stuffed axolotls at a cost of \$30 per unit rather than purchasing them for \$50 per unit without a discount or for \$49.50 per unit utilizing the most advantageous discount. The total cost of production and inventory costs for the year would be $(2400)(\$30) + \$929 = \$72,000 + \$929 = \$72,929$. The best previous alternative using an order quantity of 300 and receiving a discount resulted in a total cost of \$120,654. The savings under the EPQ model would be $\$120,654 - \$72,929 = \$47,725$. If the axolotl stuffing machine could be purchased and maintained for an amount less than this per year, then it would be a worthwhile investment for the company.

RISK IN DEMAND AND LEAD TIME

To make our inventory models more realistic (but also necessarily more complicated!) we now relax our assumption of certainty regarding demand and lead time. A model assuming conditions of risk utilizes probability distributions rather than single numbers for these states of nature. Therefore, instead of using a single number d for demand rate and L for lead time, we now have probability distributions with *mean* values of $\bar{d}$ for average demand rate and $\bar{L}$ for average lead time. This type of model can be used both for items that are ordered and for those that are produced.

While we can still calculate the EOQ or EPQ in a risk model by using the average annual demand, our demand pattern is no longer completely known. We are not sure just when we will reach 0 inventory, and we're not sure how long it will take to get our order back from our supplier (or to set up our equipment if producing). Stockouts, with their attendant costs, are now a possibility.

If lead time is average but demand is greater than usual, we experience a stockout. If lead time is average but demand is less than usual, we end up with some inventory left over when the order comes in, causing our inventory level to be higher than usual for the whole next cycle. We don't know what might happen during the next lead time, but we know we will have one cycle of extra holding costs.

Similarly, if we hold the demand rate at the average but lead time takes longer than usual, we again experience a stockout. If demand is average but lead time is less than usual, we have one cycle of extra holding cost. If we allow both the demand rate and the lead time to vary, the various combinations will sometimes result in stockouts, sometimes in extra holding cost.

It generally (but not always) costs a company more for one unit of stockout than for one cycle's worth of holding cost for a unit. They would prefer to incur a little extra holding cost in order to decrease the probability of stockouts. The way to do this is to increase the reorder level beyond the average demand during lead time. The amount by which we increase the reorder level is the average amount we will have left over at the end of the lead time. Sometimes we will have more left over and sometimes less—sometimes still going below 0 and incurring a stockout. This increase in the reorder level is called the safety stock. While some people think of safety stock as some particular items that are stuck away in the closet and brought out if they are needed, more commonly safety stock is simply the average amount of inventory left over at the end of a cycle. In the unusual situation where a company would actually prefer to have a stockout rather than carry a little extra inventory, the safety stock may be negative.

Under conditions of risk, then, our calculation of the reorder level has gone from a rather trivial computation to a complicated decision. Our new expression for the reorder level is:

$$R = \bar{d}\,\bar{L} + SS,$$

where SS is the safety stock. The problem then becomes how much safety stock to hold in our reorder level. Here we will assume that the distribution of our demand during lead time (which comes from the combination of the demand distribution and the lead time distribution) approximates a normal curve. This is often a reasonable approximation. In that case the safety stock can be expressed as the product of the standard normal variate, z, and the standard deviation of the demand during lead time distribution.

$$SS = z\sigma_{DL}$$
$$R = \overline{d}\,\overline{L} + z\sigma_{DL}$$

With a normal distribution for demand during lead time, then, we need to determine both the number of standard deviations above the mean that we want, z, and the standard deviation of demand during lead time, σ_{DL}. The number of standard deviations we desire to be above the average demand during lead time depends on how much probability we are willing to allow for a stockout to occur. The area of the demand during lead time distribution that falls above our reorder level represents the probability of a stockout occurring (of some number of units).

Service Level

If we know the stockout cost per unit as well as the holding cost per unit, it is possible to calculate the optimal probability of having a stockout using marginal cost analysis. However, the stockout cost is a very uncertain number; it is difficult to trace all the effects and costs of having a stockout. Most materials managers would find it easier to specify the desired probability of a stockout through their own mental trade-off calculations than to actually come up with a stockout cost and perform the numerical analysis. In either case we will assume here that the desired probability of a stockout has already been determined. Alternatively, we can speak of the probability of *not* incurring a stockout during a given cycle, commonly called the *service level*. Thus, we assume that the service level is specified, and we can use this probability together with a table of normal curve probabilities to determine z. For example, if the service level is specified to be 95% (5% chance of a stockout per cycle), we find a z-value of 1.65 from the normal table.

Example 8.4—Axolotl Imbedding Corp. (D)

When we used the EOQ model for Axolotl Imbedding Corp., we used a demand rate of d = 10 units per day and a lead time of L = 4 days. Now let's assume that demand is variable, with a standard deviation of two units per day, and that lead time is fixed at four days.

The average demand during lead time is $\overline{d}\,L = 40$, the same number we took as certain in original EOQ model. The standard deviation of demand during lead time will be:

$$\sigma_{DL} = \sqrt{(4)(2)^2} = 4$$

For our reorder level calculation, then, we have

$$R = \bar{d}L + SS = \bar{d}L + z\sigma_{DL}$$
$$= 40 + z(4)$$

If we desire a 90% service level, the appropriate z-value from the normal distribution would be 1.28, resulting in

$$R = 40 + (1.28)(4)$$
$$= 40 + 5.12 = 45.12$$

In practice it might be difficult to tell when we have reached the 45.12th axolotl, so the company might well round off the reorder level to 45 units.

A service level of 95% would require a z-value of 1.65, and a service level of 99% would require a z-value of 2.33. In these cases the safety stock would increase from 5.12 units to 6.60 units and 9.32 units, respectively. Because of the shape of the normal curve, we can see that adding a little more to the service level requires a large increase in the safety stock.

With a 90% service level, on the average the whole inventory pattern is raised by the amount of the safety stock, 5.12 units. Therefore, in addition to the ordering cost and holding cost we previously determined with the TC* equation, we also have the cost of holding this safety stock for the entire year. In our best case we were ordering axolotls at a cost of \$49.50, resulting in a holding cost of $H = iC = (.24)(49.50) = 11.88$. Thus, our safety stock will cost us $(11.88)(5.12) = \$60.83$ in holding costs for the year. Despite holding 5.12 units of safety stock, we will also still incur some amount of stockout cost because in 10% of our inventory cycles we will experience some degree of stockout. It is difficult to calculate the amount of expected stockout cost for the year since a stockout could be one unit short, two units short, and so on, in those cycles where a stockout is incurred. However, the cost should be similar in size to the extra holding cost of the safety stock.

CHAPTER 9

Inventory Models for Dependent Demand

OVERVIEW

When we looked at different inventory models in Chapter 8, we noted that many inventory items, particularly raw materials and work-in-process components, were called dependent-demand items. That is, their demands did not have to be forecast but rather could be determined exactly once we decided on a particular production schedule for our finished goods items. Thus, the demands for these earlier items in the production process were *dependent* on demands for later items.

The obvious question regarding these dependent-demand items is, why not use what we know about the relationships between different inventory items' demands to determine exactly how many of each item are needed and when they are needed? It makes little sense to analyze each inventory item in isolation and to apply a separate order-point type of model to each as if demands were independent. Although managers have been aware of this logic for many years, inventory items continued to be analyzed independently until computers became widely available and less costly. Then in the late 1960's and early 1970's the concept of Material Requirements Planning (MRP) was developed to handle dependent-demand inventory items. Originally, MRP was a system for calculating the quantities needed of all inventory items as well as the precise timing of purchase orders or production runs.

Besides the fact that demands for many inventory items do not need to be forecast, there is another major reason why traditional order-point models such as the EOQ model are often inadequate. These models assume that demand is smooth over time, while in real life demands are often "lumpy." There may be no demand at all for a given item for a period of time, then a sudden jump in demand, and so on. In such cases an EOQ model will result in large quantities of inventory being held through time periods when there is little or no demand. Obviously, holding costs will be unnecessarily high in such cases. Similarly, a surge in demand can easily cause a stockout under an EOQ model. MRP systems, on the other hand, can operate with *any* set of demand figures and can determine the appropriate actions to help minimize inventory costs.

A *regenerative* MRP system performs its calculations at fixed time intervals, usually once per week. Each time the system is run, it determines the necessary purchase orders and shop orders to send out, and it updates the files of the various inventory items. Several types of reports (discussed later) are also produced on a weekly basis. A *net-change* MRP system can accept new transactions at any time. For example, if a new order arrives for a finished product or if a supplier fails to send a batch of raw materials on time, these changes can be entered into the MRP system. Then the system would report changes to the production and ordering schedule rather than produce a complete revised schedule.

Installing an MRP system in a company requires compiling a large database regarding the many different inventory items and the production processes of the company. Especially in the early days of MRP, many companies experienced great frustration in attempting to implement the system. Collecting the necessary data required a great deal of time and the cooperation of many different individuals within the company. Naturally, there was usually some resistance to a change of this magnitude. Some of the data needed were just not available, and those that were collected often contained errors, producing poor results. Also, since there initially was little commercially available MRP software, companies had to hire consultants and develop their own systems from scratch. Because of these problems the failure rate of early MRP applications was high. Now, with the passage of time, the proven success of MRP in many companies and the relatively low cost and ease of adapting one of the several commercial systems available have made MRP much more attractive, even to small companies.

Recent Advances in MRP

Having amassed a large database regarding their production operations, managers began to realize that in calculating when to release purchase orders and shop orders they were only scratching the surface of the capabilities of their systems. A simple extension of the system was to produce reports showing the capacity requirements (man-hours and machine hours) of each production department in the system. With Capacity Requirements Planning (CRP) it can be determined if the current production requirements will result in an overload in any department at any time within the planning horizon. If so, ways can be found to reschedule that part of the production, to increase capacity through overtime or other temporary measures, or to change the production schedule for finished products. If a certain department shows up as a consistent bottleneck, then it will be apparent that permanent capacity expansion is needed.

We can see that MRP and CRP together can help with most short-run decisions made within an operations division of a company. However, MRP II (here the "MRP" stands for "Manufacturing Resource Planning") makes further use of the production database to provide links with other functional areas of the firm, including marketing, finance, accounting, and personnel. There are enormous benefits from all parts of the company working together through a shared database to integrate their activities toward the goals of the firm. Some of the decisions for which an MRP II system can provide information to different functional areas include:

Production—purchase orders, production scheduling and control, inventory control, capacity planning

Marketing—delivery dates for products, capacity for new orders

Finance—financial resources needed (for material, labor, overhead)

Accounting—actual cash flow projections over time, production costs

Personnel—manpower requirements over time (specific, by departments)

It is apparent that an integrated MRP II system can be a powerful tool for a company. Having a computerized database also makes it possible for any of the above functional areas to run simulations to see what might happen under certain future conditions. For example, production managers can see what might happen if a supply comes in late, a machine breaks down, or an order is canceled. Accounting can simulate changes in cash flow or in costs under similar circumstances.

Problems with MRP

All of the potential advantages of an MRP or MRP II system do not come free, of course. Many of the problems of implementing MRP in the early days persist today (although to a lesser extent). Installing an MRP system remains a major change for a company and requires a significant amount of work by operations managers. The cost of the hardware and software is not negligible, especially for small companies. Also, there still is the problem of collecting good data for the system.

The major remaining problems associated with MRP, though, pertain to the assumptions that are necessary for MRP to produce useful information. Generally, the assumption is that the various data in the database are fixed and not subject to variability. For example, each inventory item is assumed to have a certain lead time, either from a supplier of raw materials or from our own production system. If this lead time is not constant, the MRP calculations may be in error. It will be necessary to build in a safety stock in such cases, contrary to the purposes of an MRP system to provide inventory items in the correct quantities and at the times needed. If the master production schedule is subject to uncertainty due to uncertain demand forecasts, then all subsequent calculations of inventory needs will likewise be uncertain. Therefore, MRP works best in situations where demands may be lumpy, but the orders are known for some time in the future, and the relevant production and ordering data are relatively certain.

INPUTS AND OUTPUTS OF THE MRP SYSTEM

Inputs to the MRP system consist of three major files of information, while the outputs take the form of various reports and decisions made by the system. Besides these routine inputs and outputs, the system can have the capability to deal with simulations, queries, and "what-if" types of questions and to produce the corresponding special reports.

Master Production Schedule

Before the MRP system can determine the requirements for all dependent inventory items, it must know what the production plans are for the finished goods items. The demands for finished goods may come from forecasts, from orders already received, from internal requirements from other parts of the company, or most likely from a combination of all of these sources. It is necessary to project these demands for some time into the future.

Most companies generate MRP plans for a year to a year and a half into the future. However, only the first few weeks or months are considered to be a firm schedule. The more distant projections can help in the medium-range planning of capacity and ordering of raw materials. That part of the schedule considered firm is generally set to match the time it takes for a product to be produced from start to finish in the system. Once the raw materials are put into production, it would be quite disruptive to change the schedule. For instance, if it takes two months for a product to make its way through the production system, those first parts being produced now are based on finished goods demands two months in the future. It would obviously create chaos if we changed our plans for those finished goods needed within the next two months because their parts are already under production.

Most MRP systems make their plans using "time buckets" of usually one week. That is, within each bucket of time there is a certain demand for each item, a certain number may be produced, a certain number may be received, and a certain number may be ordered. We do not distinguish just when within each bucket of time these things might occur (although each production department must develop its own detailed production schedule for the week).

Rather than plan the time for each individual occurrence, we plan the number of occurrences for each unit (bucket) of time.

Given the various sources of demands for finished goods, the company comes up with a master production schedule to meet these demands. The company has great latitude in matching its master production schedule to its demands. Capacity constraints must be considered, of course, as well as the criteria of meeting due dates, providing for uncertainties through safety stock, and minimizing inventory costs.

As time passes, the planning horizon advances accordingly, as does that part of the schedule considered to be firm. If one week's report shows the scheduled production of finished goods for the first week of January through the last week of February, then the next week's report will show the second week of January through the first week of March.

Bill of Materials

In order to use our master production schedule to determine the requirements for dependent inventory items, we need to know just what parts go into the final product, as well as the sequence in which they are assembled. The bill of materials for each final product shows us this information.

The bill of materials can be visualized as a tree diagram showing which parts go into which other parts. At the top of the tree is the final product. The branches below this level show the components which are the immediate predecessors of this final product (that is, the components which are assembled to make up the final product). These components in turn are formed from other parts and components, which are shown as branches at the next lower level, and so on. A complicated product such as an automobile will include many levels of components. Figure 9.1 shows a bill of materials for a chair, a relatively simple product with only a few levels, in tree-diagram form.

A company may produce finished goods that are basically similar but differ in the selection of color, accessories, or other options. Rather than have a separate bill of materials for each possible distinct finished product (each of which may have very small demands), the company may decide to set up a single bill of materials starting from the level at which all the products are the same. Requirements can then be determined for all previous components, and the final options may be added later by means of very short-term scheduling.

The bill of materials is stored in the computer system not as a tree diagram but rather as a set of coded item numbers. The number of each item can be coded to show the level of the chart it appears on and the item on the level above into which it goes (its parent item). When an item appears at several levels (when used to produce several components), it is generally coded at its lowest level (a process called "low-level coding") in order to facilitate the accumulation of its requirements from several different parent items. Levels of

Figure 9.1
Bill of Materials and Lead Times for Chair

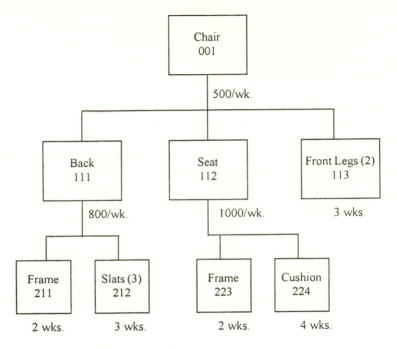

a bill of materials start from the 0 level for the final products, then level 1, level 2, and so on, as you go down the tree. For our chair example in Figure 9.1 we have assigned each item a 3-digit code. The first digit represents the level of the item in the bill of materials, the second gives the last digit of the parent item number, and the third digit numbers the items on that level. Thus, item 223 is the third item listed on level 2, and its parent item is the second item listed (on level 1). Of course, if we had more than 9 items on a given level, we would need more digits to number those items. Also, items that appear under several parents would need more complicated coding.

Given the requirements for finished goods in the Master Production Schedule and the components of the product in the bill of materials, the MRP system is able to determine requirements for all of the previous components, both the quantities and the times when needed. This process is called "exploding" the bill of materials. Requirements are determined level by level, starting from the top. At each level certain lot-sizing techniques are used to determine the best way to meet the requirements at that level. These decisions then serve as inputs to determine the requirements at the next lower level, and so on. The exploding process, as well as several techniques for lot sizing, will be illustrated later in the chapter.

Inventory Status File

Information on each inventory item is stored in the inventory status file. Two kinds of information are needed for each item—ordering information and status information. Ordering information for an item that is ordered from a supplier would include that supplier's address and telephone number, the lead time for obtaining a shipment of that item, the item's price, any quantity discounts offered by the supplier, any restrictions on the size of the batch ordered, shipping costs, any particular lot-sizing techniques appropriate for that item (such as an EOQ), any safety stock required, and perhaps an indication of other items from that same supplier that should be ordered at the same time. For items produced in our own shop we would have information on cost, production time, capacity of that department, safety stock, and any lot-sizing techniques that are appropriate.

Status information on each item would include both current and projected quantity figures for that item. These quantities would include the number demanded during each time period, the number scheduled to be received, the number on hand in inventory, and the number scheduled to be ordered. The calculations made in the exploding and lot-sizing process are entered into the inventory status file of each item, showing current conditions and future projections. When it comes time to place an order for an item (either a purchase order or a shop order) as determined by the MRP system, the system automatically processes that order.

Outputs of the MRP System

The original and most basic purpose of the MRP system was to generate the purchase orders and shop orders mentioned above. Today, though, MRP and MRPII systems are being used to generate increasingly sophisticated outputs. Capacity requirements and detailed load schedules can be produced for each work center. If anything goes wrong, such as a batch of supplies not arriving on time, a change in a customer's order, or a machine breaking down, the system can produce exception notices to show deviations from the original plans. A process called "pegging" can trace through the bill of materials to show the effects that changes in one item will produce upon other items. Reports can evaluate the delivery performance of suppliers, as well as the performance of work centers within the company regarding stockouts and meeting the production schedule.

HOW MRP WORKS

In the bill of materials in Figure 9.1 we have also included the production capacity for items we produce ourselves and the lead times for items that we order. For the chair, item 001, for example, our chair assembly department can

Figure 9.2
Exploding the Chair

Week

Item 001 Chair	0	1	2	3	4	5	6	7	8	9	10
Gross Requirements		450	310	380	240	350	620	150	420	640	360
Scheduled Receipts		330	310	380	240	470	500	210	500	500	360
Inventory On Hand	120	0	0	0	0	120	0	60	140	0	0
Planned Order Releases		310	380	240	470	500	210	500	500	360	

Item 111 Back

Gross Requirements		310	380	240	470	500	210	500	500	360	
Scheduled Receipts		230	380	240	470	500	210	500	500	360	
Inventory On Hand	80	0	0	0	0	0	0	0	0	0	
Planned Order Releases		380	240	470	500	210	500	500	360		

Item 211 Frame

Gross Requirements		380	240	470	500	210	500	500	360		
Scheduled Receipts		360	240	470	500	210	500	500	360		
Inventory On Hand	20	0	0	0	0	0	0	0	0		
Planned Order Releases		470	500	210	500	500	360				

Item 212 Slat

Gross Requirements		1140	720	1410	1500	630	1500	1500	1080		
Scheduled Receipts		890	720	1410	1500	630	1500	1500	1000		
Inventory On Hand	250	0	0	0	0	0	0	0	0		
Planned Order Releases		1500	630	1500	1500	1000					

assemble 500 chairs per week. In other words, the lead time for assembling any number of chairs up to 500 is one week. (While 300 chairs would certainly take less than a week to produce, we are using time buckets of one week, so no smaller time periods are indicated.) Similarly, for each item that we order we have shown the lead time. For simplicity we are assuming that we can order whatever quantities we want from our suppliers without affecting these lead times.

Status Information

At the top of Figure 9.2 is the status information in the inventory status file for the chair, item 001. The current time is the end of week 0 (regenerative

MRP systems typically are run on Friday evening). The planning horizon in our example is ten weeks into the future. We begin with the gross requirements for the next ten weeks and the current inventory on hand.

Gross requirements are the projected demands for this chair for the next ten weeks. Note that in this example we do indeed have quite lumpy demands for our final product. The weekly demands range from 150 to 640 in the next 10 weeks, with no particular trend.

Scheduled receipts are those quantities which we expect to receive during each of the next ten weeks. For a given week the scheduled receipts may arrive at any time within that one-week time bucket (just as the demands may occur at different times within the week). Some authors prefer to distinguish between scheduled receipts of those items *already* ordered (open orders) and those which we *plan* to order over the course of the planning horizon. We will indicate both types of receipts in the same row of the inventory status file. The scheduled receipts row of the table thus represents the decisions we make regarding how we will meet our demands for that item.

Inventory on hand refers to the quantity of items left over at the *end* of each week. These inventories will be projected over the span of the planning horizon. Thus, the projected inventory on hand at the end of a given week is equal to the inventory on hand at the end of the previous week, plus any scheduled receipts and minus any gross requirements that are projected to occur within that week.

Planned order releases in our table show us when we expect to send an order to a supplier or to ourselves for that item. The figures in this row represent no new decisions; they just reflect the decisions made for scheduled receipts with adjustments made for the lead times. In other words, the planned order releases are just the scheduled receipts backed up in time by the amount of the lead time. If we decide that we need to receive an order in week 10, and the item's lead time is two weeks, then we need to plan to release the order in week 8.

Constructing the Master Production Schedule

In Figure 9.2 we started with the gross requirements for our final product, item 001. These numbers have presumably come from the company's aggregate plan, which has then been disaggregated to show the individual products. In other words, the company has already decided whether to use level production, production to meet demand, overtime strategies, and so on, in setting up the aggregate plan. We are now trying to adapt our short-run schedule to this plan.

First we have filled in the scheduled receipts for our final product, item 001. We are making several assumptions in this example. First, we are trying to meet our demands as much as possible in the week they occur. That is, we are trying to keep our inventory at the end of each week at 0. However, we are constrained by our capacity limitations, and we will assume that any temporary increases in capacity, such as using overtime, are undesirable. Also, we assume that stockouts are unacceptable because of their cost. These assumptions will apply to all inventory items in this example.

Looking at the capacity limitations of departments or work stations in this manner is called rough-cut capacity planning. The aggregate plan has already considered capacities in a broader sense, but now we must check each department in the short term (one week). In a simple system like this one, with only one product, this process is rather easy. However, in more complex situations a CRP (Capacity Requirements Planning) module in an MRP II system can aid in the rough-cut capacity planning.

For our chair, then, we run into our capacity limitation of 500 per week in weeks 6 and 9. In order to avoid stockouts it is necessary to produce the excess quantities needed in the previous week in each case. Therefore, 120 units of the 620 needed in week 6 have been shifted to week 5 and added to the 350 units required then; 140 of week 9's units required will be produced early also. However, week 8 already requires 420 units, so only 80 more can be added. The remaining 60 units needed in week 9 will have to be received in week 7, along with the 150 already required. These shifts will result in some inventories on hand at the end of weeks 5, 7, and 8. Also, the original inventory of 120 units in week 0 will reduce week 1's scheduled receipts to 330.

In order to receive the numbers of chairs determined above, we need to start producing each quantity one week earlier (since lead time is one week for up to 500 chairs). Therefore, we move the numbers in the Scheduled Receipts row back one week earlier in the Planned Order Releases row; this is the order we send to the chair assembly department at that time so that the chairs will be finished as scheduled. Since item 001 is the final product, the Planned Order Releases row represents the master production schedule for that product.

Exploding the Bill of Materials

The planned order releases of one item may then be used to determine the gross requirements of items at the next lower level that go into that item. For example, if we send ourselves an order to start producing a batch of some item, then it is necessary for the previous components all to be present at that time. Thus, the gross requirements of an item are just the planned order releases of the parent item (or possibly the sum of several parent items), adjusted for the number of components needed for each one of the parent item. Having determined these new gross requirements for the level below the finished product, we then apply some type of lot-sizing technique to determine the scheduled receipts. These lead to the planned order releases, which lead to the gross requirements for the next lower level, and so on. This is the exploding process. Note, however, that at each level the calculations are not mechanical; lot-sizing decisions must be made before the exploding process can continue to the next lower level. If we have predetermined the best lot-sizing technique for a particular item, we can program that technique into the system.

The requirements for item 111, the back, are the same as the planned order releases for the chair, since each chair has exactly one back. In order for us to release an order to start producing 310 chairs in week 1, we must have 310 backs available in week 1 to assemble into chairs. The requirements for seats (item 112) and front legs (item 113) would similarly be determined from the chair's planned order releases. The capacity of 800 per week in the back-producing department does not restrict us at all since no weekly requirement exceeds 500. In fact, because the chair assembly capacity is 500 per week, it makes little sense to have a greater capacity in the back department.

Since the lead time to produce up to 800 backs is one week, we have scheduled our planned order releases one week before our scheduled receipts. We can see that our effective planning horizon for backs is less than that of the chairs. We can forecast no requirements beyond week 9, and we can plan no order releases beyond week 8.

Both the frame, item 211, and the slat, item 212, derive their gross requirements from the planned order releases of the back, their parent item. The difference in requirements results from the fact that three slats are required for each back. Therefore, the requirements for slats are three times the planned order releases for backs. Both of these items are ordered from suppliers and have no limit on their order size. Thus, it is possible to receive just what we need each week and to keep our inventories at 0 after using up the initial inventories of each item. Because of the 2-week and 3-week lead times of these items, our effective planning horizon is shortened considerably. If we had some forecasts for the chair beyond week 10, however tentative, we could fill in some more tentative plans for ordering frames and slats.

Safety Stock

Holding safety stock violates the basic premise of MRP—providing exactly the parts needed when they are needed. However, uncertainty in several of the figures used in determining requirements may make it desirable to hold some safety stock to avoid stockout costs. Companies usually try to restrict the use of safety stock mainly to the finished goods level. Here safety stocks can make up for uncertainty in the demand forecasts. By holding safety stock at the finished goods level, the company reduces its need for safety stock at lower levels. Whole finished goods may be held in inventory, but previous components can still be planned exactly to meet these finished goods requirements.

At lower levels, though, there may still be a need for safety stock in some circumstances. If lead times are quite variable, or if there is sometimes a problem with scrappage, defective items, or absenteeism among the workers, this uncertainty could justify some safety stock. In the case of variable lead times, rather than thinking in terms of holding safety stock, the company may respond by planning for a longer lead time than average. The effect is exactly the same, however.

LOT-SIZING TECHNIQUES

As the MRP system explodes the bill of materials to determine the requirements of successively lower levels, it must decide how much of each item to order or to produce before proceeding to the next lower level. Generally, the system will use one particular method of determining the lot size at each different level of the bill of materials. The rule used to determine the lot size at one level may not be the same as the rule used at another level. In other words, the process that works best for finished goods lot sizes may not be appropriate for raw material lots. To attempt to minimize the inventory costs at all levels simultaneously would be an enormous undertaking. The relationships between demands at different levels make the problem very complicated. Also, the optimization process would need to be aimed at a moving target—demand figures that are constantly changing. For these reasons a company is usually satisfied to determine some simple method of lot sizing that it believes will tend to minimize inventory costs at a given level of the bill of materials. We will examine a few of the most commonly used of these methods of lot sizing.

Lot-for-Lot Method

The lot-for-lot method simply matches the order or production quantity to the demand for a certain time period. The idea is to meet the demand exactly within that time period so that there is no inventory remaining at the end of the time period. Note that this is the method we used for all inventory items in our chair example. Since our time buckets spanned a one-week period, we attempted to meet each weekly demand exactly. However, constraints in our production capacity and in the quantities we might order sometimes prevent us from achieving this goal.

The lot-for-lot method is obviously a very simple one to apply. It also can be very effective in minimizing costs in those situations where the holding costs are high relative to the ordering or setup costs. Basically, the aim of the lot-for-lot method is to minimize holding costs by allowing frequent (usually weekly) orders or production runs. To be effective, then, this method requires a situation where ordering and setup costs have been cut to the bone.

EOQ and EPQ

Although MRP is largely a response to the inadequacies of the traditional EOQ-type model, there are still situations where the EOQ (or EPQ) may be the most effective lot-sizing technique. The EOQ will minimize inventory costs when certain assumptions apply. If an inventory item's requirements are smooth and predictable rather than lumpy, then an EOQ model will minimize the total of the ordering and holding costs.

Period Order Quantity (POQ)

In cases where there is some demand for an item nearly every week, but where these weekly demands might vary somewhat, many companies find it convenient to apply the period order quantity (POQ). The POQ is calculated by first determining the EOQ and then dividing it by the average weekly demand. The result (after rounding) is the average number of weeks covered by the EOQ (or EPQ). Orders are then placed for this fixed time period. For example, if an EOQ for an item was 100 units, and the average weekly demand was 30 units, the company would order every three weeks (100/30 = 3.33 ≈ 3). The item's actual projected requirements for the next three weeks would be grouped together and ordered. The inventory level would thus return to 0 every three weeks rather than every week as in the lot-for-lot method. We can see that this technique is a simple one to apply, and it does tend to balance ordering and holding costs. It avoids the problem of an EOQ model in handling lumpy demands because the actual demands are used to determine the order, and it can be used in situations where the lot-for-lot method's assumption of negligible ordering costs does not apply. It also has the advantage of a limited demand horizon (three weeks in this example) rather than the yearly demand used in the EOQ. Seasonal fluctuations might make a shorter horizon much more accurate.

Part-Period Algorithm

The part-period algorithm is capable of adjusting the ordering decision to any set of lumpy demands. Weekly demands are grouped together in such a way that the total ordering cost approximately equals the total holding cost for that order. This can result in irregularly spaced orders, unlike the POQ.

The first step is to determine the break-even number of part-periods (parts held x the number of periods held) that will balance ordering and holding costs. For example, if the ordering cost for an item is $40 and the holding cost is $.50 per unit per week, we divide $40 by $.50 to get a break-even point of 80 part-periods. That is, if we hold 80 parts for one week, or 40 parts for 2 weeks, or 20 parts for 4 weeks, or whatever combination that produces 80 part-periods, then we will have a holding cost of $40, equal to the ordering cost. We would be just as happy to order 80 units one week ahead of the time when they are needed if we can combine them with another order to save one ordering cost as to order them separately and incur the ordering cost.

We then look ahead at the future requirements and accumulate them together into a single order until the total number of part-periods ordered in advance is approximately equal to our break-even number. The next period's demand will have to be met by a separate order, and then we will again look ahead to the following demands to determine whether we want to add them to that order.

The part-period algorithm as described above can also be enhanced by incorporating "look-ahead" and "look-back" features. As it is, it does not consider all possible groupings of the item's requirements, and therefore it does not guarantee an optimal solution.

A Comparison of Lot-Sizing Techniques

Let's reconsider the ordering decisions we made for item 211, the frame of the chair, in our previous example (Figure 9.2). For this item we will assume that the ordering cost is $48 per order and that the holding cost is $ .03 per unit per week ($1.56 per unit per year).

Lot-For-Lot

In our initial example of the exploding process we used the lot-for-lot method for all parts of the chair. In Figure 9.2 we can see that we have scheduled an order to be received during each of the next 8 weeks. We know that the lot-for-lot method works best when ordering or setup costs are negligible. However, here the ordering cost is $48 per order, so the cost over the eight-week horizon would be (8)($48) = $384. We were able to keep our inventories at 0 (at the end of each week, at least), so we will have no holding cost. The total eight-week inventory cost for this method, then, is $384.

Economic Order Quantity

To calculate the EOQ, we need an estimate of the annual demand for the chair frame. The gross requirements for the next eight weeks total 3160 units, or an average of 395 units per week. For a 52-week year we can project an average annual demand of (52) (395) = 20,540 units per year. Then we have:

$$\text{EOQ} = \sqrt{2SD/H}$$
$$= \sqrt{(2) (48) (20,540)/1.56}$$
$$= 1124 \text{ units}$$

Therefore, we will order 1124 units whenever we reach our reorder level. Since the lead time is 2 weeks, and the weekly demand averages 395 units, we have:

$$R = L\bar{d} = (2) (395) = 790$$

This reorder level includes no safety stock. We are given no stockout cost or desired service level, so we will assume that no safety stocks are kept at this level, only at the finished goods level, in this example.

Because we always order 1124 units regardless of our weekly demands, we will most likely reach our reorder level sometime in the middle of a week. Since our time buckets are one whole week, though, we will not be able to indicate exactly when during the week the order was sent (or received). Figure 9.3 shows

Figure 9.3
Lot-Sizing Techniques

Lot Sizing Using the EOQ

Week

Item 211 Frame	0	1	2	3	4	5	6	7	8	9	10
Gross Requirements		380	240	470	500	210	500	500	360		
Scheduled Receipts		1124	0	1124	0	0	1124	0	0	1124	
Inventory On Hand	20	764	524	1178	678	468	1092	592	232		
Planned Order Releases	1124	0	0	1124	0	0	1124				

Lot Sizing Using the POQ

Week

Item 211 Frame	0	1	2	3	4	5	6	7	8	9	10
Gross Requirements		380	240	470	500	210	500	500	360	395*	
Scheduled Receipts		1070	0	0	1210	0	0	1255*	0		
Inventory On Hand	20	710	470	0	710	500	0	755*	395*		
Planned Order Releases	0	1210	0	0	1255*	0					

Lot Sizing Using the Part-Period Algorithm

Week

Item 211 Frame	0	1	2	3	4	5	6	7	8	9	10
Gross Requirements		380	240	470	500	210	500	500	360	395*	395*
Scheduled Receipts		1070	0	0	1210	0	0	1255*	0		
Inventory On Hand	20	710	470	0	710	500	0	755*	395*		
Planned Order Releases	0	1210	0	0	1255*	0					

the revised inventory status file for item 211 using the EOQ model. We will assume that an order has already been placed and will arrive in week 1 (or else we would have a massive stockout!).

We see that orders were scheduled to be placed in weeks 1, 4, and 7, when the inventory level dropped below the reorder level of 790. The inventory costs incurred with this method over the next 8 weeks would include:

Ordering costs = (3 orders) ($48/order) = $144.00
Holding costs = (5528 units) ($ .03/unit/week) = $165.84
Total inventory costs = $309.84

For this 8-week period, at least, the EOQ performs better than the lot-for-lot method.

Period Order Quantity

Having already determined the EOQ to be 1124 units, we can calculate the POQ by dividing this number by the average weekly demand:

POQ = EOQ/d
    = 1124/395 = 2.85 ≈ 3 weeks

Therefore, we will group our gross requirements for three weeks at a time and place an order every three weeks. Figure 9.3 shows the results of this policy.

Note that our third order received encompasses weeks 7, 8, and 9. However, we do not yet have a requirements figure for week 9. Therefore, for comparability to the other methods we have included an average demand figure for week 9 in order to determine the approximate size of that order and the resulting inventories. All numbers in Figure 9.3 that are based on this estimate are indicated with an asterisk. With this approximation, then, we have the following inventory costs for the 8-week period:

Ordering costs = (3 orders) ($48/order) = $144.00
Holding costs = (3540 units) ($ .03/unit/week) = $106.20
Total inventory costs = $250.20

The POQ results in 3 orders over the 8-week period, just as does the EOQ. However, ordering based on the actual requirements for the next three weeks makes the inventories substantially smaller overall, resulting in a significant cost savings.

Part-Period Algorithm

We calculate the break-even number of part-periods for item 211 from the ratio of the ordering cost to the holding cost per unit per week: $48/$ .03 = 1600 part-periods. Therefore, whenever we need to place an order for a certain week's requirements, we will include the requirements of future weeks until the total number of part-periods ordered in advance is approximately 1600.

With only 20 units on hand in week 0, it is obvious that we need to receive an order in week 1 for at least 360 units (380 required-20 on hand). If we order week 2's requirements of 240 units one week early to combine them with week 1's order, we will be holding 240 units for one period, for a total of 240 part-periods. Since this is still well below the break-even point, we also consider adding week 3's requirements to this order due in week 1. Week 3's 470 units will thus be held for 2 periods, for a total of 940 part-periods. The total of part-periods due to week 2's and week 3's requirements would then be 1180, still less than 1600. If we order week 4's requirements of 500 units to arrive three weeks early, they will add 1500 part-periods to our total, resulting in 2680 part-periods. If we stop after adding week 3's requirements, our total of 1160 part-periods is closer to the break-even point of 1600 than if we include week 4's requirements. Therefore, our decision is to include week 2's and week 3's requirements in our order due for week 1, but not to include week 4's requirements. The table below shows these calculations for determining our first order.

EXAMPLE OF PART-PERIOD ALGORITHM CALCULATIONS

	Include Week 2	Include Weeks 2 & 3	Include Weeks 2, 3, & 4
Part-Periods:	$(240)(1) = \underline{240}$ 240	$(240)(1) = 240$ $(470)(2) = \underline{\ 940}$ 1180	$(240)(1) = \ \ 240$ $(470)(2) = \ \ 940$ $(500)(3) = \underline{1500}$ 2680

Since 1180 is closer to 1600 than is 2680, we will include weeks 2 and 3 in this first order, and we will need to schedule another order to arrive in week 4. We then look ahead to the requirements in the next few weeks to see if we would like to receive them along with this order. Week 5's requirements of 210 parts ordered one week early will contribute 210 part-periods; 1000 more part-periods will result from including week 6's 500 units two weeks early, for a total of 1210 part-periods. If we also include week 7's 500 units received three weeks early, the resulting 1500 part-periods would give us a total of 2710 part-periods, well beyond our break-even point. Since 1210 is much closer to 1600, we will include only weeks 5 and 6 in our order to be received in week 4.

Our next order will be needed in week 7, then. Week 8's 360 units held for one week would contribute 360 part-periods and would certainly be included in our order for week 7. After week 8, though, we again run into the problem of having no gross requirements determined. As we did when applying the POQ, we will see what would happen if the next weeks' requirements are equal to the weekly average of 395. In that case ordering week 9's 395 units two weeks early would add 790 part-periods, resulting in a total of 1150 part-periods. Week 10's 395 units held for 3 weeks would add 1185 more part-periods, for a total of 2335. Since 1185 is closer to 1600 than is 2335, we would include only week 8 and week 9 in our order due for week 7.

Of course, the order determined above for week 7 is only tentative at this point. We included hypothetical requirement figures in order to compare this technique with our other lot-sizing techniques. When we have a number for the actual requirements for week 9, we can determine the actual order needed in week 7. However, even if it exceeds our hypothetical number of 395 somewhat, the total number of part-periods will still be close to the desired 1600. It is even possible that week 10's requirement could be included if the actual requirements for weeks 9 and 10 are small.

In any case, we can calculate our inventory costs from these hypothetical ordering decisions. The results appear in Figure 9.3. It turns out that our ordering pattern is exactly the same as we got using the POQ. This, however, is a co-incidence that results from a particular set of requirements figures over a very short time span. If we continue to apply the part-period algorithm to future requirements, we expect to see some orders that include just one week's demand, some including two weeks, three weeks, four weeks, and so on, not always the three-week grouping of the POQ policy.

The inventory costs for the part-period algorithm in this example would, of course, be the same as those using the POQ, a total of $250.20. However, in the long run we would expect the part-period algorithm to result in somewhat lower costs because it bases its ordering decisions on the actual upcoming re-quirements rather than following a rigid ordering schedule. The POQ, though, would obviously be a much easier system to administer and seems to perform fairly well in this example.

Summary of Lot-Sizing Techniques

We have applied four different lot-sizing techniques to our example of the chair frame—the lot-for-lot method, the EOQ, the POQ, and the part-period algorithm. These are among the most commonly used techniques. Most com-panies tend to rely on the lot-for-lot method for parts that they produce them-selves. As we saw, this method is easy to apply and is effective when setup costs are small. A major virtue of this method is that we don't need precise calculations of the ordering or setup cost and holding cost of each inventory item. In practice these numbers may be difficult to determine reliably.

For parts purchased from suppliers the EOQ and part-period algorithm are commonly used, with a few companies using the POQ. Besides these common techniques, though, there are many other more complicated techniques that have been proposed in the literature.

CHAPTER 10

Production Scheduling and Control

OVERVIEW

The problem of inventory control is closely connected to the problem of production scheduling and control. The main purpose of inventories of raw materials and work-in-process items is to counteract the effects of uneven production. If production were made completely smooth, we theoretically would need no in-process inventories. Of course, even the smoothest production system is subject to unpredictable problems such as machine breakdowns and late deliveries of supplies. Still, we strive constantly to make our production systems more repetitive to take advantage of the many benefits in efficiency, including lower inventories.

Companies whose business is less repetitive by nature still are often able to separate at least part of their operations system from the rest and organize that part to operate repetitively. Such a company operates partly as a mass producer and partly as a job shop, using different methods of production scheduling and control in each part.

It is difficult to discuss production scheduling and control, then, without discussing inventory control at the same time. Methods such as MRP and MRP II, which were discussed primarily as inventory control techniques, also are involved in production scheduling and control. These systems generate orders to work centers and provide reports to help control the work in the system. Similarly, we will be discussing Just-in-Time (JIT) systems in Chapter 11; such systems also have an effect on both inventory and scheduling.

What is it that makes a "good" schedule in general? In all types of systems, service or manufacturing, mass production or job shop, there are several goals that a schedule should meet. First of all, the schedule must be feasible—it must be possible with the facilities and labor force available, and it must be flexible enough to remain feasible as conditions change slightly. For the sake of the customers, the schedule must meet any due dates promised or, if none, to minimize the completion times. For the sake of the efficiency of the operation, the schedule should provide a high utilization of the facilities, avoiding costly idle time, especially in the short term. Finally, the schedule should enhance efforts in the major areas of inventory control and quality control; it should help keep inventory costs low and provide the opportunity to devote the attention necessary to produce high-quality goods or services.

Mass Production Systems

In the extreme mass production systems, where there is a continuous flow into, through, and out of the operations system, there is really no scheduling to be done. In such a situation the design of the system is paramount, for it must have the necessary capacity and the necessary efficiency to be competitive. Appropriate machines and workers must be selected, and the system must be balanced to ensure a smooth flow, as we discussed in Chapter 3.

Production control in such a repetitive system consists of making sure that the components of the system, the machines and the workers, are all doing their part to keep the system running as designed. Machine maintenance and worker motivation and safety become primary concerns.

Few operations systems, however, operate at this extreme of repetitiveness. As we move along the continuum toward less repetitive systems (intermittent production), we begin to experience the need for active production scheduling and control decisions. Systems that are largely repetitive can often benefit from a JIT system, as discussed later in the chapter. In many companies the use of group technology (cellular manufacturing) or flexible manufacturing systems can help to make parts of the system more repetitive and less in the need of complicated scheduling and controlling techniques. Whatever parts of the system remain relatively nonrepetitive can benefit from techniques used in job shops.

Job Shop Systems

The most interesting and most complicated scheduling problems occur in job shop systems. Since new jobs come in all the time at random, job shops have a constant scheduling problem. Besides the unpredictability of the arrival of new jobs to be done, the uniqueness of each job means that the time estimates for the various tasks required may not be completely reliable. Besides these difficulties, unexpected absenteeism, machine breakdowns, and so on, necessitate constant rescheduling. Further, each time a schedule is made, there is a huge number of ways to juggle the various jobs and to sequence the different tasks within jobs. All of these uncertainties create an extremely complicated and continual scheduling problem for a job shop.

We noted in Chapter 1 that scheduling is also a crucial operations problem for job shops because their profitability depends to a great extent on good utilization of their facilities. The heavy investment in machinery and in inventory necessary in most job shops requires careful attention to their efficient use.

When a job is accepted, a *routing* sheet must be prepared, showing the sequence of operations required, the specific work centers where it is to be sent, the part numbers, and the specifications of the production processes. Next, a major part of the scheduling process is *loading*, or actually sending a job to a work center. The method of *infinite loading* sends all jobs to the next work center as soon as possible without considering the capacities of the work centers. It then is necessary to decide the exact sequencing of jobs at each work center, a process called *dispatching*. The method of *finite loading* determines ahead of time just when to send each job to a given work center in order to meet the capacity constraints of the work centers. The process of *expediting* monitors the progress of important jobs and attempts to speed their completion. Together these processes constitute the production scheduling and control function of a job shop.

The most general situation in a job shop is that we have a set of jobs that we have accepted which we must match over some span of time to a set of work centers or facilities that we have available in our shop. Each job needs to be routed through a number of our work centers before it is completed. Besides this very complicated general situation, though, we sometimes have special scheduling problems that are more structured and which can be handled by specialized analytical techniques. We will discuss both the general scheduling problem and a few special cases of job shop scheduling.

Because of the complex nature of job shop scheduling, it is useful to create visual aids to depict the production schedule and the progress of the work. Several types of Gantt charts, originated by Henry Gantt, may be used for this purpose. There are many large schedule boards available commercially which use such things as magnetic cards and markers to show the status of work in the shop. Computer-generated reports can also be distributed to appropriate personnel in place of such large schedule boards.

Gantt charts have a horizontal scale showing time for a certain distance into the future. The vertical scale can show a variety of things. A Gantt load chart shows the various work centers on the vertical scale, and the chart itself shows the planned work assigned to each center in the near future. The current progress of the different jobs can be indicated as time progresses, and compared to the original schedule. Alternatively, the vertical scale can show the various steps of a single job (a Gantt progress chart) and the time each step is scheduled to be performed.

Service Systems

Service systems face a somewhat different type of scheduling problem than manufacturing systems. Jobs are generally of shorter duration, they don't consist of a lot of identical parts, and the work involved is performed largely by humans rather than by machines. Therefore, the problem is to schedule human workers in such a way that customers are served speedily without allowing too much wasteful idle time among the workers.

In service systems where customers arrive at random and they need service immediately, such as in a bank or a post office, the scheduling of service personnel can be analyzed with queuing theory, the theory of waiting lines. This topic is well covered in management science texts.

In other service systems where service need not be so immediate, such as in a hospital (other than the emergency room), some of the same scheduling techniques used in job shops may be useful. For example, Gantt load charts can show the utilization of the various work centers. The use of reservations or other priority rules can help determine the proper sequencing of customers and provide for efficient utilization of the system's resources. Inventories of supplies in a service system can be treated much as inventories of raw materials in a job shop.

FINITE LOADING IN A JOB SHOP

Finite loading requires that we consider the capacities of our facilities before we send them jobs. Thus, the whole scheduling process from the start of a job to its completion is a centralized decision as opposed to leaving priority decisions to the work centers as the jobs progress through the system. Obviously, this type of loading is very complex if we attempt to determine an "optimal" schedule. Even if we succeed in this lofty goal, we will need to redo our schedule continually as new jobs come in and as work deviates from its schedule.

Criteria

In trying to define what an optimal schedule means, we might consider several candidates for our goal. For example, we might try to minimize the *average completion time* of the set of jobs we are adding to our schedule. Besides pleasing the greatest number of customers, this goal will also enable us to minimize our own idle time in the near future by pushing jobs back as near to the present time as possible. Our idle time will thus be pushed farther into the future on the average, and we expect that new jobs coming in will enable us to utilize that time as well.

A second possible goal would be to minimize the *overall completion time* of our set of jobs, that is, get the last job done as early as possible. If we had a number of jobs from one customer, for example, this might be the best goal to satisfy that customer.

If we have agreed to due dates for our jobs, then we would probably want to use a criterion that would include these due dates. Of course, it would be best if we could always meet our due dates. Also, it may or may not be beneficial to finish *before* the due dates. A quantitative criterion that we might use would be to minimize the *average time beyond due dates*. Meeting due dates would then result in 0 time beyond the due dates; if getting done early is desirable, we can count this as a negative time beyond the due date in our average.

If our jobs have different *priorities* because of their importance to our company, we can simply set up a schedule to finish jobs in the order of their priorities. This criterion can also be used in combination with others when only some of the jobs have higher priorities.

Scheduling Options

Besides our choice of criteria, we also need to know just what scheduling options are available to us for a given set of jobs. For example, is it possible to *split a lot* at a particular work center? Splitting a lot means that we produce part of a lot during one stretch of time, then shift to another job, and finally come back to finish the original lot. In some cases the cost of setting up twice for a particular job may be prohibitive. If setup costs are small, though, splitting lots will give us a great deal more flexibility in our scheduling and enable us to achieve a higher utilization of our facilities, while completing jobs earlier for our customers.

Somewhat similar to splitting lots is *lap-phasing*, or sending part of a lot ahead to the next work center before the entire lot is finished. At the extreme each piece can be sent ahead to the next work center after it is completed, much as in an assembly line. If lap-phasing is possible, we do not have to wait for an entire lot to finish at one work center in order to send it along to the next; the job can be worked on almost simultaneously at several work centers. Of course, many jobs do not consist of a large number of identical parts and thus would not lend themselves to lap-phasing. Even where feasible, lap-phasing would be limited by the availability and cost of transportation between work centers.

In most manufacturing situations a job will include *time between steps*; that is, a job will not proceed from work center to work center without any delays. Ordinarily, each job, upon completion at one work center, will wait for a while to be transported to the next work center, followed by a certain amount of time in transport, and finally a period of waiting at the new work station before it is worked on. However, in some cases we may not have this flexibility. Especially in the case of food or chemical products, it may be necessary for the steps of the production process to follow each other without delay. Developing photographs, for example, requires such timely processing.

While it is obviously impossible to insert a bolt before drilling the hole, in many cases we have some *flexibility in sequencing* the steps of the production process. To the extent that we do have this flexibility, the complexity of our scheduling problem increases.

Another factor increasing the complexity of scheduling would be the case where a job might require *different times on different machines*. A job shop may have several welders, for example, perhaps some newer, faster, or more sophisticated than others. A given job might require different times, either for setup or for processing, on these different machines. Also, different jobs may be affected to different extents by the choice of machine. Later we will examine a special case of this situation, where we have a set of some number of jobs to assign to an equal number of machines in order to achieve the greatest total efficiency.

Example 10.1—Scene Creators, Inc.

Scene Creators is a company that produces scenery and props for motion pictures. They have just received the following three jobs:

Job A: 2 days Work Center 1, 4 days Work Center 3, 2 days Work Center 4

Job B: 3 days Work Center 1, 2 days Work Center 2, 3 days Work Center 3, 3 days Work Center 4

Job C: 4 days Work Center 2, 3 days Work Center 4, 2 days Work Center 3 (time requirements include setup times)

Let's assume that the jobs all come from the same movie, so our objective is to minimize the overall completion time of these three jobs. Even though in real life there would ordinarily be work already scheduled for our four work centers, we will assume that in this case these are our only three jobs. Otherwise, though, we will keep the example manageable by making several assumptions that reduce our flexibility. We will assume that we are not able to split any lots, and lap-phasing is also not an option. The jobs must progress through the work stations in the sequence listed, with no flexibility. We will further assume that it is acceptable for a job to have time gaps between steps at the different work centers. If we were to relax some of these assumptions, our options would quickly expand beyond the point where we could conveniently analyze the problem by hand. Even as it is, we will see that we have a number of choices to make in our schedule.

Below we see a Gantt load chart of our four work centers over the next 18 days. Since we are concerned with the overall completion time of our three jobs, it seems reasonable in our initial solution to schedule the longest job first. Job B requires 11 days of work, while jobs A and C require only 8 and 9 days, respectively. By putting job B on our schedule first (all four steps), then job C, and finally job A, we arrive at the initial solution shown.

GANTT LOAD CHART SHOWING INITIAL SOLUTION

										Day								
	1	2	3	4	5	6	7	8	9	10	11	12	13	14	15	16	17	18
WC 1	B	B	B	A	A													
WC 2				B	B	C	C	C	C									

WC 3	B	B	B	A	A	A	A			C	C
WC 4		B	B	B	C	C	C	A	A		

Completion Times: job A—Day 16
job B—Day 11
job C—Day 16

While starting by scheduling job B seemed like a good idea at the time, we can see now that it leads us to a very poor solution, with an overall completion time of 16 days. We are unable to begin job C in work center 2 until day 6 because of its 4-day duration and our assumption that we cannot split a lot. For this reason both job A and Job C are delayed unnecessarily. As a result, we see that we are left with a great deal of idle time in our facilities in the near future.

However, if we begin job C in work center 2 on day 1, we will need to push job B back by only one day, while completing job A and job C a little earlier. This new solution, with an overall completion time of 15 days, appears below:

GANTT LOAD CHART SHOWING REVISED SOLUTION

	Day																	
	1	2	3	4	5	6	7	8	9	10	11	12	13	14	15	16	17	18
WC 1	B	B	B	A	A													
WC 2	C	C	C	C	B	B												
WC 3							B	B	B	A	A	A	A	C	C			
WC 4					C	C	C			B	B	B		A	A			

Completion Times: job A—Day 15
job B—Day 12
job C—Day 15

We see that in our revised solution the cause of the late completion time of jobs A and C is that job A must wait so long for work center 3. The only way to remedy this situation is to start job A before job B at work center 1 so that job A can then begin work at work center 3 much earlier. With this change we arrive at the solution shown on the following page. After staring at this solution for a while (since we aren't using a computer to try all possible alternatives), we can convince ourselves that this is the optimal solution. Job B is the last job done, but after it is put into production on day 3, it progresses through the system with no delays. Therefore, the only way to finish job B any earlier would be to reverse the change we just made in placing job A ahead of job B at work center 1. We already know that solution is worse.

What if we used a different criterion in our example problem? If the three jobs to be scheduled came from three different customers, it might be more relevant to minimize the *average* completion time rather than the overall completion time. Our solution above yields an average completion time of (9 + 13 + 12)/3 = 34/3 = 11.33 days (much better than either of the first two solutions).

GANTT LOAD CHART SHOWING OPTIMAL SOLUTION

Day

	1	2	3	4	5	6	7	8	9	10	11	12	13	14	15	16	17	18
WC 1	A	A	B	B	B													
WC 2	C	C	C	C		B	B											
WC 3			A	A	A	A		B	B	B	C	C						
WC 4					C	C	C	A	A		B	B	B					

Completion Times: job A—Day 9
job B—Day 13
job C—Day 12

This is surely a very good initial solution, but is it optimal under the new criterion?

Because of the very restrictive assumptions we have placed upon this problem, there really aren't too many reasonable alternatives remaining. We certainly don't want to move job A ahead of job C at work center 4, since we would save only one day on job A while delaying jobs B and C one day each. However, if we schedule job C ahead of job B at work center 3, our average completion time improves. Both are ready to begin on day 8, so work center 3 will finish the two jobs on day 12 in any case. However, by putting job C ahead of job B, we save 3 days on job C's completion time, while delaying job B by only 2 days. We have discovered the general principle that, if all else is equal, placing the shorter job first will decrease the average completion time.

The chart below shows our new optimal solution, with an average completion time of $(9 + 15 + 9)/3 = 33/3 = 11$ days. Note that the overall completion time of the three jobs is now 15 days again, not as good as our previous solution for that criterion.

Real scheduling problems would, of course, be much larger and more complex than this example and would require the use of a computer to analyze the many alternatives.

OPTIMAL SOLUTION FOR MINIMUM AVERAGE COMPLETION TIME

Day

	1	2	3	4	5	6	7	8	9	10	11	12	13	14	15	16	17	18
WC 1	A	A	B	B	B													
WC 2	C	C	C	C		B	B											
WC 3			A	A	A	A		C	C	B	B							
WC 4					C	C	C	A	A				B	B	B			

Completion Times: job A—Day 9
job B—Day 15
job C—Day 9

Forward and Backward Scheduling

The previous example problem illustrated the process of forward scheduling. Starting from the present, we use finite loading to schedule our work as near to the present as possible in order to finish jobs quickly and to make good use of our facilities. In cases where we have predetermined due dates, however, we could also schedule backward from these due dates. Each step of a job would be scheduled as late as possible without causing the job to extend beyond the due date.

In backward scheduling the logic is very similar to that used in MRP. Requirements (in this case capacity requirements at the various work centers) are projected backward from the final product requirements. MRP itself, though, is generally not used in extreme job shop systems where the work consists of many small, unrepeated jobs. It is more suited to situations where there are relatively few, commonly used, bills of materials.

The advantage of backward scheduling is that materials can be ordered to arrive at the latest time possible, cutting down on holding costs of inventory. With forward scheduling there are more likely to be gaps between processing steps, increasing the holding costs. The obvious disadvantage of backward scheduling is that if there is any delay in the production process, the job will be finished late. Also, if new jobs arrive, it may be more difficult to fit them into the schedule; with forward scheduling the capacity in the future is unlimited, while with backward scheduling the capacity prior to any given due date may well be insufficient. If we then are forced to rearrange our existing schedule, our carefully timed schedule of material arrivals and earlier production steps will be disrupted.

INFINITE LOADING IN A JOB SHOP

With infinite loading we send each job to the next work center on its routing sheet as soon as it is ready. At that point the job joins a queue of jobs waiting to be processed at that work center. To determine the proper sequencing of jobs waiting in the queue, workers apply a particular *priority dispatching rule*. These simple rules eliminate the need for a detailed analysis of the sort we undertook with finite loading, and new jobs can easily be accommodated at any time without trying to determine a new optimal schedule. Several of the most common priority dispatching rules are discussed below.

First-Come, First-Served

Because of its simplicity and perceived fairness, this is a very commonly used rule both in manufacturing and service systems. In manufacturing applications the first job to arrive at a given work center would be the first to be processed.

Shortest Processing Time

We have seen in our finite loading example that scheduling the shorter jobs first generally minimizes the average completion time of a set of jobs. By putting the shortest job first, we cause the other jobs to wait as little as possible. In many simulations of job shops under different conditions this rule has often proven to be the best. In service systems the shortest processing rule can also be used when it does not violate the appearance of fairness to customers. To avoid this problem and still serve customers with shorter jobs quickly, it is sometimes possible to use separate service facilities dedicated to quick jobs, such as express lanes in a supermarket.

In systems with frequent arrivals of jobs, and where setups are not a problem, it is even possible to look at shortest *remaining* processing time and allow short new jobs to interrupt jobs in progress.

Longest Processing Time

Obviously, putting longer jobs first *increases* the time that other jobs must wait. However, working on a longer job first will at least "get it out of the way." It is also possible that longer jobs might be considered more important (more profitable) than shorter jobs. Further, in a busy job shop that uses the shortest processing time rule, the longer jobs may be delayed indefinitely because of a constant stream of shorter jobs receiving priority.

Shortest Setup Time

When each new job requires a time-consuming and costly setup of equipment at a work center, the setup time may become the overriding consideration. Also, it is quite possible that the setup times for jobs in the queue are dependent on which job has just finished processing. That is, job A may require one hour of setup time when it follows job B through a certain work center but two hours of setup time when it follows job C. Therefore, the job chosen next depends on the previous job processed.

Due Dates

So far, none of our possible priority dispatching rules has paid any attention to the times the various jobs are due. A very simple rule to follow would be to schedule jobs according to their due dates. However, this rule by itself does not consider how much work remains to be done before the due date.

Minimum Slack Time

A job's slack time is equal to (time remaining until due date) minus (time required for work remaining). A job that is already bound to run beyond its due date will have a negative slack. The job with the least slack can withstand the least delay if it is to meet its due date and thus should be scheduled first. Either minimum slack time or minimum slack time per number of operations remaining may be used to assign priorities.

Critical Ratio

Rather than take the difference between the time remaining until the due date and the work remaining to be done, we can take the ratio of these numbers: Critical Ratio = (time remaining until due date)/(time required for work remaining). We would choose the job with the smallest critical ratio. Of course, this calculation tells us pretty much the same thing as the slack time calculation. A critical ratio less than 1 means the same thing as a negative slack time—the job is already projected to go beyond its due date.

Artificial Priorities

A company may assign different degrees of importance to jobs for reasons other than the timing factors which we have considered. Large jobs or jobs with high profit margins may be considered more important, or certain preferred customers may have their jobs scheduled first.

SCHEDULING n JOBS IN A TWO-STEP PRODUCTION PROCESS

In some job shop situations all products go through the same basic process even though the jobs differ quite a bit in the exact work done at each work center. In the simplest case consider a production system where all jobs must go through two work centers in the same order and where lap-phasing is not an option. For example, at Big Bertha's Body Shop cars generally go through the body department, where the body is smoothed, filled, and sanded, and then through the paint department. Currently, she has 6 cars in the shop ready to begin repair; time estimates are as follows:

Job	Body	Paint
A	2.0 hrs.	4.5 hrs.
B	2.5	4.0
C	4.0	3.5
D	1.5	3.0
E	3.0	2.0
F	2.5	3.0

A technique known as Johnson's Rule will be applied to determine the proper sequencing of the 6 jobs through the system. This rule will minimize the overall completion time of the jobs, thereby also minimizing the idle time of the two work centers. The process may be described as follows:

1. Pick the shortest processing time on the list, regardless of whether it is in the first work center or the second. If it is in the first work center, schedule that job as early as possible. If it is in the second work center, schedule that job as late as possible. Repeat this process with those jobs remaining unscheduled until all jobs are scheduled.

2. If there is a tie between two or more jobs for the shortest processing time,

   a. If job X has that shortest time at the first work center and job Y has that time at the second work center, schedule job X as early as possible and job Y as late as possible.

   b. If job X has that shortest time *both* at the first work center and at the second work center, schedule job X either as early as possible or as late as possible.

   c. If job X and job Y both have that shortest time at the same work center, break the tie by choosing the job which takes *longest* at the other work center.

Let's apply Johnson's Rule to Big Bertha's Body Shop. The shortest time requirement overall is the 1.5 hours of job D at the body department. Since the body department is the first phase of production, we will schedule job D as early as possible (first):

	1st	**2nd**	**3rd**	**4th**	**5th**	**6th**
Job:	D					

Eliminating job D, then, the lowest time overall is 2.0 hours, both for job A at the body department and for job E at the paint department. Therefore, we will place job A as early as possible and job E as late as possible:

	1st	**2nd**	**3rd**	**4th**	**5th**	**6th**
Job:	D	A				E

Of the three remaining jobs the shortest time requirement is 2.5 hours, shared by jobs B and F, both at the body department. To break the tie, then, we note that job B's time at the paint department is 4.0 hours, longer than job F's 3.0 hours. Therefore, we choose job B to schedule as early as possible (since the 2.5 hours was at the body department, the first step). Job F is next, of course, and we again would like to schedule it as early as possible (fourth). That leaves just job C to occupy the fifth position. Our optimal sequence of jobs is:

	1st	**2nd**	**3rd**	**4th**	**5th**	**6th**
Job:	D	A	B	F	C	E

The chart below shows how our schedule would actually appear on the load chart. Because we have put jobs first which require shorter processing during the first phase of production (the body department) and generally longer times during the second phase (the paint department), we hope that we will send jobs from the first phase to the second phase before the second phase is completed on previous jobs. Therefore, jobs will be waiting at the second phase of production, avoiding idle times there. Of course, we avoid any idle times at the first phase of production by starting one job immediately after another. Thus, by getting the second phase of production started as soon as possible and keeping it busy, we minimize the overall time that jobs are in the system. After just 1.5 hours we start work in the paint department; since there are 20 hours of work to be done in that department (and no idle time), we finish after 21.5 hours.

GANTT LOAD CHART FOR OPTIMAL SEQUENCE

	Hour																		
	1	2	3	4	5	6	7	8	9	10	11	12	13	14	15	16	17	18	19
Body	D	D/A	A	A/B	B		B	F	F	F/C	C	C	C	C/E	E	E	E/		
Paint		/D	D	D	D/A	A	A	A	A	B	B	B	B	F	F	F	C	C	C

	20	21	22
Paint (cont.)	C/E	E	E/

ASSIGNING n JOBS TO n FACILITIES

Sometimes the situation arises when we have a number of jobs to be done, each of which could be done by any of a set of machines, or perhaps by any of a set of workers. We would like to decide which job should be done by which machine or worker in order to achieve the greatest overall efficiency—shortest time, least cost, and so on. This is a one-time, or static, decision: no new jobs arriving will be considered.

If the number of jobs is equal to the number of facilities available, the problem can be solved by applying the assignment method of linear programming. (Even if the number of jobs does not equal the number of facilities, a dummy job or facility can be added to solve the problem.) The assignment method is a special case of the transportation method, which is itself a special case of linear programming. Because this problem is so highly structured, it is not necessary to use such linear programming algorithms as the simplex method to solve it, or even the common methods for transportation problems. A simpler, almost magical-looking algorithm (known as the Hungarian method after the Hungarian mathematician Honig) can be used instead.

Suppose that Phil's Phurniture Phactory has five jobs (A, B, C, D, and E) that need sawing. There are five saws of various types available with different blades and fixtures (S1, S2, S3, S4, and S5). Phil has estimated the hours it would take to perform each job on each saw, with the results as shown in Figure 10.1. If we were to consider all possible assignments of jobs to saws, we would

Figure 10.1
Hungarian Method for the Assignment Problem

Original Hours Required

Saw	A	B	C	D	E
S1	3	4	2	5	2
S2	4	5	1	3	3
S3	4	6	3	4	2
S4	5	5	4	5	4
S5	3	3	3	4	3

Job

⇒

After Subtracting in Rows

Saw	A	B	C	D	E
S1	1	2	0	3	0
S2	3	4	0	2	2
S3	2	4	1	2	0
S4	1	1	0	1	0
S5	0	0	0	1	0

Job

After Subtracting in Columns

Saw	A	B	C	D	E
S1	1	2	0	2	0
S2	3	4	0	1	2
S3	2	4	1	1	0
S4	1	1	0	0	0
S5	0	0	0	0	0

Job

⇒

Crossing Out 0's

Saw	A	B	C	D	E
S1	1	2	0	2	0
S2	3	4	0	1	2
S3	2	4	1	1	0
S4	1	1	0	0	0
S5	0	0	0	0	0

Job

After Adding and Subtracting

Saw	A	B	C	D	E
S1	0	1	0	1	0
S2	2	3	0	0	2
S3	1	3	1	0	0
S4	1	1	1	0	1
S5	0	0	1	0	1

Job

⇒

Crossing Out 0's Again

Saw	A	B	C	D	E
S1	0	1	0	1	0
S2	2	3	0	0	2
S3	1	3	1	0	0
S4	1	1	1	0	1
S5	0	0	1	0	1

Job

need to consider n! = 5! = 120 different alternatives. As n increases, the alternatives skyrocket.

We would like to minimize the average number of hours required for the five jobs. To apply the Hungarian method to this problem, we proceed as follows:

1. Subtract the smallest number in each row from all entries in that row. (Adding or subtracting a constant to a row or column will not change the optimal assignment. This process will ensure at least one 0 in each row.)

2. Subtract the smallest number in each column from all entries in that column (many are 0). This will ensure at least one 0 in each column as well.

3. Draw lines through rows and/or columns in order to cross out all the 0's with as few lines as possible. (If it is not obvious how to draw the minimum number of lines, use the following procedure. If a row has only one 0 in it, cross out the *column* containing that 0. Likewise, if a column has only one 0, cross out the *row* containing that 0.)

4. If the number of lines drawn is equal to the number of rows or columns, the problem is finished; see step 6. If the number of lines drawn is less than the number of rows or columns, proceed to step 5. (We will never need *more* lines than the number of rows or columns since we could just draw a line through each row or through each column.)

5. When the solution is not optimal, subtract the smallest uncrossed number from all uncrossed entries. Add this same number to all entries where lines intersect. Leave other entries alone. Return to step 3.

6. When the solution is optimal, we still need to interpret just what the solution is. If any row or column has just one 0, that 0 indicates that that row is assigned to that column. Eliminating that row and column, then, look for other rows or columns with just one 0. If at some point no row or column has just one 0, then we have alternative optima. Pick one 0 from a row or column with two 0's and proceed as before. (The other solution can be determined also by picking the other 0.)

Applying this technique to Phil's problem, we first subtract the smallest number in each row from all entries in that row. This and succeeding steps are shown in Figure 10.1.

After subtracting the smallest number in each column from all entries in that column, we arrive at the third table in Figure 10.1. At this point we are ready to start crossing out the 0's. The fourth table shows one way to cross out the 0's with the fewest lines (there is another equally good way).

Since all the 0's can be crossed out with only four lines, we have not yet arrived at the final solution. Therefore, we apply step 5, subtracting 1 from all the uncrossed numbers and adding 1 to all the numbers crossed twice (fifth table).

We now repeat the process of crossing out the 0's with as few lines as possible. The result in the sixth table shows that now 5 lines are necessary. Therefore, the solution is optimal. Since there is only one 0 for S4, it is assigned to job D. Saw S5 is also assigned to job B because of the single 0 in column B. With these rows and columns eliminated, it is easy to see the remaining assignments as listed below. The average time spent per job in our optimal solution is $14/5 = 2.8$ hours.

FINAL SOLUTION FOR
PHIL'S PHURNITURE PHACTORY

Saw	Job	Hours
S1	A	3
S2	C	1
S3	E	2
S4	D	5
S5	B	3
		14

CHAPTER 11

Just-in-Time Systems

OVERVIEW

The idea of Just-in-Time (JIT) systems is one of several concepts that have been popularized by Japanese managers recently. Generally, the principles behind these ideas have been rather well-known for years, but Japanese companies have taken them to lengths previously thought unattainable. In Chapter 1 we discussed JIT's principle of demand-flow manufacturing as a strategic weapon in today's marketplace. This central concept of JIT holds that lead times should be reduced throughout the production system so that each worker receives just what is needed when it is needed. Thus, work-in-process inventories are seen as an evil that wastes money and space, and also conceals bottlenecks in the system.

In the case of JIT systems the goal is just the same as it was for the classical EOQ model of inventory control and for the more recent development of MRP. In all these cases operations managers seek to balance the ordering or setup costs with the holding costs of inventory in order to achieve the lowest total inventory cost. However, each approach is based on certain assumptions and therefore works best only under certain conditions. For example, we have seen that the EOQ model applies to fairly smooth but independent demands, while MRP applies to lumpy, dependent demands. JIT works best in highly repetitive production situations where relatively few end products are produced, and the production sequence can be fixed with very little variation.

While the traditional EOQ model is also a demand-flow, or "pull," system, it separates the function of inventory management from the function of production control. In JIT, though, interconnections between production and inventory levels are recognized and dealt with.

THE JIT PHILOSOPHY

The inventory aspect of JIT, though, is part of a much larger philosophy. The idea here is to reduce the lot size as far as possible, preferably to just 1 unit at a time. If this could be accomplished, each item would be produced or ordered only when needed, or "just in time." Raw material and work-in-process inventories would be reduced to 0. Of course, this implies a very large number of setups for production of items and of orders for raw materials.

For this strategy to be optimal if only inventory costs are considered, it is obvious that the ordering or setup costs would have to be reduced virtually to 0. Indeed, that is part of the philosophy of JIT. In plants with JIT systems workers constantly strive to reduce setup times. Setups that traditionally have taken several hours in auto plants have been reduced to a few minutes in plants using JIT. Of course, in order to allow for such quick setups, the product must be designed with setup times in mind.

One of the main virtues of the JIT approach is that by minimizing in-process inventories, any inefficiencies or imbalances in the system are brutally exposed and can then be corrected. Cost savings result not only in the inventory area but in several other facets of the operations system. When work-in-process inventories are large, they can absorb fluctuations in work flow caused by breakdowns, poor quality, and improper work station capacities. These hidden inefficiencies can persist for a long time without attracting any attention. However, for JIT to work properly, there must be a perfect balance in capacity all along the production pipeline, and any breakdown or quality lapse becomes immediately noticeable. In fact, individual workers often have the authority to shut down the assembly line, thereby causing everyone's work to screech to a halt, if something goes wrong. Then workers all cooperate to fix the problem as quickly as possible and resume production.

It is apparent that the role of the production worker in such a system is a little different than was traditional in the United States. Workers are given more responsibility for controlling the flow of production, for maintenance of their machines, and for the quality of their output. They also are generally trained to be very flexible and capable of performing a variety of work duties rather than one repetitive job over and over. This allows for much better utilization of workers than when everyone's job is very narrowly defined. Such worker-management relations have so far been easier to achieve in Japan where there has been a tradition of company loyalty and often guaranteed lifetime employment. In the United States, on the other hand, the traditional labor union-management relationship has been much more confrontational. Still, this "team concept" has been increasingly implemented in U.S. plants with some success.

The philosophy of JIT also encourages efforts to make the production process more repetitive. In particular, JIT lends itself to the use of cellular manufacturing (group technology), since cells can be used to produce several different but similar products with minimal setup times. Cells (U-shaped, for example) also contribute to improved efficiency in utilizing floor space, cutting down on travel distances between work centers and thereby improving the quick responses needed in JIT. Of course, carrying the cellular manufacturing idea to the extreme by creating flexible manufacturing systems where feasible will cut down on setup times even more through computerization.

Effects of JIT on Quality Control

A good JIT system can contribute to the quality control effort. Because of the small lot sizes involved, problems with quality are discovered very soon after production rather than at some distant time in the future. Therefore, the problem can be corrected quickly before too many parts are affected. Indeed, the problem must be corrected quickly or all work centers down the line will have no parts to work on. This urgency encourages the workers to monitor their own quality closely and to join together to correct problems when they do arise. Workers are also expected to take greater initiative in performing preventive maintenance, which can further improve quality.

A common thread throughout the JIT philosophy and that of Total Quality Management (see Chapters 1 and 13) is to strive constantly to improve the system. The goal is a system that produces things correctly the first time, rather than having to fix them later.

Effects of JIT on Suppliers

If a company succeeds in smoothing out its production and reducing work-in-process inventories, it naturally would like to extend these results to its raw material inventories. Ideally, it would like to treat its suppliers just like its own supplier work centers: raw materials would be sent in small standard quantities only when required by demander work centers. Such cooperation with suppliers is a rather radical idea, but Japanese companies have been successful in developing very close relationships with a small number of carefully chosen suppliers. These suppliers can be tied into the company's computer system, and the plant can be located very near its suppliers in order to facilitate very quick deliveries.

Before asking a supplier to cooperate in sending small, frequent orders whenever demanded, however, the company must have its own production system running smoothly. It would be unfair to transfer its inefficiencies (and its inventories!) to its suppliers by asking them to provide quite variable quantities of products at a moment's notice.

It is also necessary, of course, for a supplier's quality control to be as stringent as the company's. Receiving defective raw materials from suppliers would have a devastating effect on the company's JIT system. Therefore, it is in the company's interest to work with its suppliers to help them achieve the high quality desired.

JIT Compared to MRP

The main distinction between JIT and MRP is that MRP is a "push" type of production control system, while JIT is a "pull" system. That is, MRP relies on a predetermined production schedule derived by exploding the bill of materials to determine requirements for all parts and components. These parts are produced according to this schedule, and the parts are pushed ahead to the next work center upon completion. When they arrive, they create a workload for the demander work center. JIT, on the other hand, pulls parts through the system only when they are needed, through signals such as kanbans. Thus, MRP can be seen basically as a planning device, while JIT serves mainly as a controlling device. We have also seen that JIT is part of a larger philosophy of production encompassing such ideas as an emphasis on quality, cooperation with suppliers, and increased responsiblity for workers.

MRP is a concept that can be applied to a broad range of operations, while JIT consists of a specific set of principles. For example, MRP can be used in cases where demand is lumpy as well as smooth, while JIT is useful only in repetitive production systems. Forecasts for MRP need not be quite as certain as in JIT systems. MRP can utilize large lots as well as the small lots utilized in JIT. MRP can include such ideas as safety stock and several types of lot-sizing techniques, while JIT avoids safety stock and uses constant small lot sizes. MRP systems can sometimes operate with much looser control than in JIT systems. JIT systems strive to make production control very simple, while MRP systems can often be rather complicated and expensive.

The main difficulty in an MRP system is the necessity to specify lead times for each item. For things to work smoothly, these lead times must be fixed and known. However, the degree of congestion on the floor can have an effect on lead times. If there is any variability in lead times, they will probably be set at the highest possible number to avoid a late batch, thus increasing inventories when lead times turn out to be shorter. As opposed to JIT systems, there is little incentive with MRP to improve lead times with new methods—this would only lead to troublesome changes in the system's relationships.

However, it is possible for a company to use both MRP and JIT if the system is repetitive enough. The JIT ideas of cooperation with suppliers and worker involvement can be incorporated into an MRP system. The company can always strive for cheaper and quicker setups to enable the use of small lot sizes. JIT systems can incorporate the data collection, materials coordination, and tracking methods of MRP while maintaining a pull method of order releases. Also, a production system may have some parts that are rather repetitive, lending themselves to JIT, while other areas, such as final assembly, are less predictable and can benefit from MRP.

For less repetitive systems, though, MRP (and especially the enhancements of MRP II) may still be valuable, while JIT would not be applicable. Even here, though, the JIT philosophy of narrowing the product line and making production as repetitive as possible can be used to change the nature of existing production systems to some extent.

JIT IN ACTION

Production Control with Kanbans

Beginning with Toyota, Japanese companies have traditionally accompanied their JIT programs with very simple, low-tech methods of production control on the floor. Visible signals, such as cards (kanbans) or lights, are used by one work center to request production of parts from the previous work center.

The original kanban system used by Toyota makes use of two types of kanbans, a production card and a move card. In Figure 11.1 we see the way the system works. Parts are moved between work centers in standard containers which hold only a small, predetermined number of parts. When a work center empties one of these containers, it sends the empty container to the supplier work center accompanied by a move card (step 1). At the supplier work center the move card is removed and placed in a finished container of parts, thus authorizing the moving of this container to the demander work center (step 2).

The finished container of parts previously was accompanied by a production card. When the move card is placed into this container, the production card is removed and added to the work schedule of the supplier work center (step 3). Thus, the production card authorizes the production of another container of items. When the new container is filled, the production card is placed back into the full container at the storage area of the supplier work center (step 4), waiting for a move card to arrive again to claim the container.

In summary, then, move cards are sent from demander work centers to supplier work centers to claim containers of parts. When a container is taken, a production card is removed and used to signal a new batch of production at the supplier work center. Therefore, a work center doesn't begin production of a new batch of items until a previously produced batch is taken away. Of course, most work centers are both suppliers and demanders, receiving move cards in their role of supplier and sending move cards in their role as demander.

Most companies using JIT today use an even simpler system involving just the move cards. A move card is sent along with an empty container to the supplier work center. There the move card is placed in a full container and returned to the demander work center. However, rather than using a production card, the supplier station takes the empty container as a signal to begin production in order to refill it. The production of the supplier work center is generally predetermined, but, if demand is less than planned, the lack of empty containers arriving will serve as a signal to slow down production (since there is no provision for storing large quantities of items). Similarly, inventory at the demander work center is limited by the number of containers and move cards in the system.

Figure 11.1
Two-Card Kanban System

Supplier Work Center   Demander Work Center

1. Empty container with Move card sent from demander to supplier.

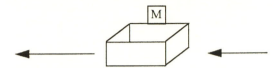

2. Move card removed and placed in full container, which is then sent

    from supplier to demander.

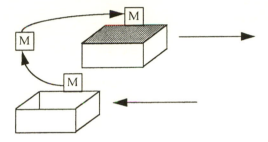

3. Production card removed from full container before container is sent

    and placed on work schedule.

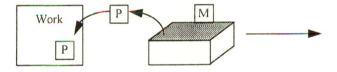

4. New container filled; Production card placed in full container.

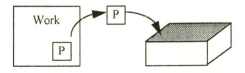

The total inventory available in the storage area of any work center thus depends on the number of kanbans circulating in the system. For example, when a demander work center sends back an empty container to a supplier work center, they may still have several containers left to work from while awaiting the production of the new batch. Alternatively, several containers of parts may be stored at the supplier work center awaiting removal by demander work centers. To decrease the work-in-process inventory, the company needs only to reduce the number of containers and kanbans in the system. A common practice in companies using JIT systems is to systematically reduce the number of kanbans in the system when things are working smoothly. This may expose underlying inefficiencies and imbalances in the system, which may then be corrected. When things again are working smoothly, the number of kanbans is reduced further, and so on. The goal is to reduce the number of kanbans to the absolute minimum so that the system is perfectly coordinated and there is no work-in-process inventory at all.

Drawbacks of JIT

As mentioned, JIT is best suited to systems which are very repetitive. Indeed, it has sometimes been found that in situations with much variability in supply and demand, JIT is even less likely than MRP to achieve low inventories. Similarly, the production system needs to be balanced—any imbalances or bottlenecks will be readily apparent under JIT, and if these cannot be fixed, results will continue to be poor.

As a reactive system, JIT does not plan well. Even in a balanced system demands can change. In fact, most companies strive to increase their sales steadily over time. When this occurs, though, the JIT system experiences a painful readjustment period. Without some kind of tracking system, such as MRP, the JIT system will not adjust to even the most obvious changes in demand until after the fact.

CHAPTER 12

Project Planning with PERT

OVERVIEW

A special type of scheduling and controlling problem is the scheduling of large, one-time projects. Examples of such projects would be building projects, relocation or overhaul of a plant, and production of large or unique items such as battleships or space shuttles. Because of the uniqueness of such projects the data required for planning may be rather sketchy, and it may be necessary to do some estimating. Also, given the expense and time requirements of such large projects, it is obvious that careful planning and control are necessary in order to maintain profitability.

Unfortunately, because of "cost-plus" contracts often awarded by the government or other large contractors, the incentive for economy is often lost, resulting in the large cost overruns that we read about. On the other hand, when the contract does call for a fixed payment or offers other incentives for early completion or cost control, companies that find themselves with costs out of control have been known to cut corners in production and to falsify test data. In any case, it is apparent that careful planning and control of costs are crucial for these large, expensive projects.

We have seen the use of the Gantt chart for scheduling in a job shop where jobs are generally different from each other. However, the tasks required for these jobs are usually well-known even though the particular job may be unique. With large projects, though, the time requirements and the necessary sequencing of tasks may be much more uncertain. Also, the project is generally much larger and more complicated than jobs in a job shop. Therefore, for these large projects a technique is needed that will go beyond the Gantt chart to show the sequencing requirements of the tasks. This type of scheduling problem lends itself to the use of *network models*.

In 1958 the U.S. Navy was planning the construction of the Polaris nuclear submarine missile system. This was a very large, complicated, and expensive project that needed a better planning and controlling technique than was currently available. Along with the consulting firm of Booz, Allen, and Hamilton, they devised the system called PERT (Program Evaluation and Review Technique), a type of network model for scheduling. At the same time, but independently, the DuPont Company, along with the Remington Rand Corp., was trying to devise a scheduling technique for the construction and maintenance of chemical plants. Their technique, called CPM (Critical Path Method), had much in common with PERT. Although there are some differences between the two methods, which will be noted later, today the two are used almost interchangeably, combining the features of each.

The early applications of PERT and CPM were very successful in saving time and money. Therefore, the techniques quickly became popular for large projects. However, the collection of data and subsequent analysis necessary in these techniques makes them rather expensive to use. For that reason we see their use mainly in large, expensive projects where their potential cost savings can justify their use. It is quite possible, though, to perform a PERT type of analysis on a much smaller scale for one-time projects within a company, such as redesigning an assembly line or installing a new information system.

As mentioned, the information needed for a PERT analysis is rather extensive. First, we need a list of all the activities that must be performed throughout the project. In other words, we need a complete understanding of everything that must be done to complete the project. However, a PERT analysis can be performed at different levels of detail. The major steps of a project can be analyzed with PERT, and then each of these can be broken down into smaller, more detailed tasks. A PERT analysis can then be made of these smaller tasks. This process can be repeated for several levels of detail.

Second, we need to know the sequencing requirements for all of the activities. Which activities need to follow which other activities? Which can be performed simultaneously?

Finally, we need time estimates for all of the activities. Keep in mind that this is a unique project, so we may never have performed some of these activities before. Their time must then be estimated. This is one difference between the original PERT and CPM methods. PERT assumed a probability distribution for the duration of each activity, while CPM assumed a single number.

With all of these information requirements, it is apparent that we need a rather complete understanding of the project (at least through estimates) before we can proceed with a PERT analysis. For large, expensive projects, though, the cost savings are well worth the effort.

SEQUENCING DIAGRAMS

In order to visualize the sequencing, or precedence, requirements of the activities in the project, it is helpful to draw a diagram. Both PERT and CPM use a network model to show these requirements; however, the type of diagram used is another of the differences between the two techniques. The original PERT technique used an "activities-on-arrows" diagram (AOA), while CPM used an "activities-on-nodes" diagram (AON). We used the AON type of diagram in Chapter 3 for diagramming the sequencing requirements for assembly line balancing.

As the name indicates, AOA diagrams place activities on arrows (see Figure 12.1). At each end of the activity arrow is a circle, or node. These nodes represent points in time, or instants, when an activity is starting or ending. The arrow itself represents the passage of time required for that activity to be performed. In fact, with a little effort AOA diagrams can be superimposed on a time scale with the arrows drawn the correct length to indicate the time requirement. AON diagrams simply place the activities within the nodes, and the arrows are used only to indicate sequencing requirements.

In AOA diagrams, if we wish to show that activity B must follow activity A, we simply let B's starting node be the same as A's ending node. That is, the instant when A is finished is also the instant when B can start. It is possible that several activities must follow one activity (B and C must follow A, for example). In this case both B and C start from A's ending node. It is also possible that several activities must precede another activity (C must follow A and B, for example). In that case these preceding activities all come together at the same ending node, which is the starting node of the following activity.

The only other possible sequencing situation is illustrated in example 5 in Figure 12.1. In this case two activities (C and D) have a common predecessor (A) but also differ in their dependence on activity B. We would like to bring A and B together to the same ending node, as we did in example 4, to precede activity D. However, if we do that, we will be placing activity B before activity C, which is not a requirement. Unless the requirements are exactly the same, then, C and D must start from separate nodes. Therefore, we start C from A's ending node, as usual, and we bring a dummy activity from A's ending node to B's ending node. This dummy activity, represented by a dotted line, indicates an activity that requires 0 time but is there only for sequencing requirements. In this case activity A is done at its ending node, and this ending node precedes B's ending node (by 0 time), so at B's ending node both A and B are finished.

AON diagrams are a bit simpler to construct. We just draw an arrow for each precedence requirement. There is no need for dummy activities in AON diagrams.

With AOA diagramming the entire project starts with a single beginning node, from which all activities with no predecessors may start. The diagram then works its way from left to right, ending with a single ending node, where all activities with no followers come together. AON diagrams generally have no

Figure 12.1
AOA and AON Diagramming

AOA   AON

1. Activity A

2. B must follow A

3. B & C must follow A

4. C must follow A & B

5. C must follow A
   D must follow A & B

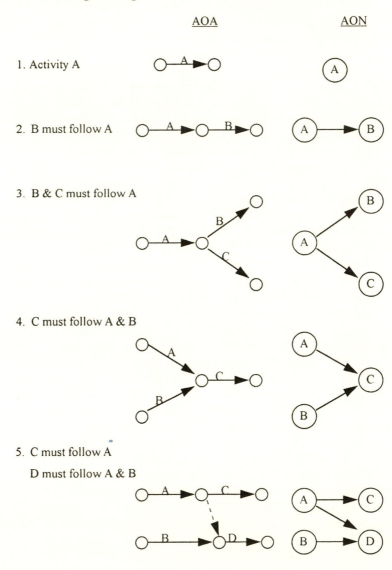

particuilar starting or ending nodes for the whole project. Whatever activities are able to start immediately appear on the left of the diagram, and whatever activities have no followers appear on the right.

Diagramming Examples

The following examples illustrate the diagramming techniques of AOA and AON. Although each example contains eight activities, the diagrams get progressively more difficult, at least for the AOA type of diagram. Sequencing requirements are given by listing which activities each activity must follow (as we did in Chapter 3).

Example 1:

Activity	Must Follow
A	—
B	—
C	—
D	A
E	B
F	B, C
G	D, E, F
H	E, F

In example 1 we need to use two dummy activities in the AOA diagram (see Figure 12.2). First, we start A, B, and C from the starting node of the project. Next, we need to join B and C together for activity F, but we need to preserve B's ending node for E. Since we are not using C's ending node for any other activity, we bring a dummy from B's ending node to C's ending node. Similarly, G follows D, E, and F, while H follows only E and F. In both cases E and F are required, so we bring them together directly and use that node to start H. That node is then joined with D's ending node to form G's starting node. Since G and H have nothing following them, they come together at the project's ending node.

The AON diagram begins with activities A, B, and C on the left and ends with activities G and H on the right.

Example 2:

Activity	Must Follow
A	—
B	—
C	—
D	A
E	A, B
F	A, B, C
G	D, E, F
H	F

Figure 12.2
Diagramming Examples

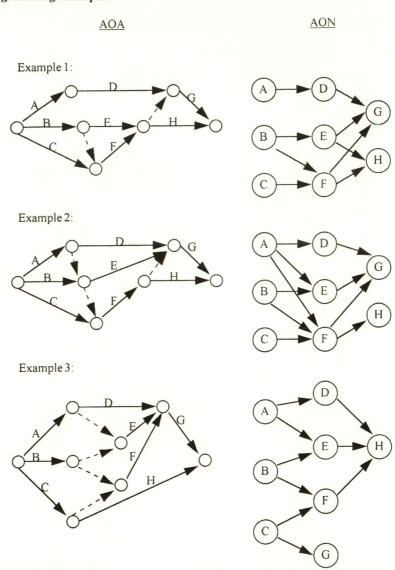

Example 2 has an interesting set of sequencing requirements involving activity A. We need a node where A is by itself, another with both A and B, and a third where A, B, and C meet. Therefore, we draw a dummy activity from A's ending node to B's ending node for E's start. We then join this node to C's ending node with another dummy for F's starting node.

Example 3:

Activity	Must Follow
A	—
B	—
C	—
D	A
E	A, B
F	B, C
G	C
H	D, E, F

With just a few minor changes from example 2 we have made example 3 much more challenging. The problem is that we now have four activities (D, E, F, and G) that must follow some different combination of activities A, B, and C. We know that D, E, F, and G must therefore start from four different nodes. However, A, B, and C have only three ending nodes between them. It is obvious that activity D must start at A's ending node, and activity G must start at C's ending node. Where do we put E and F, though? We need to join A and B together for E and to join B and C together for F. These activities can only be brought together at new nodes that we create.

The AON diagram for example 3, however, is very easy to construct. The lack of dummy activities in AON diagrams always makes them quite a bit easier to draw and to interpret. Why, then, would anyone use AOA diagrams? There appear to be two reasons. First, they were used in the original PERT technique, and they continue to be used through tradition. Second, the AOA diagrams do give a better sense of the flow of time throughout a project. For these reasons it is useful to be able to construct and to interpret AOA diagrams. However, for the remainder of the chapter our examples will use AON diagrams

The Critical Path

Generally, the first step of a PERT analysis after constructing the sequencing diagram is to determine the *critical path*. Paths in the diagram represent sequences of activities that must be performed, one after the other, in order to complete the project. The critical path is the path that takes the longest time to complete. This path will determine the overall length of the project. Activities that are not on the critical path may be delayed to some extent without delaying the project's completion.

It is important to determine the critical path for several reasons. First, the organization would like to know how long the project will take. A company submitting a bid for a project must specify the length of the project as well as the cost. Government bodies may require this information, and the company needs to know the length for its own planning.

Second, identifying the critical path makes it possible to focus attention on the critical activities throughout the project in order to keep the project on schedule. Also, if the project needs to be shortened for the purpose of submitting a bid or simply for the company's own benefit, the critical activities are the ones that must be shortened. There are several ways that a company might shorten activities on the critical path, including working overtime, hiring more workers, subcontracting, or shifting resources from noncritical activities to critical activities.

Besides identifying the critical path, the company is also interested in other paths that are close to being critical. If the times required for various activities begin to differ from the estimates, these other paths might become critical. Also, if we shorten the critical path, some other path might become critical.

To find the critical path, it is theoretically possible to list all of the paths and their lengths. However, this is not a practical way of determining the critical path for larger projects. The number of paths may get quite large, and even to list them would require the aid of a computer. Fortunately, there is a much more efficient way of determining the critical path, along with other useful information.

BOUNDARY TIME TABLE

We will now construct a time table that will give us information on the starting and finishing times of each activity. As we calculate these times, we will also discover the critical path and the overall length of the project. The columns of the table are defined as follows:

D = duration of each activity

ES = early starting time of each activity

    = the earliest an activity can possibly start

LS = late starting time of each activity

    = the latest an activity can start without delaying the project

EF = early finishing time of each activity

    = the earliest an activity can possibly finish

    = ES + D

LF = late finishing time of each activity

    = the latest an activity can finish without delaying the project

    = LS + D

TS = total slack of each activity

    = the amount of time each activity can delay without delaying the project (if other activities start at their ES)

    = LS − ES = LF − EF

Figure 12.3
Boundary Time Table

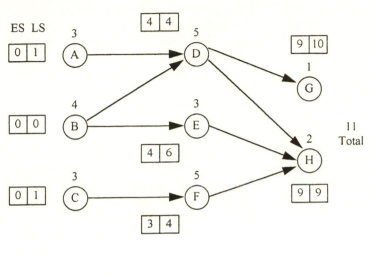

Activity	D	ES	LS	EF	LF	TS
A	3	0	1	3	4	1
B	4	0	0	4	4	0
C	3	0	1	3	4	1
D	5	4	4	9	9	0
E	3	4	6	7	9	2
F	5	3	4	8	9	1
G	1	9	10	10	11	1
H	2	9	9	11	11	0

To construct the boundary time table we first calculate the ES and LS of each activity by working on our sequencing diagram. Figure 12.3 shows a sequencing diagram for a project with eight activities. Alongside each activity we have shown the duration, and we have placed two boxes for the ES and LS.

All activities on the left of the AON diagram (those with no predecessors) have an early starting time of 0, the time when the project begins. We then work from left to right, adding the durations of the activities to determine when succeeding activities can start. For example, activity D can start when both A and B are completed. A can start at 0 and takes 3 weeks, so it can finish as early as time 3. Likewise, B can start at 0 and takes 4 weeks, so it can finish as early as time 4. Since activity D must wait for both A and B to finish, its early starting time is 4. Thus, the general rule for calculating an activity's early starting time is to take the *latest* early finishing time of all its predecessors.

Continuing from left to right, we find that G can finish as early as 10 and H as early as 11. Therefore, we know that the project will take 11 weeks.

To obtain the late starting times, we work backwards from the project completion time of 11 weeks to see how late each activity can start and still allow the project to finish by 11. We work from right to left, subtracting the durations of the activities. For example, activity H has a duration of 2 weeks, so in order to finish by 11, it must start by time 9. Since G only requires 1 week, it can start as late as 10.

Activity F must finish before H can start. Since H can start no later than 9 and F requires 5 weeks, F must start no later than time 4. Activity D precedes both G and H. Therefore, it must finish in time for both to start. Since G has a late starting time of 10 and H has a late starting time of 9, then, D must finish no later than 9. Its LS must be $9 - 5 = 4$. The general rule here is that an activity's LS is calculated from the *earliest* LS of following activities minus the activity's duration.

We perform all of these calculations on our sequencing diagram and then transfer them to our boundary time table to obtain the ES and LS columns. Next, it is a simple operation to add each activity's duration to its ES and LS to obtain its EF and LF. Finally, we can subtract each activity's EF from its LF to determine its total slack.

With our slack times it is easy to determine the project's critical path. The critical path simply consists of those activities with 0 slack. In other words, these activities are the ones whose durations add up to 11 weeks in this case, so they have no slack if the project is to be completed in 11 weeks. These activities must start as soon as they can start. If there is more than one critical path, it will be necessary to refer to the sequencing diagram to see which of the critical activities are on which path.

The slack times also tell us which activities are close to being critical. Here activities A, C, F, and G have only one week of slack. This means that the longest path through each of these activities must take 10 weeks. For activity A, for example, we see that it is a part of path ADG, requiring 9 weeks, and of ADH, requiring 10 weeks. Activity E, on the other hand, appears only in path BEH, which requires 9 weeks, so it has a slack of 2 weeks. If we wanted to shorten our project, perhaps we could switch some resources from activity E to a critical activity.

Note, however, that these figures in the TS column are not necessarily independent from each other. For example, we see that activity C has 1 week of slack, and so does activity F. However, this is the *same* 1 week of slack. Both activities appear only in path CFH, which requires 10 weeks. Therefore, we can not delay *both* by 1 week since then CFH would require 12 weeks. Activities on the same path, then, have slack times that are interdependent.

The boundary time table provides a great deal of information. We know when the earliest time is that we will need to provide workers and materials for each activity. We can use the chart as a controlling device to make sure that activities are completed on time. The slack column tells us the critical path, near-critical paths, and those activities which we can delay quite a bit without delaying the project.

WORKER DEPLOYMENT CHARTS

When we originally made our time estimates for each activity, we must have had some particular size of work crew in mind (along with other resources, such as materials and equipment). We can visualize the assignment of workers to activities throughout the project by means of a worker deployment chart. In the table below we have reproduced our boundary time table, and we have added a column showing the number of workers originally assumed for each activity.

BOUNDARY TIME TABLE WITH CREW SIZES

Activity	D	ES	LS	EF	LF	TS	Crew Size
A	3	0	1	3	4	1	4
B	4	0	0	4	4	0	3
C	3	0	1	3	4	1	5
D	5	4	4	9	9	0	2
E	3	4	6	7	9	2	5
F	5	3	4	8	9	1	3
G	1	9	10	10	11	1	6
H	2	9	9	11	11	0	4

Our worker deployment chart has a horizontal scale showing time from 0 through the end of the project (eleven weeks). The vertical scale shows the number of workers assigned. Each activity is represented by a rectangle with a width equal to the activity's duration and a height equal to the number of workers deployed.

Initially we will assume that each activity begins as early as possible (at its ES) and finishes at its EF. If we begin placing activities on the chart in alphabetical order, we get the result at the top of Figure 12.4. We can rearrange the rectangles to put the critical activities on the bottom and to put larger blocks underneath smaller blocks.

We might also like to smooth out the number of workers throughout the length of the project (because of space limitations, for example). One way to avoid large gaps in the chart would be to slide some activities to the right, utilizing their slack. The second chart in Figure 12.4 shows a worker deployment

Figure 12.4
Worker Deployment Chart

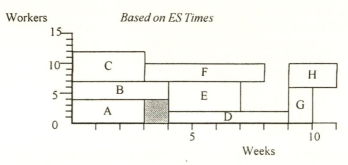

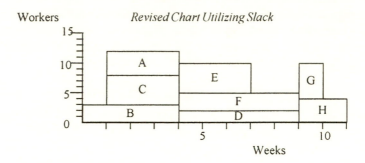

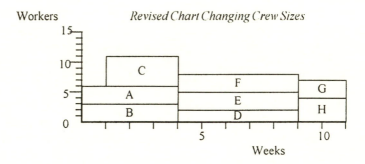

chart with the critical activities on the bottom and with some activities starting later than their ES (but no later than their LS) in order to smooth out the chart.

Depending on the activity, we may also be able to change the number of workers on some activities, with proportional changes in the durations. For example, if it takes one worker 4 days to mow a golf course, it should take two workers only 2 days. This type of activity can easily be split into jobs for several workers with no loss in efficiency. Some jobs, though, such as applying wallpaper to a room, cannot be split without losing efficiency.

In our example we will assume that the activities involved are completely flexible regarding the number of workers and durations; the total work as measured in man-weeks remains constant in all cases. We can use this flexibility to further smooth out the work force requirements throughout the project. In fact, we could shorten the whole project by adding workers if we wanted to. In this example, though, we will maintain a project length of 11 weeks and try only to smooth out the work force. We will also restrict ourselves to using whole numbers of workers and of weeks.

Specifically, we propose three changes to our duration/worker combinations. Activity A's 12 man-weeks of work will be accomplished through 3 workers for 4 weeks rather than 4 workers for 3 weeks. Activity E's 15 man-weeks will now be performed by 5 workers working 3 weeks rather than 3 workers for 5 weeks. Finally, activity G will accomplish its 6 man-weeks through 3 workers working 2 weeks rather than 6 workers for 1 week. The resulting chart is shown on the bottom of Figure 12.4. If we relaxed our assumption regarding whole numbers, we could also flatten activity C a bit.

VARIABILITY IN PERT

As was mentioned earlier, one difference between the original PERT technique and the CPM technique is the way that each estimates the duration times of the activities. While CPM uses a single, deterministic, estimate of the duration, PERT assumes a probability distribution for each activity's duration. The type of distribution assumed in PERT is a rather uncommon one, the *beta distribution*.

The beta distribution may be skewed either to the left or to the right, or it may be a symmetrical distribution similar to the normal curve. Unlike the normal distribution, though, the beta distribution has a lowest value, a, and a highest value, b. These two points, along with the peak of the curve, or mode (m), are the three parameters that identify a particular beta distribution. In the context of PERT, then, these parameters may be defined as follows:

a = optimistic time = shortest possible duration of an activity

m = most likely time

b = pessimistic time = longest possible duration of an activity

In order to conduct a PERT analysis, then, we will need to make these three time estimates for each activity's duration.

When constructing our boundary time table, determining the critical path, and so on, we will need to use a single time estimate for each activity's duration. This figure will be the mean duration time, as calculated by the following formula:

$$D = (a + 4m + b)/6$$

We can see that this is just a weighted average of the three time estimates, with the extreme points weighted by a factor of 1 and the mode by a factor of 4.

Although we will use these mean durations in our calculations, we realize that each activity is subject to some variability. The standard deviation of the duration of activity i is calculated from the following formula:

$$\sigma_i = (b - a)/6$$

In other words, the standard deviation is 1/6 of the range.

The variability of a sequence of activities, such as the critical path, depends on the variability of each of the activities on that path. If we assume that the durations of the activities are independent random variables, then the variance of the total path's duration is the sum of the variances on that path. Defining σ_p as the standard deviation of the critical path, we have:

$$\sigma_p^2 = \Sigma \, \sigma_i^2$$
$$\sigma_p = \sqrt{\Sigma \, \sigma_i^2}$$

In this formula the summation refers to all the activities on the critical path.

Boundary Time Table Calculations

In Figure 12.5 we have an example of a PERT analysis starting from the original three duration estimates for each activity. We have then calculated the mean durations in the D column. For example, the duration of activity A was calculated from $D = (2 + 4(4) + 6)/6 = 24/6 = 4$. The rest of the boundary time table has then been completed as usual. Then, after identifying the critical path as ACH from the TS column, we have also calculated the variances of the durations of the critical activities. For example, A's variance is calculated as follows:

$$\sigma_A^2 = (b - a)^2/(6)^2 = (6 - 2)^2 \, /36 = 16/36$$

Probability Calculations

By adding the variances of the durations of the critical activities, we find that $\sigma_p^2 = 16/36 + 4/36 + 25/36 = 45/36 = 5/4$. Therefore, $\sigma_p = \sqrt{5/4} = 1.118$ weeks. The critical path thus has a mean length of 11.5 weeks, with a standard deviation of 1.118 weeks. As the number of activities on the critical path increases, the distribution of the total duration of the critical path approaches a normal curve. We can use this approximation to estimate such things as confidence intervals for the length of the critical path and the probability of completing that path by any given time of interest.

Figure 12.5
Boundary Time Table for Variable Activity Durations

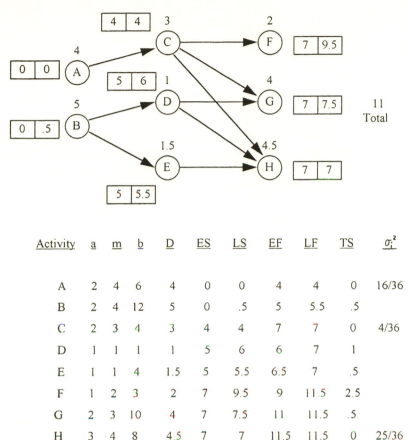

Activity	a	m	b	D	ES	LS	EF	LF	TS	σ_i^2
A	2	4	6	4	0	0	4	4	0	16/36
B	2	4	12	5	0	.5	5	5.5	.5	
C	2	3	4	3	4	4	7	7	0	4/36
D	1	1	1	1	5	6	6	7	1	
E	1	1	4	1.5	5	5.5	6.5	7	.5	
F	1	2	3	2	7	9.5	9	11.5	2.5	
G	2	3	10	4	7	7.5	11	11.5	.5	
H	3	4	8	4.5	7	7	11.5	11.5	0	25/36

However, if there are other paths that are close to being critical, they might actually become critical as activity durations vary from their means. It is possible to calculate the joint probability of completing several paths by a certain due date or to calculate a confidence interval based on the variance of several paths. Here, though, we are concentrating only on the critical path and ignoring other paths.

If we would like to construct a 95% confidence interval for the completion time of the critical path, we look up the z-value needed in the normal table and find that $z = 1.96$ standard deviations on either side of the mean. Our confidence interval, then is:

$$11.5 \pm 1.96(1.118) = 11.5 \pm 2.19 = 9.31\text{---}13.69 \text{ weeks}$$

We are 95% sure that this path will be completed somewhere between 9.31 and 13.69 weeks.

Suppose that we had a due date of 12 weeks for the project, after which we would have to pay substantial penalties. We can calculate the probability of finishing within 12 weeks as follows:

$$z = (12 - 11.5)/1.118 = .5/1.118 = .45$$

From the normal table we see that the area between the mean and a z-value of .45 is .1736. Therefore, the probability of finishing the critical path within 12 weeks is .5000 + .1736 = .6736. With only about a 2/3 chance of meeting the deadline, the company might well look into ways to shorten some of the critical activities (or at least keep a very close watch over them).

CHAPTER 13

Quality Control

OVERVIEW

The assurance of quality, while mainly the responsibility of operations management, transcends departmental boundaries in an organization. Especially in recent years, quality has come to be seen as a powerful marketing tool. With ever-increasing availability of information and the heightened competition from companies around the world, consumers no longer will put up with products of inferior quality. The peace of mind and convenience of high-quality products are often more important to customers than price.

Also, for a company really to pursue quality as a primary goal, it is necessary that the whole company become involved, especially including the top management. Putting quality first represents a rather radical shift in emphasis from traditional practices among both management and labor. Both groups must be convinced that emphasizing quality is in their own best interest.

What Is Quality?

In order to pursue quality as a primary goal, an organization must obviously have a clear understanding of just what it is. First of all, quality can refer to many different measurable aspects of a product or service. For instance, a product's strength, its average life, its weight, its incidence of repairs, its size, or its appearance may be the primary measure of its quality, depending on the product. Similarly, a service may be judged on the length of time it takes, its accuracy, how long it lasts, the attitude of the server, and so on.

Unfortunately, however, the typical consumer's view of quality is not the definition most relevant to an organization. That is, the consumer generally thinks of quality as the *level* attained on some of the above factors by a particular product or service. In that sense, a lightbulb that lasts 1000 hours is of higher quality than one that lasts 800 hours, and a bolt that can withstand 5000 pounds of pressure is of higher quality than one that can only withstand 3000 pounds. It is certainly ridiculous, though, for all products to be manufactured to the highest possible *level* of quality. Not all cars need to be Rolls-Royces, and not all watches should be Rolexes. If that were the case, there would be an awful lot of people walking around wondering what time it is. Obviously, there is a market for all different levels of those factors that go into people's perceptions of quality.

The relevant concept of quality, then, is not the level attained, but rather the *adherence to* whatever *standards* the organization is aiming at. If the company is manufacturing lightbulbs that last 800 hours, it should strive to ensure that all its lightbulbs do in fact last that long. Then those customers who judge that an 800-hour lightbulb is the best buy for them will be glad to purchase from that company.

Service organizations likewise benefit by focusing on adherence to their pre-determined standards. A Motel 6 can succeed by providing consistent comfort, convenience, and cleanliness without attempting to match the furnishings, personal services, or ambiance of a Hyatt or Hilton. Customers simply want to get what they paid for, no matter how cheap or expensive the product or service.

Organizing for Quality

Traditionally, manufacturing companies have had a quality control department serving as a staff group within the operations system. That is, quality control personnel typically perform in an advisory capacity to the line managers of the operations system. On the other hand, their job requires them to work closely with workers all throughout the system. This process, along with their specialized expertise, often results in a certain amount of functional authority over workers in the operations system. Thus, a quality control inspector may be able to tell a worker to stop and readjust a machine that is producing too many defects.

Along with (and occasionally instead of) this centralized approach to quality control, we are increasingly seeing the responsibility for quality distributed throughout the system. We have seen how the Japanese concept of Just-in-Time management often includes individual responsibility for preventive maintenance and for product inspection. If a company makes a substantial commitment to increased quality, it is necessary to get just about everybody involved. The program will not be a success without the cooperation of everyone, and the increased workload in quality-assurance activities would be impossible to dump on a centralized staff department. Thus, the involvement of individual workers becomes a necessity.

Quality Costs

The question always arises as to how much quality assurance effort is enough. The short answer is that we should keep increasing the quality effort until it no longer pays for itself. As the level of effort put into quality assurance increases, the costs generally increase proportionally. This effort may include actual inspections, programs to educate and to train workers concerning quality, time spent working with suppliers, and so on.

As these efforts bear fruit, though, there is a corresponding savings in the costs of defects. These costs would include internal costs, such as repair costs, lost wages when the production line must be shut down, and excessive scrappage costs. In addition, there may be external costs of poor quality, such as extra repairs under warranty and lost future sales due to defects in the product or service. Therefore, the company theoretically should continue increasing its quality efforts until the cost savings no longer exceed the costs of the effort.

Quality Inspection

Quality may be inspected at various points along the production or service process. Generally, it is desirable to inspect any incoming raw materials from suppliers before putting them to use and possibly ruining any future effort. If a particular step of the process is especially difficult, an inspection after that step might be worthwhile. Also, at some point in a production process earlier work may become hidden, so an inspection immediately before that point would be needed. If a step in the process is particularly expensive, it would be good to inspect previous work before undertaking that expense and perhaps having to scrap the result because of a previous error. In most cases it is desirable to inspect the final product before sending it to the customer in order to avoid the external costs of defects mentioned above.

The inspection performed at each of these points in the process can be either a 100% inspection or the inspection of a random sample of items. While a 100% inspection is certainly more thorough, it is not always the better choice. First, even a 100% inspection may result in some errors due to imperfections in the testing process itself. Conversely, a small sample may still be quite accurate if conducted correctly. Second, some inspection processes require the destruction of the item tested, such as testing the tensile strength of a metal bolt or the bursting strength of a cardboard box. A 100% inspection in such cases might not be the best idea. Finally, the most obvious argument against 100% inspection is simply the inspection cost itself. If the inspection cost is proportional to the number of items inspected, a small sample will result in significant savings. For these reasons a company will often choose to inspect somewhat less than 100%.

Statistical Quality Control

Making a quality determination based on a sample is called *statistical quality control*. When measuring quality, we will collect data that may be classified into two types—variables and attributes. Variables are those aspects of quality that we ordinarily think of as being "measured"—weight, length, temperature, and so on. Whatever factor we are measuring may vary along a (usually continuous) scale, and a particular item's measurement may assume any value on that scale. In such cases we simply record the item's weight, length, or whatever, and end up with a series of numbers for our sample. When working with variables, we then would ordinarily calculate such statistics as the mean and standard deviation of our sample.

Attributes, on the other hand, are categories into which we classify our items, rather than values along some scale. Examples of attributes would be categories such as "male" or "female"; "freshman," "sophomore," "junior," or "senior"; "good" or "defective"; "too small," "acceptable," or "too large." Our data would consist simply of a tally of the number of items falling into each category. The relevant statistics we could calculate from our data would just be the frequencies or proportions of items that we observed in each category.

Attribute data are generally easier and cheaper to collect but then provide less information to us. Sometimes a particular inspection could lend itself to either type of data. For example, we could measure the voltage between two points of a circuit and then record either the actual number observed (variable data) or whether the voltage is acceptable or unacceptable (attribute data).

We may also distinguish two types of quality control efforts under the general category of statistical quality control. First, *acceptance sampling* is the process of taking a sample from a batch of items in order to determine whether to accept that batch or not. This "yes-no" type of decision is especially useful in deciding whether a batch of the company's own work-in-process is fit to be sent along to another step in the process.

Acceptance sampling may utilize either variable data or attribute data. Using variable data, we would simply perform a hypothesis test regarding whether the mean of the variable was where it was supposed to be. If our sample mean fell outside of predetermined limits based on the sample size, standard deviation, and level of significance we chose, we would reject the entire batch. Similarly, with attribute data, if the total number (or proportion) of defects in our sample was greater than some predetermined level, we would reject the batch.

The second type of statistical quality control effort we might undertake is the use of *process control charts*. Rather than make a single "yes-no" or "accept-reject" type of decision, we keep track of our quality over a period of time on charts. This approach lends itself especially to monitoring our own selected production or service processes over time. It is hoped that this monitoring will allow us to catch a process before it goes completely out of control. If our charts indicate a gradual worsening of quality or some nonrandom type of behavior in the process, we search for an "assignable cause" for the aberrations and correct the problem as quickly as possible.

Process control charts may also utilize either variable or attribute data. If our data are in the form of variables, we keep track of the mean and variability of the factor measured. If the data are attributes, we just chart the proportion of defective items over time. It is probably most common, though, for acceptance sampling to use attribute data for the purpose of making a quick "accept-reject" decision and for process control charts to use variable data in order to monitor the process most accurately.

TOTAL QUALITY MANAGEMENT

American businesses have adopted a series of catchphrases over recent years, including "zero defects," "quality is free," and "total quality management," all emphasizing the importance of greater attention to quality assurance. Japanese companies, on the other hand, have been more successful in actually applying such concepts. In any case, there is a definite trend to devote more time and money to quality assurance in the belief

The idea of total quality management (TQM) emphasizes planning for quality, including designing the product in such a way that consistent quality is more easily obtained and more easily measured. The impetus for a company to devote significantly more resources to quality through a TQM program comes from a trend that most companies are now experiencing—an increased competitive pressure that leads to higher costs associated with poor quality.

Several aspects of a total quality management program fit in very well with a JIT materials control program. Japanese companies especially have instituted such an integrated program involving greater attention to quality and to smooth material flow. By making the production process more repetitive as in JIT, it is easier to design and to control for quality. Greater repetitiveness also allows greater automation, which in turn helps to eliminate human errors affecting quality. The use of very small lots in JIT helps to detect any quality problems before they become disastrous. Finally, the preventive maintenance and problem-solving emphases of JIT directly contribute to improved quality. With the help of such concepts, largely promoted by W. Edwards Deming, Japanese manufacturing has gone from being a synonym for poor quality to the leading exponent of high-quality goods.

All of this is not to say, however, that these popular programs are cure-alls or are universally accepted. Successful companies have generally been large, highly repetitive manufacturers. It is easy to forget the many small (and generally less repetitive) manufacturers and the service operations throughout the world that don't have large design staffs, large computer systems, and so on, needed to emulate such companies as Toyota. However, the principles of a total quality management system, as described below, are sound. Some of them may be applied to a given system even when not all of them are relevant.

Planning for Quality

Probably the most basic principle of a total quality management program is that quality is something that you design in, not something that you inspect in. The product must be designed in such a way that it can be produced consistently without losing sight of the design aspects demanded by the customer. Also, the production process or the service process must be designed with quality in mind. Again, greater repetitiveness is the goal. The ideal is to do it right the first time, not to have to detect errors through inspection and then correct them.

A fairly recent idea is the *quality audit*, where an external consultant (usually) performs an audit of the company's plans for quality and its success in carrying them out. Such an idea is a good example of the rather radical shift in emphasis that a company must undergo in making quality a primary goal of the organization.

The Role of Inspection

Even though the ideal is to reduce the need for inspection through planning, there is still a place for inspection within a TQM program. In fact, 100% inspection is common for finished goods to avoid sending out defective products. However, sampling may still be more appropriate at other steps of the process, sometimes just inspecting the first and last item of a batch to see if there has been any problem from the changeover from the previous batch. The techniques of statistical quality control still are useful in a TQM program, although the simplification of the production process tends to reduce the costs of 100% inspection.

Organizational Implications

As with JIT, a TQM program tends to decentralize the responsibility for quality assurance. Workers are responsible for their own inspection. Quality results are prominently displayed through charts, lighted displays, and so on. The worker, in fact, often has the authority to stop the production line if there is a problem with quality. When that happens, other workers in the work group help to find and solve the problem quickly. Thus, every worker is responsible for quality, not just some separate quality control department. In fact, some theorists go so far as to advocate the elimination of the centralized quality control department.

Despite this decentralization, strong support from top management is still needed. It is responsible for promoting quality assurance as the overriding philosophy of the organization and for designing the appropriate systems to promote quality. Some sort of a centralized quality control department might also be desirable for the purpose of training the workers in quality control techniques and in performing the final inspection.

Problem-Solving Emphasis

When a problem is discovered by a worker, the response is not to find someone to blame, but rather to work together to find the reason for the problem and to correct it. Workers are part of a work group, or team, so a sense of teamwork develops. This cooperative spirit also carries over to relationships with suppliers. Just as a JIT program promotes working with suppliers to ensure steady, predictable deliveries, a TQM program fosters helping the supplier to provide materials of the appropriate quality.

Quality Circles

Quality circles is another idea that originated in the United States but was made popular in Japan. Originally, a quality circle was a group of workers that met regularly for the purpose of suggesting ways to improve quality. This idea is in keeping with the decentralization of responsibility for quality and with the problem-solving emphasis of TQM. These groups of workers were trained in group decision-making and were given power to collect data for their analyses. Their recommendations would then go to their superiors, who were not a part of the circle.

In time, quality circles began to expand their focus to other problems within the organization besides quality. Some became general gripe sessions, but in any case the workers were given increased input into the decision-making process and increased responsibility for the company's success. Thus, they have sometimes helped motivate workers as well as generate useful ideas.

Quality circles have had mixed results in the United States. Middle managers have sometimes resisted the suggestions made to them by their subordinates. They may be reluctant to adopt a suggestion which they have not been a part of. Occasionally, a quality circle will solve all of the relatively easy problems and leave nothing for themselves to do; keeping them going costs money with little prospect for further benefits.

International Quality Standards: ISO 9000

ISO 9000 refers to a list of quality standards developed by the International Organization for Standardization (ISO) based in Geneva, Switzerland. By adopting these standards, a firm can demonstrate to its potential customers that it is undertaking appropriate quality procedures and attaining a certain level of performance. The benefit is that these standards are applied uniformly to companies throughout the world, rather than each company promoting its own standards.

In order to become certified, a production facility must document its procedures to demonstrate its adherence to the standard. After an outside auditor confirms its compliance, the facility becomes registered as fulfilling that standard (subject to periodic audits in the future). ISO 9000 does not guarantee the outputs of a facility, but does confirm that the facility is at least following consistent procedures to assure quality.

ACCEPTANCE SAMPLING

Acceptance sampling is a hypothesis test regarding some measure of quality. A sample of n items is selected randomly from a batch of N items. If the measure of quality is a variable, then the sample mean and standard deviation are calculated for that variable. If the measure of quality is an attribute, then the number observed in each category of the attribute is recorded. In either case the sample results are compared to a predetermined decision rule to decide whether to accept or reject the batch. This process will be described in some detail for attributes sampling (probably the more common), and an example will be given for variables sampling.

Acceptance Sampling by Attributes

Although an attribute can be broken down into several possible categories, we will generally be concerned with the number of good items and the number of defective items. In our sample of n items, we will define x as the number of defective items found in the sample.

If we are sampling without replacement randomly and placing our results into these two categories, the probability distribution that describes the results is the *hypergeometric distribution*. However, this distribution is not well-known, and it is not easily reduced to tables. If the sample size n is small relative to the batch size N, and if the proportion of defects in the batch (p) is small (10% or less), then the Poisson distribution will be a good approximation. We will be using this approximation in our calculations below.

In a single sampling inspection plan the decision to accept or reject the batch is based on a (surprise!) single sample. The number of defects found in the sample (x) is compared to a predetermined cutoff number c. Our decision rule is to accept the batch whenever x is less than or equal to c and to reject the batch if x is greater than c. In order to implement a single sampling plan, we need to determine the sample size n and the cutoff point c.

The probability of getting c or fewer defects in a sample of size n can be approximated by the Poisson distribution for different values of p, the proportion of defects in the entire batch. If we have some proportion p of defects in the batch and take a sample of size n, we expect to find an average of np defects in our sample. This value of np expected defects is the parameter we need to look up the probability of getting c or fewer defects using the Poisson distribution (see Poisson table in the Appendix). We can find such probabilities for any given value of p for a certain sample size n and cutoff point c. The graph of all such probabilities is called an *operating characteristic curve*, or OC curve. Figure 13.1 shows the OC curve for a single sampling plan of n = 50 and c = 2. We have defined P_a = P(accepting the batch) = P(x ≤ c). The following table shows the points from the Poisson table that have been plotted on the OC curve:

p	np = 50p	Pa = P(x ≤ 2)
.01	.5	.9856
.02	1.0	.9197
.03	1.5	.8088
.04	2.0	.6767
.05	2.5	.5438
.06	3.0	.4232
.07	3.5	.3208
.08	4.0	.2381

Now let's see what happens if we choose different values for n and c. If we reduce c, we are obviously less likely to find c or fewer defects in our sample, regardless of the proportion of defects in the batch. Therefore, reducing c makes it harder to accept and easier to reject batches of any given quality. This effect is also shown in Figure 13.1, where we have reduced c to 1 while maintaining a sample size of 50. The points plotted are as follows:

p	np = 50p	Pa = P(x ≤ 1)
.01	.5	.9098
.02	1.0	.7358
.03	1.5	.5578
.04	2.0	.4060
.05	2.5	.2873
.06	3.0	.1991
.07	3.5	.1359
.08	4.0	.0916

If we were to increase our sample size and also increase our cutoff point proportionally, we would have an OC curve that has a steeper slope. This makes the sampling plan more discriminating, as the probability of accepting batches of good quality (low p) remains high, but the probability of accepting batches of poor quality (high p) drops off sharply. Figure 13.1 shows the OC curve for n = 100 and c = 4 plotted from the points below:

Figure 13.1
Operating Characteristic Curves

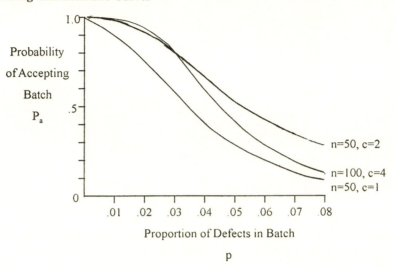

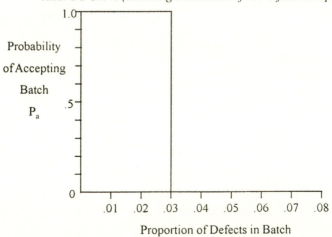

Ideal OC Curve (assuming a maximum of 3% defects acceptable)

p	np = 100p	Pa = P(x ⩽ 4)
.01	1.0	.9963
.02	2.0	.9473
.03	3.0	.8153
.04	4.0	.6288
.05	5.0	.4405
.06	6.0	.2850
.07	7.0	.1730
.08	8.0	.0996

The ideal OC curve would be one that is perfectly vertical at some level of quality p (bottom of Figure 13.1). Batches with a proportion of defects less than or equal to that p would always be accepted, and those with more would always be rejected. Such a curve, unfortunately, would require 100% inspection with no inspection errors. Larger sample sizes can help us approach this curve, but they are also more costly.

How do we determine which OC curve, and consequently, which combination of n and c, is acceptable? We first specify some arbitrary level of quality that is very good (a low p). This quality level is called the Acceptable Quality Level, or AQL. We would like to accept batches with this quality level most of the time. If we reject a good batch, we are making a Type I error. The probability of a Type I error is called α, or the *producer's risk*, since it is the probability that the producer sends a good batch which nevertheless is rejected.

We need to decide what level of α is acceptable for the specified AQL. This depends largely on the economic consequences of such an error. If we reject a batch of goods from a supplier, a typical agreement would be to ship it back to the supplier, where they would give the batch a 100% inspection to determine the actual proportion of defects. If it turns out that the batch is really good, then we will generally have to pay for the shipping and the inspection. When we specify the desired α for the AQL, we have one point of our OC curve.

Next we pick a level of quality that is rather poor (a high p). This number is called the Lot Tolerance Percent Defective (LTPD). We hope that most of the time such a batch would be rejected. If we accept a batch of poor quality, we are making a Type II error. The probability of such an error is called β, or the *consumer's risk*, since it is the probability of the consumer accepting a bad batch. We need to determine the desired level of β just as we did with α, by looking at the economic consequences of such an error (extra repairs later on, more scrappage, dissatisfied customers). Specifying β for the LTPD gives us a second point on the OC curve.

Now we work backwards to see which combination of n and c give us an OC curve that hits both of our points. Only one curve will probably come close to both. We can perform a trial-and-error process plotting points as before for each n and c combination, or we can find the necessary n and c values from published tables.

Outgoing Quality

For a given sampling plan (n and c) we can calculate the average proportion of defects that get passed along, the *average outgoing quality* (AOQ). This calculation depends on certain assumptions. If we find some defective items in our sample, but no more than c defects, we will accept the batch. However, the defects we find will surely be fixed before sending the batch along. When a batch is rejected (more than c defects in the sample), let's assume that we inspect the entire batch and fix all defects, so none are passed along.

It the batch is accepted, then, the average number of defects passed along is $0n + p(N-n)$, or just $p(N-n)$, because there are 0 defects remaining in sample of n items, and the remaining $N-n$ uninspected items have their original proportion of p defects. If we reject a batch, no defects are passed along. Since the probability of accepting a batch is P_a and the probability of rejecting is $(1 - Pa)$, we have:

$$AOQ = \frac{p(N - n)Pa + 0(1 - Pa)}{N}$$
$$= pPa \, (N - n)/N$$

If we make other assumptions, our formula must be modified accordingly, but it is constructed similarly.

We can see that the AOQ formula depends on p, the incoming quality, and on P_a, the probability of accepting a batch with that quality, which in turn depends on p and the OC curve. Let's return to our example of $n = 50$ and $c = 2$ and calculate a few points of the AOQ curve. We will assume that the overall batch size N is 1000 items. Therefore, the constant part of the AOQ formula, $(N-n)/N$ is equal to $(1000 - 50)/1000 = 950/1000 = .95$. The AOQ formula can then be restated as $AOQ = .95pP_a$. Figure 13.2 shows the calculations of several points and the resulting AOQ curve.

We see that the AOQ curve rises to a peak and then declines. This peak occurs at an AOQ of about 2.6% defects for an incoming quality of about 5%. This peak is called the Average Outgoing Quality Limit (AOQL). Regardless of the incoming quality level, this is the worst average quality being passed along.

Acceptance Sampling by Variables

Consider a lightbulb that is supposed to have a life of at least 1000 hours. We are perfectly happy if it lasts more than 1000 hours; we are only concerned if the life is less than 1000 hours. Therefore, we will try a one-tailed test of the mean life of the bulbs. Assume that we take a sample of $n = 100$ bulbs and get a sample mean of 990 hours with a standard deviation of 40 hours. The standard error of the mean is

$$s/\sqrt{n} = 40/\sqrt{100} = 4 \text{ hours}$$

Figure 13.2
Average Outgoing Quality

p	$np = 50p$	$P_a = P(X \leq 2)$	$AOQ = .95pP_a$
.01	.5	.9856	.0094
.02	1.0	.9197	.0175
.03	1.5	.8088	.0231
.04	2.0	.6767	.0257
.05	2.5	.5438	.0258
.06	3.0	.4232	.0241
.07	3.5	.3208	.0213
.08	4.0	.2381	.0181

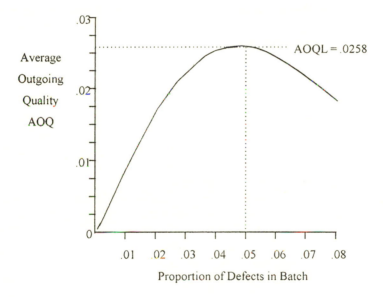

Proportion of Defects in Batch

Therefore, our sample mean is $(990 - 1000)/4 = 2.5$ standard errors below the hypothesized mean of 1000. If we allow a level of significance of $\alpha = .05$, our rule would be to reject the hypothesis when z is more than 1.65 standard errors below the hypothesized mean (from the normal table). Therefore, our sample leads us to reject the batch of lightbulbs.

PROCESS CONTROL CHARTS

An ongoing process, whether in a production or service operation, can be monitored by process control charts. By charting some measure of quality over time and comparing the results with predetermined limits, we in effect can perform an ongoing hypothesis test of quality similar to the example above. Moreover, we can sometimes catch a problem developing before it has reached the limits. The kinds of charts relevant for process control again depend on the type of data we are using.

Control Charts for Variables

$\bar{X}$ Chart

As in acceptance sampling with variables, the obvious statistic to calculate from our data is the sample mean ($\bar{X}$). In order to set up limits for our chart, we need to take some samples during a time period when the process is performing normally. Let's assume that during this period we take k samples, each including n items. From our samples we can calculate the overall process mean $\bar{\bar{X}}$ by averaging the sample means:

$$\bar{\bar{X}} = \Sigma \ \bar{X}/k$$

In process control charts it is traditional to set limits that are 3 standard errors above and below the overall mean. These very wide limits include 99.73% of the normal curve, leaving an α of just .0027. In other words, there is just a .0027 chance of getting a sample mean outside of these limits if the process really is under control (performing normally).

We can calculate these limits if we have calculated the standard error of the mean from the standard deviation and the sample size. However, a good approximation of the standard deviation can be made using the average sample range, $\bar{R}$, a much simpler calculation (highest − lowest value in the sample). Tables have been constructed (see Control Chart Factors in the Appendix) which incorporate this approximation into a number called A. Using this approximation, our limits become:

$$LCL = \bar{\bar{X}} - A\bar{R}$$
$$UCL = \bar{\bar{X}} + A\bar{R}$$

where LCL = Lower Control Limit and UCL = Upper Control Limit.

Let's consider a company that produces yardsticks. These should, of course, be exactly 36" long. During a 12-day period the company took a daily sample of 10 yardsticks and measured them. Their results follow.

Day	Deviations from 36.00 (Inches)										X̄	R
1	.10	.05	−.04	.12	−.03	.08	−.08	.06	−.05	.01	.022	.20
2	.02	−.03	−.06	.04	.01	−.07	.10	−.05	−.03	−.02	−.009	.17
3	.06	.07	.04	.05	−.03	.03	.03	−.02	.06	−.08	.021	.15
4	.15	.10	−.06	.08	.07	−.04	−.02	.05	.06	.09	.048	.21
5	−.07	−.04	−.03	.04	−.01	−.02	.05	−.01	.00	.08	−.001	.15
6	.01	−.07	.06	.11	.03	−.02	.02	.05	−.07	.04	.016	.18
7	.06	.03	.00	−.04	−.01	.08	.06	−.05	.03	.06	.022	.13
8	.04	−.01	.05	.07	.03	−.02	−.08	.09	.04	.05	.026	.17
9	.03	−.03	−.05	−.08	.04	−.03	.02	.08	.09	−.04	.003	.17
10	.05	.00	.04	−.02	.04	−.05	.03	.07	−.05	.03	.014	.12
11	.07	.09	.04	.01	−.03	.08	−.04	−.05	.03	.04	.024	.14
12	−.06	.04	.13	−.05	.01	.02	.06	−.03	.08	−.02	.018	.19
											.204	1.98

$$\overline{\overline{X}} = 36.00 + .204/12 = 36.00 + .017 = 36.017$$
$$\bar{R} = 1.98/12 = .165$$

Using our overall mean $\overline{\overline{X}}$ of 36.017", our average range $\bar{R}$ of .165", and an A value of .31 from the table, we obtain the following control limits:

$$LCL = 36.017 − (.31)(.165) = 36.017 − .051 = 35.966$$
$$UCL = 36.017 + (.31)(.165) = 36.017 + .051 = 36.068$$

Figure 13.3 shows our $\overline{X}$ chart for the 12 samples, along with the control limits.

In the future we will continue to take samples of 10 items and plot the mean on the $\overline{X}$ chart. Whenever this mean falls outside our control limits, the process is out of control and must be corrected. Also, if there is any nonrandom pattern observed, such as means tending toward one of the limits, we might be able to catch a problem before a sample mean falls outside the limits.

R Chart

Even though the $\overline{X}$ chart gives us a great deal of information about our process, it doesn't tell the whole story. While the sample mean may be within our control limits, we don't know anything about the individual yardsticks. For this we need some measure of variability, or dispersion. However, we already have measures of R, the sample range. If this range gets too large, we know that individual yardsticks are straying far from the mean. The R chart, which also has control limits of three standard errors, can tell us when the ranges are out of control.

Our Control Chart Factors in the Appendix has a column called B to help calculate 3-standard-error limits for R:

$$LCL = \bar{R} − B\bar{R}$$
$$UCL = \bar{R} + B\bar{R}$$

Figure 13.3
Control Charts for Yardsticks

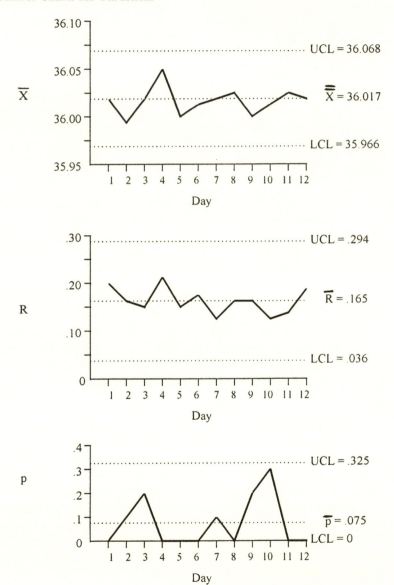

Using our example value of .165 for R̄ and the B value of .78 from the table, we have:

LCL = .165 − (.78)(.165) = .165 − .129 = .036
UCL = .165 + (.78)(.165) = .165 + .129 = .294

Figure 13.3 shows the R chart with the control limits calculated. Again, in the future whenever the sample range R falls outside of the limits, the company will seek to find an assignable cause and correct it.

Control Limits versus Tolerance Limits

At this point we need to clarify just what it means to be "in control." Notice that the overall mean length of yardsticks was 36.017". We would prefer that the process produce yardsticks averaging exactly 36". Still, 36.017" is what we get when the process is under control. If we're not satisfied with that figure, we need to find a way to improve the process.

Being "in control," then, simply means that the process is continuing in the same way that it normally does. This says nothing about whether the output of the process is good or bad. For this determination we need to refer to the tolerance limits that define a good yardstick. These could vary quite a bit depending on the target market of these particular yardsticks.

Ordinarily, we would hope that the control limits would be well within the tolerance limits of the process. Then, when the sample mean was within the control limits, the individual items varying around the mean would still be within the tolerance limits. For example, if these yardsticks were considered acceptable if they were between 35.90" and 36.10", only a few in our samples would be unacceptable. While neither the X̄ chart nor the R chart looks directly at how the individual items compare to the tolerance limits, in the next section we will discuss a control chart that does.

Control Charts for Attributes

As we did with acceptance sampling, we will concentrate here on classifying each item into one of two categories, "acceptable" or "defective." We could easily convert our variable of yardstick length into an attribute by defining the tolerance limits of the process. However, there could be any number of other qualities that we might inspect similarly. For instance, suppose that this company has an inspector that checks the yardsticks for warpage and then classifies them as "good" or "bad." The relevant statistic we could calculate from our sample, then, would be the proportion of items that are defective, p. We can construct a p chart in much the same way that we constructed X̄ and R charts in order to track the proportion of defective yardsticks.

It is not necessary to refer to any tables to construct control limits for a p chart because the standard error of a proportion depends on the proportion itself.

From our sample data in the period when the process is under control we will calculate $\bar{p}$, the average proportion of defects, as follows:

$$\bar{p} = \Sigma\ p/k$$

Defining σ_p as the standard error of a proportion, we have:

$$\sigma_p = \sqrt{\bar{p}(1-\bar{p})/n}$$

Therefore, for 3-standard-error control limits,

$$LCL = \bar{p} - 3\sqrt{\bar{p}(1 - \bar{p})/n}$$
$$UCL = \bar{p} + 3\sqrt{\bar{p}(1-\bar{p})/n}$$

Let's assume that the following data represent the proportion of warped yard-sticks found in each daily sample:

Day	p = proportion warped
1	0
2	.1
3	.2
4	0
5	0
6	0
7	.1
8	0
9	.2
10	.3
11	0
12	0
	.9

The overall average proportion of defects, $\bar{p}$, is $.9/12 = .075$. (Again, this may not be considered good, but that's what they're getting when things go normally.) Control limits for the p chart are:

$$LCL = .075 - 3\sqrt{(.075)(.925)/10} = .075 - .25 = 0$$
$$UCL = .075 + 3\sqrt{(.075)(.925)/10} = .075 + .25 = .325$$

(Note that we can't have a lower control limit less than 0.)

The completed p chart is shown in Figure 13.3. In the future we would be happy to see the graph staying near the lower control limit, but, of course, a value near to or above the upper control limit would be a cause for concern.

CHAPTER 14

Putting It All Together: Developing World-Class Operations

OVERVIEW

In the preceding chapters we have tried to accomplish several goals:

1. To discuss the various problem areas that must be addressed in managing the operations of an organization.

Since operations systems vary widely from service to manufacturing systems, from job shops to mass production, from small to large, and so on, this discussion has necessarily been rather general, while providing some analytical techniques for specific types of systems. While there has been a great deal of innovation in the techniques used to address these problem areas recently, the areas that need to be analyzed remain constant over the years. Therefore, a good background in understanding the problems to be solved is quite valuable, even though we expect continued rapid theoretical developments in the field.

2. To present some of the basic quantitative tools available to analyze the problem areas mentioned.

The focus of this book has been on the *analysis* of operations management problems, not just the presentation of the latest buzzwords. Some of the techniques discussed are the tried and true methods that have been used for decades, while some represent the latest theory, such as TQM and JIT. But what good does it do to learn any quantitative techniques, even the latest ones, when new ones are sure to arrive very frequently in the coming years?

It is certainly true that an operations manager cannot afford to remain stagnant in theoretical knowledge. It is hoped that this introduction will spur operations managers to keep up with new developments in the field as well as to branch out into more narrow areas of existing theory that are beyond the scope of this book. However, there are at least two good reasons for studying the basic quantitative tools of the field. First, the changes in operations management theory, like those in most fields, are generally evolutionary rather than revolutionary. That is, new theories build upon old ones; understanding the basic techniques will make it much easier to keep up with the new ones.

Second, and perhaps more important, learning quantitative techniques can be a powerful means to a deeper understanding of the problem areas themselves. It has been rightly said that the main benefit of quantitative techniques is not in solving problems but in communicating them. Putting problems in the framework of a quantitative model will, of course, lose some of the reality of the problem, but it will make it much easier to get a mental picture of the problem, which will lead to much greater insight into the problem. Then the structure of the model will also greatly enhance the communication of the problem, or "transfer of insight," to other people.

3. To whet the reader's appetite for further study in the field.

As mentioned, we have only scratched the surface of the analytical tools available in operations management, and we have only discussed the larger, more universal problem areas. Several more narrow topics, such as purchasing, industrial engineering, and maintenance, have been left for those directly involved in those fields; there are entire books devoted to these more narrow areas. Similarly, there are sources such as professional journals with the latest theories in those topics that we introduced in this book. The goal here has been to convey some of the importance and interest of the field of operations management so that readers will be encouraged to enter this rewarding field and to seek out further sources.

While parroting the latest buzzwords is definitely not one of the goals of this book, it is useful to discuss the current state of the art of operations management and to consider some of the potential future directions of the field in general terms. In doing so, the temptation is to focus on large, multinational corporations to the exclusion of other types of operations systems. It seems that most of the current literature does fall into this trap, probably because of the visibility and economic clout of these corporate giants. However, there are innumerable small manufacturers that just don't get too excited about things like JIT, MRP, and TQM. Further, more than half of the workers in the United States work in the service sector, where the concerns are a bit different. With this disclaimer, then, let's look at three pillars upon which rest much of the current discussion of the state of the art of operations management.

World-Class Manufacturing

This term has been used to embody a set of complementary ideas that can help a company to compete successfully in the international market and to become a model in its industry. While each author would likely produce a slightly different list of the principles involved, there is general consensus on the characteristics necessary for a world-class manufacturer. As discussed in more detail in Chapter 1, these would include such principles as a sincere desire to meet the needs of customers, a focus on quality with continuous improvements, providing facilities that are flexible and are also being continually improved, reducing the throughput time of the product, improving productivity through the reduction of waste (in time, materials, and labor), a high degree of coordination with marketing and engineering, and the development of competitive advantages.

Companies that have undertaken the attainment of world-class manufacturing have found that awareness of these desirable characteristics is not enough to bring them into fruition. In taking these goals seriously, they must greatly expand their training of current employees as well as seek out highly educated new employees.

Computer-Integrated Manufacturing (CIM)

Computer-Integrated Manufacturing, along with the similar concept of Computer-Integrated Service Systems (CISS), reflects the pervasive influence of computers in modern operations systems. CIM systems consist of several integrated modules, or subsystems, containing hardware and software components. It is safe to say that whenever a new development in the use of computers comes along, that development will be applied to the improvement of operations systems. Such developments would include the use of Local Area Networks (LAN's) of linked microcomputers, special purpose remote-use computers that relay data back to the main system, bar-code scanners, and so on.

In a CIM system there are several standard modules that link the operations system to the other major functional areas of the firm, as well as several modules of interest within the operations system. The marketing module would help in the area of forecasting and product specifications, both major inputs into operations system planning. A Computer-Aided Design (CAD) module could then help develop specific products to meet the specified demands. Accounting and finance modules would then provide cost and cash-flow projections.

Within the manufacturing module there would be smaller modules concerned with scheduling, inventory management, quality control, and routing, each of which would have implications for the others. If we compare the CIM modules mentioned here with the generalized operations system depicted in Figure 1.1, we find an almost perfect match. In other words, a CIM uses computer technology to link the components within the operations system to each other and to the other major functional areas that have interactions with the operations management system.

The Internationalization of Operations Management

In the last couple of decades the field of operations management has become increasingly internationalized in two main ways. First, there has been an increase in the number of multinational firms. American clothing companies have facilities in Asia and Mexico; Japanese auto manufacturers have plants in the United States. The explosion in communications technology has made it possible to tie together far-flung facilities of a single company, allowing the company to utilize resources that may be more plentiful or less expensive in other locations and to more effectively market the company's products to diverse customers.

The second aspect of internationalization has been in the area of operations management theory. Whereas in the nineteenth century and the first half of the twentieth century most of the theoretical developments in the field came from England and the United States, recently major advances have come from all parts of the world. Japan especially has been active in popularizing modern ideas of quality and inventory control.

This high degree of internationalization in operations management (increasingly, even for smaller firms) has certain implications for managers. An operations manager can become more valuable by developing the skills necessary for conducting business in various settings. These would include language skills and a certain amount of flexibility, understanding, and resourcefulness in dealing with different cultures.

In addition, there are implications for multinational companies. In the area of quality control the ISO 9000 standards are a way of standardizing quality efforts around the world and of certifying the attainment of shared standards. In a similar vein, companies find it increasingly necessary to come to some agreement on design standards within a given industry so that their products will be compatible with others throughout the world. For example, there is currently a struggle to determine the appropriate standards for the newest television technology in an attempt to avoid the earlier problems with competing VCR technologies. Finally, there is a similar desire to standardize computer and telecommunication systems to ensure compatibility. Computer programs have been developed to help in these standardization efforts by performing conversions of such things as language and currency in commercial transactions across countries.

COMPETING IN THE FUTURE: TECHNOLOGY, STRATEGY, AND ANALYSIS

We close by considering some current and future trends that will affect the way operations managers approach the important problem areas discussed in this book. As in the earlier chapters, we will consider problem areas grouped into long-run decisions, medium-run decisions, and short-run decisions. Within each category we will briefly discuss three topics: technological advances that will affect the problem areas addressed, strategic considerations that affect a company's choices regarding those problems, and the implications of technology and strategy on the way operations managers will perform their analysis of these problems in the future. Within the topic of strategic considerations we will mention the different strategical arenas appropriate to different types of operations systems, ranging from service systems and job shops to mass production systems.

Long-Run Decisions

Technological Advances. In planning a new operations system or in making major changes in a system there are several recent developments that can be useful. Certainly a CIM system can aid in such decisions as planning a network of facilities throughout the world and in designing a plant layout. The recent concept of group technology, or cellular manufacturing, presents a way to manufacture nonstandard products while taking advantage of the repetitiveness that does exist to improve efficiency. A number of planning decisions can be made with the help of Computer-Integrated Software Engineering (CISE). This system includes modules for Computer-Aided Design (CAD), Computer-Aided Engineering (CAE), which is a way of testing a design by simulation on a computer, and Computer-Aided Process Planning (CAPP), which takes the completed design and determines an efficient way to produce it.

Strategic Considerations. In choosing a location, mass production systems generally face a much larger strategic issue than do job shops. In a large mass production system, especially a multinational one, transportation costs between multiple sites and positioning for access to resources and to markets become important strategic considerations.

In designing a production system and a layout for that system, job shops and service systems can develop competitive advantages in quality, flexibility, and speed. In such systems costs can be high for such things as material handling, setups, providing some excess capacity (in labor and equipment) as a cushion, and often being forced to use outside suppliers. Any improvement in these areas can be very beneficial. On the other hand, mass production systems are faced with designing a fast, efficient, high-quality system with low overhead costs in order to compete against other high-volume producers.

Implications for Analysis. It is obvious that decisions regarding the designs of operations systems are becoming increasingly computerized, especially for large mass production systems. While they may include algorithms or heuristics similar to those of our simple models, CIM modules for location, product design, process design, and layout analysis can incorporate a great deal more data. Thus, the use of CIM is indispensable for designing efficient systems for large, repetitive manufacturers. However, smaller firms of all types can still reach good decisions using these models and graphical tools. Intermittent production systems especially can benefit from the use of cellular manufacturing to utilize the cost savings of repetitiveness wherever possible.

Medium-Run Decisions

Technological Advances. In forecasting and planning production or service levels for the next year or so, there have been no startling breakthroughs. However, there has been and probably will continue to be a gradual improvement in the sophistication and accuracy of forecasting and tracking methods. Operations managers are receiving increasing quantitative training and are able to understand more complex statistical methods; the software is widely available. Also, it is becoming easier to monitor and keep track of demand data in a timely manner through such technology as Point-of-Sale (POS) systems and smart warehouses, which can record items' usage. The use of Decision Support Systems (DSS) can facilitate aggregate planning analysis through linear programming models.

Strategic Considerations. Repetitive manufacturing systems have the greatest need for forecasting models in order to set the appropriate capacity for the system in the medium run. Job shops and service systems are more dependent on actual orders before they can plan capacity. Over time a job shop can develop a feel for the average and the peak capacities needed, as well as any seasonal fluctuations.

The less repetitive systems generally have more flexibility in applying certain aggregate planning strategies, such as using overtime, subcontracting, and adding shifts. Large mass producers are more likely to use a level production strategy because of the likelihood that all available shifts are already utilized and the low probability of finding a subcontractor with the appropriate efficiency and available capacity to help out. It is difficult to change the level of production very quickly in a large, repetitive operation, and finished goods inventories are more acceptable to mass producers because of the low probability of obsolescence in the short term. At the same time, large mass producers often have some capability to level their demands through pricing strategies and complementary product mix strategies. These options are not as readily available for nonrepetitive systems.

Implications for Analysis. Accurate forecasts can make a real difference in the profitability of a firm. The appropriate statistical techniques are available for operations of all types and sizes, so there is no real reason not to use them. However, the problem is that no statistical technique can predict random fluctuations. If these fluctuations are large relative to the numbers being forecast, the forecasts will not be of much use. Therefore, the emphasis should be on finding ways to reduce these fluctuations in demand. Attention should also be directed to timely monitoring of demand so that forecasts can be made quickly with the best data possible.

One of the principles of world-class manufacturing systems is flexibility in production. If a large, repetitive manufacturer can increase its flexibility, it can more fully utilize the array of aggregate planning strategies available rather than being stuck with some fixed level of production. This flexibility can pay off in lower costs of finished goods inventories and back orders.

Short-Run Decisions

Technological Advances. There are many new technologies utilizing advances in computerization and automation in the day-to-day operations of manufacturing and service systems. Many of these are also components of a CIM or CISS system. For example, computers are being used to a greater extent in monitoring quality and in putting together day-to-day production schedules. In inventory control, Automated Storage and Retrieval Systems (ASRS) can respond to computer controls and mechanically move inventory items using bar codes. Also, Electronic Data Interchanges (EDI) link a firm's ordering system to a supplier's computer for automatic ordering of supplies. Automated Guided Vehicles (AGV) can rout batches of items mechanically between work centers. The rapidly advancing field of Artificial Intelligence/Expert Systems (AI/ES) can aid in making complicated decisions in such areas as scheduling and routing.

Strategic Considerations. In the area of quality control a nonrepetitive system is concerned with the *level* of quality. A reputation for high quality can be an effective marketing tool. There is not enough volume to use statistical quality control, so the focus is on careful documentation of the production process and tooling for each new job to meet the desired quality level. Mass production systems, on the other hand, focus on the consistency of their quality and do utilize statistical quality control. Their goal is to monitor quality from the start of the process at the raw material level and then throughout the process in order to avoid costly scrappage and rework.

In a job shop a certain amount of raw material and component inventories is acceptable because of the advantage of being able to quickly respond to orders for various final products. There are no finished goods inventories since all products are made to order. Relationships with suppliers are necessarily less formal than those of mass producers. MRP, a push system of control, is useful in less repetitive systems. In repetitive systems, however, raw material and work-in-process inventories are to be avoided, and a JIT system is more beneficial.

Scheduling in a job shop or service system is heavily dependent on labor because of the labor-intensity of the system. Schedules must be adjusted frequently to maintain good utilization and to respond to new orders. In repetitive systems scheduling is a more centralized operation and more dependent on machine capacities. Schedules are more stable in the short run, less subject to change.

Implications for Analysis. In large, repetitive systems technological advances are making it possible to fine-tune the system for efficiency considerably more than in the past. To compete internationally, such a system must be quick on its feet and willing to take advantage of appropriate technologies as they become available. Much more of the short-run decision-making is therefore routinized by the computer. Larger job shops and service systems can also make use of certain technologies, such as AI/ES for scheduling, but human analysis of the type we have described remains a large part of the effort.

Areas under the Normal Curve

(from the Mean to z)

z	.00	.01	.02	.03	.04	.05	.06	.07	.08	.09
0.0	.0000	.0040	.0080	.0120	.0160	.0199	.0239	.0279	.0319	.0359
0.1	.0389	.0438	.0478	.0517	.0557	.0596	.0636	.0675	.0714	.0753
0.2	.0793	.0832	.0871	.0910	.0948	.0987	.1026	.2064	.1103	.1141
0.3	.1179	.1217	.1255	.1293	.1331	.1368	.1406	.1443	.1480	.1517
0.4	.1554	.1491	.1628	.1664	.1700	.1736	.1772	.1808	.1844	.1879
0.5	.1915	.1950	.1985	.2019	.2054	.2088	.2123	.2157	.2190	.2224
0.6	.2257	.2291	.2324	.2357	.2389	.2422	.2454	.2486	.2517	.2549
0.7	.2580	.2611	.2642	.2673	.2704	.2734	.2764	.2794	.2823	.2852
0.8	.2881	.2910	.2939	.2967	.2995	.3023	.3051	.3078	.3106	.3133
0.9	.3159	.3186	.3212	.3238	.3264	.3289	.3315	.3340	.3365	.3389
1.0	.3413	.3438	.3461	.3485	.3508	.3531	.3554	.3577	.3599	.3621
1.1	.3643	.3665	.3686	.3708	.3729	.3749	.3770	.3790	.3810	.3830
1.2	.3849	.3869	.3888	.3907	.3925	.3944	.3962	.3980	.3997	.4015
1.3	.4032	.4049	.4066	.4082	.4099	.4115	.4131	.4147	.4162	.4177
1.4	.4192	.4207	.4222	.4236	.4251	.4265	.4279	.4292	.4306	.4319
1.5	.4332	.4345	.4357	.4370	.4382	.4394	.4406	.4418	.4429	.4441
1.6	.4452	.4463	.4474	.4484	.4495	.4505	.4515	.4525	.4535	.4545
1.7	.4554	.4564	.4573	.4582	.4591	.4599	.4608	.4616	.4625	.4633
1.8	.4641	.4649	.4656	.4664	.4671	.4678	.4686	.4693	.4699	.4706
1.9	.4713	.4719	.4726	.4732	.4738	.4744	.4750	.4756	.4761	.4767

Appendix A

z	.00	.01	.02	.03	.04	.05	.06	.07	.08	.09
2.0	.4772	.4778	.4783	.4788	.4793	.4798	.4803	.4808	.4812	.4817
2.1	.4821	.4826	.4830	.4834	.4838	.4842	.4846	.4850	.4854	.4857
2.2	.4861	.4864	.4868	.4871	.4875	.4878	.4881	.4884	.4887	.4890
2.3	.4893	.4896	.4898	.4901	.4904	.4906	.4909	.4911	.4913	.4916
2.4	.4918	.4920	.4922	.4925	.4927	.4929	.4931	.4932	.4934	.4936
2.5	.4938	.4940	.4941	.4943	.4945	.4946	.4948	.4949	.4951	.4952
2.6	.4953	.4955	.4956	.4957	.4959	.4960	.4961	.4962	.4963	.4964
2.7	.4965	.4966	.4967	.4968	.4969	.4970	.4971	.4972	.4973	.4974
2.8	.4974	.4975	.4976	.4977	.4977	.4978	.4979	.4979	.4980	.4981
2.9	.4981	.4982	.4982	.4983	.4984	.4984	.4985	.4985	.4986	.4986
3.0	.4987	.4987	.4987	.4988	.4988	.4989	.4989	.4989	.4990	.4990

APPENDIX B

Cumulative Poisson Probabilities

P(x ≤ c) for a Given Mean (np)

					np					
c	.5	1.0	1.5	2.0	2.5	3.0	3.5	4.0	4.5	5.0
0	.6065	.3679	.2231	.1353	.0821	.0498	.0302	.0183	.0111	.0067
1	.9098	.7358	.5578	.4060	.2873	.1991	.1359	.0916	.0611	.0404
2	.9856	.9197	.8088	.6767	.5438	.4232	.3208	.2381	.1736	.1246
3	.9982	.9810	.9344	.8571	.7576	.6472	.5366	.4335	.3423	.2650
4	.9998	.9963	.9814	.9473	.8912	.8153	.7254	.6288	.5321	.4405
5	1.0000	.9994	.9955	.9834	.9580	.9161	.8576	.7851	.7029	.6160
6		.9999	.9991	.9955	.9858	.9665	.9347	.8893	.8310	.7622
7		1.0000	.9998	.9989	.9958	.9881	.9733	.9489	.9134	.8666
8			1.0000	.9998	.9988	.9962	.9901	.9786	.9597	.9319
9				1.0000	.9997	.9989	.9967	.9919	.9829	.9682
10					.9999	.9997	.9990	.9972	.9933	.9863
11					1.0000	.9999	.9997	.9991	.9976	.9945
12						1.0000	.9999	.9997	.9992	.9980
13							1.0000	.9999	.9997	.9993
14								1.0000	.9999	.9998
15									1.0000	.9999
16										1.0000

Appendix B

np

c	6.0	7.0	8.0	9.0	10.0	12.0	14.0	16.0	18.0	20.0
0	.0025	.0009	.0003	.0001	.0000	.0000	.0000	.0000	.0000	.0000
1	.0174	.0073	.0030	.0012	.0005	.0001	.0000	.0000	.0000	.0000
2	.0620	.0296	.0138	.0062	.0028	.0005	.0001	.0000	.0000	.0000
3	.1512	.0818	.0424	.0212	.0103	.0023	.0005	.0001	.0000	.0000
4	.2850	.1730	.0996	.0550	.0292	.0076	.0018	.0004	.0001	.0000
5	.4457	.3007	.1912	.1157	.0671	.0203	.0055	.0014	.0003	.0001
6	.6063	.4497	.3134	.2068	.1301	.0458	.0142	.0040	.0010	.0002
7	.7440	.5987	.4530	.3239	.2202	.0895	.0316	.0100	.0029	.0008
8	.8472	.7291	.5925	.4556	.3328	.1550	.0620	.0220	.0070	.0021
9	.9161	.8305	.7166	.5874	.4579	.2424	.1094	.0433	.0154	.0050
10	.9574	.9015	.8159	.7060	.5830	.3472	.1757	.0774	.0304	.0108
11	.9799	.9466	.8881	.8030	.6968	.4616	.2600	.1270	.0549	.0214
12	.9912	.9730	.9362	.8758	.7916	.5760	.3584	.1931	.0917	.0390
13	.9964	.9872	.9658	.9261	.8645	.6815	.4644	.2745	.1426	.0661
14	.9986	.9943	.9827	.9585	.9165	.7720	.5704	.3675	.2081	.1049
15	.9995	.9976	.9918	.9780	.9512	.8444	.6694	.4667	.2866	.1565
16	.9998	.9990	.9963	.9889	.9730	.8987	.7559	.5660	.3750	.2211
17	.9999	.9996	.9984	.9947	.9857	.9370	.8272	.6593	.4686	.2970
18	1.0000	.9999	.9993	.9976	.9928	.9626	.8826	.7423	.5622	.3814
19		1.0000	.9997	.9989	.9965	.9787	.9235	.8122	.6509	.4702
20			.9999	.9996	.9984	.9884	.9521	.8682	.7307	.5591

np

c	6.0	7.0	8.0	9.0	10.0	12.0	14.0	16.0	18.0	20.0
21			1.0000	.9998	.9993	.9939	.9712	.9108	.7991	.6437
22				.9999	.9997	.9970	.9833	.9418	.8551	.7206
23				1.0000	.9999	.9985	.9907	.9633	.8989	.7875
24					1.0000	.9993	.9950	.9777	.9317	.8432
25						.9997	.9974	.9869	.9554	.8878
26						.9999	.9987	.9925	.9718	.9221
27						.9999	.9994	.9959	.9827	.9475
28						1.0000	.9997	.9978	.9897	.9657
29							.9999	.9989	.9940	.9782
30							.9999	.9994	.9967	.9865
31							1.0000	.9997	.9982	.9919
32								.9999	.9990	.9953
33								.9999	.9995	.9973
34								1.0000	.9998	.9985
35									.9999	.9992
36									.9999	.9996
37									1.0000	.9998
38										.9999
39										.9999
40										1.0000

APPENDIX C

Control Chart Factors

Sample Size	Factor For X̄ Chart	Factor For R Chart
n	A	B
2	1.88	2.27
3	1.02	1.57
4	.73	1.28
5	.58	1.11
6	.48	1.00
7	.42	.92
8	.37	.86
9	.34	.82
10	.31	.78
11	.29	.74
12	.27	.72
13	.25	.69
14	.24	.67
15	.22	.65
16	.21	.64
17	.20	.62
18	.19	.61
19	.19	.60
20	.18	.59

Bibliography

CHAPTER 1

Barrier, Michael. "When 'Just In Time' Just Isn't Enough." *Nation's Business*, November 1992.

Hayes, Robert H., and Gary P. Pisano. "Beyond World Class: The New Manufacturing Strategy." *Harvard Business Review*, January–February 1994.

Jacob, Rahul. "Beyond Quality and Value." *Fortune*, Autumn–Winter 1993.

Krajewski, Lee J., and Larry P. Ritzman. *Operations Management: Strategy and Analysis*, 3rd ed. Reading, Mass.: Addison-Wesley Publishing Co., 1993.

Rohan, Thomas M. "Starting Over: Business Slump Spurs a Renovation." *Industry Week*, February 4, 1985.

Sheridan, John H. "JIT Spells Good Chemistry at Exxon." *Industry Week*, July 1, 1991.

Teresko, John. "Decentralization Yields Solutions." *Industry Week*, March 20, 1989.

Wartzman, Rick. "A Whirlpool Factory Raises Productivity—And Pay of Workers." *Wall Street Journal*, May 4, 1992.

CHAPTER 2

Evans, James R. *Applied Production and Operations Management*, 4th ed. St. Paul, Minn.: West Publishing Co., 1993.

Groebner, David F., and Patrick W. Shannon. *Management Science*. New York: Dellen Publishing Co., 1992.

Haigh, Robert. "Selecting a US Plant Location: The Management Decision Process in Foreign Countries." *Columbia Journal of World Business*, Fall 1990.

Love, Robert F., James G. Morris, and George O. Weslowsky. *Facilities Location: Models and Methods*. New York: North-Holland, 1988.

Lyne, Jack. "Quality-of-Life Factors Dominate Many Facility Location Decisions." *Site Selection Handbook*, August 1988.

Sprackland, Teri. "Texas Instruments Supplies Europe With Homegrown Chips." *Electronic Business*, December 10, 1990.

Sugiura, Hideo. "How Honda Localizes Its Global Strategy." *Sloan Management Review*, Fall 1990.

CHAPTER 3

Francis, Richard L., Leon F. McGinnis, Jr., and John A. White. *Facility Layout and Location: An Analytical Approach*, 2nd ed. Englewood Cliffs, N.J.: Prentice-Hall, 1992.

Hyer, Nancy Lea. "The Potential of Group Technology for U.S. Manufacturing." *Journal of Operations Management*, May 1984.

Milas, Gene H. "Assembly Line Balancing . . . Let's Remove the Mystery." *Industrial Engineering*, May 1990.

Moffat, Susan. "Japan's New Personalized Production." *Fortune*, October 22, 1990.

Pesch, Michael J., Lary Jarvis, and Loren Troyer. "Turning Around the Rust Belt Factory: The $1.98 Solution." *Production and Inventory Management Journal*, 1992.

Weiss, Howard J., and Mark E. Gershon. *Production and Operations Management*. Boston: Allyn and Bacon, 1989.

Woodruff, David. "A Dozen Motor Factories—Under One Roof." *Business Week*, November 20, 1989.

CHAPTER 4

Carlisle, Brian. "Job Design Implications for Operations Managers." *International Journal of Operations and Production Management*, 1983.

Christopher, William F., and Carl G. Thor, eds. *Handbook for Productivity Measurement and Improvement*. Portland, Ore.: Productivity Press, 1993.

Cunningham, J. Barton, and Ted Eberle. "A Guide to Job Enrichment and Redesign." *Personnel*, February 1990.

Lee, Sang M., and Marc J. Schniederjans. *Operations Management*. Boston: Houghton Mifflin Co., 1994.

Powell, Cash. "Process Reengineering at Westinghouse." *Target 10*, May–June 1994.

Sanders, Mark A., and Ernest J. McCormack. *Human Factors in Engineering and Design*, 6th ed. New York: McGraw-Hill, 1987.

CHAPTER 5

Argote, Linda, and Dennis Epple. "Learning Curves in Manufacturing." *Science*, February 1990.

Niebel, Benjamin W. *Motion and Time Study*, 8th ed. Homewood, Ill.: Richard D. Irwin, 1988.

Ramsey, George F., Jr. "Using Self-Administered Work Sampling in a State Agency." *Industrial Engineering*, February 1993.

Rutter, Rick. "Work Sampling: As a Win/Win Management Tool." *Industrial Engineering*, February 1994.

Sakamoto, Shigeyasu. "Key to Productivity: Work Measurement, An International Survey Report." *MTM Journal of Methods—Time Measurement*, 1987.

Schonberger, Richard J., and Edward M. Knod, Jr. *Operations Management: Serving the Customer*, 3rd ed. Plano, Tex.: Business Publications, 1988.

CHAPTER 6

Bowerman, Bruce L., and Richard T. O'Connell. *Forecasting and Time Series: An Applied Approach*, 3rd ed. Belmont, Calif.: Duxbury Press, 1993.

Chambers, John C., Satinder K. Mullick, and Donald D. Smith. "How to Choose the Right Forecasting Technique." *Harvard Business Review*, July–August 1971.

Hanke, John E., and Arthur G. Reitsch. *Business Forecasting*, 4th ed. Boston: Allyn and Bacon, 1992.

Jain, Chaman. "Developing Forecasts for Better Planning." *Long Range Planning*, October 1993.

Mason, Robert D., and Douglas A. Lind. *Statistical Methods in Business and Economics*, 8th ed. Homewood, Ill.: Richard D. Irwin, 1993.

Picconi, Mario J., Albert Romano, and Charles L. Olson. *Business Statistics: Elements and Applications*. New York: HarperCollins, 1993.

Render, Barry, and Jay Heizer. *Principles of Operations Management*. Boston: Allyn and Bacon, 1993.

Stevenson, William J. *Introduction to Management Science*, 2nd ed. Homewood, Ill.: Richard D. Irwin, 1992.

CHAPTER 7

Anderson, David R., Dennis J. Sweeney, and Thomas A. Williams. *An Introduction to Management Science*, 8th ed. St. Paul, Minn.: West Publishing Co., 1997.

Connell, Bertrum C., Everett E. Adam, Jr., and Aimee N. Moore. "Aggregate Planning in a Health Care Food-Service System with Varying Technologies." *Journal of Operations Management*, No. 1 (1984).

Fisher, Marshall L., Janice H. Hammond, Walter Obermeyer, and Anath Raman. "Making Supply Meet Demand in an Uncertain World." *Harvard Business Review*, May–June 1994.

Fogarty, Donald W., Thomas R. Hoffman, and Peter W. Stonebraker. *Production and Operations Management*. Cincinnati, Ohio: South-Western Publishing Co., 1989.

Posner, M. E., and W. Szwarc. "A Transportation Type Aggregate Production Model with Backordering." *Management Science*, February 1983.

Proud, John F. *Master Production Scheduling: A Practical Guide to World Class MPS*. Essex Junction, Vt.: Oliver Wight, 1994.

Turbain, Efraim, and Jack R. Meredith. *Fundamentals of Management Science*, 6th ed. Burr Ridge, Ill.: Richard D. Irwin, 1994.

CHAPTER 8

Adam, Everett E., Jr., and Ronald J. Ebert. *Production and Operations Management*, 4th ed. Englewood Cliffs, N.J.: Prentice-Hall, 1989.

Davis, Samuel G. "Scheduling Economic Lot Size Production Runs." *Management Science*, August 1990.

Fogarty, Donald W., John H. Blackstone, and Thomas R. Hoffman. *Production and Inventory Management*, 2nd ed. Cincinnati, Ohio: South-Western Publishing Co., 1990.

Harris, Fred Whitman. "How Many Parts to Make at Once." *Operations Research*, November–December 1990.

Plane, Donald R. *Management Science: A Spreadsheet Approach*. Danvers, Mass.: Boyd and Fraser Publishing Co., 1994.

Tersine, Richard J. *Principles of Inventory and Materials Management*, 4th ed. Englewood Cliffs, N.J.: Prentice-Hall, 1993.

Willis, T. Hillman, and Jerry D. Shields. "Modifying the ABC Inventory System for a Focused Factory." *Industrial Engineering*, May 1990.

CHAPTER 9

Heizer, Jay, and Barry Render. *Production and Operations Management*, 3rd ed. Boston: Allyn and Bacon, 1994.

Johnson, Alicia. "Is Any System Letter-Perfect?" *Management Review*, September 1986.

LaForge, R. C. "MRP and the Part-Period Algorithm." *Journal of Purchasing Management*, Winter 1982.

Orlicky, Joseph. *Material Requirements Planning*. New York: McGraw-Hill, 1975.

Sivula, Chris. "Georgia-Pacific's MRPII Test." *Datamation*, November 15, 1989.

Wallace, Thomas F. "MRP II and JIT Work Together in Plan and Practice." *Automation*, March 1990.

Wight, Oliver W. *The Executive's Guide to Successful MRP II*. Williston, Vt.: Oliver Wight, 1982.

CHAPTER 10

Ashton, James E., and Frank X. Cook, Jr. "Time to Reform Job Shop Manufacturing." *Harvard Business Review*, March–April 1989.

Berry, W. L., R. Penlesky, and T. E. Vollman. "Critical Ratio Scheduling: Dynamic Due-Date Procedures under Demand Uncertainty." *JIE Transactions*, March 1984.

Chase, Richard B., and Nicholas J. Aquilano. *Production and Operations Management: Manufacturing and Services*, 7th ed. Chicago: Richard D. Irwin, 1995.

Kanet, J. K., and J. C. Hayya. "Priority Dispatching with Operation Due Dates in a Job Shop." *Journal of Operations Management*, May 1982.

Mabert, V. A. "Static vs. Dynamic Priority Rules for Check Processing in Multiple Dispatch–Multiple Branch Banking." *Journal of Operations Management*, May 1982.

Schachter, H. L. "Shop Floor Control: How Much Is Enough." *Production and Inventory Management Review*, December 1981.

Vollman, Thomas E., William L. Berry, and D. Clay Whybark. *Manufacturing Planning and Control Systems*, 3rd ed. Homewood, Ill.: Richard D. Irwin, 1992.

CHAPTER 11

Billesback, Thomas J., and Marc J. Schniederjans. "Applicability of Just-in-Time Techniques in Administration." *Production and Inventory Management Journal*, 3rd Quarter 1989.

Dilworth, James B. *Operations Management*, 2nd ed. New York: McGraw-Hill, 1996.

Karmarkat, U. "Getting Control of Just-in-Time." *Harvard Business Review*, September–October 1989.

Kenney, Martin, and Richard Florida. *Beyond Mass Production: The Japanese System and Its Transfer to the U.S.* New York: Oxford University Press, 1993.

Koziol, David S. "How the Constraint Theory Improved a Job-Shop Operation." *Management Accounting*, May 1988.

LaPlante, Alice. "Inventory Solution from Henry Ford's Day Is Just as Valid Today." *Infoworld*, November 23, 1992.

O'Boyle, Thomas F. "Gulf War Affects Firms as Shipments Lag." *Wall Street Journal*, January 31, 1991.

White, Richard E. "An Empirical Assessment of JIT in U.S. Manufacturers." *Production and Inventory Management Journal*, No. 2 (1993).

CHAPTER 12

Andrew, R., and A. Corominas. "SUCCESS 92: A DSS for Scheduling the Olympic Games." *Interfaces*, September–October 1989.

Cleland, David I. *Project Management: Strategic Design and Implementation*, 2nd ed. New York: McGraw-Hill, 1994.

Dreger, J. Brian. *Project Management: Effective Scheduling*. New York: Van Nostrand Reinhold, 1992.

Kermer, Harold. *Project Management for Executives*. New York: Van Nostrand Reinhold, 1984.

Littlefield, T. K., and P. H. Randolph. "PERT Duration Times: Mathematical or MBO." *Interfaces*, November–December 1991.

Rogers, Tom. "Project Management: Emerging as a Requisite for Success." *Industrial Engineering*, June 1993.

Stevenson, William J. *Production/Operations Management*, 5th ed. Chicago: Richard D. Irwin, 1996.

Taylor, Bernard W. III. *Introduction to Management Science*, 5th ed. Englewood Cliffs, N.J.: Prentice-Hall, 1996.

CHAPTER 13

Anderson, David R., Dennis J. Sweeney, and Thomas A. Williams. *Statistics for Business and Economics*, 6th ed. St. Paul, Minn.: West Publishing Co., 1996.

Aquilano, Nicholas J., Richard B. Chase, and Mark M. Davis. *Fundamentals of Operations Management*, 2nd ed. Chicago: Richard D. Irwin, 1995.

Berenson, Mark L., and David M. Levine. *Basic Business Statistics: Concepts and Applications*, 5th ed. Englewood Cliffs, N.J.: Prentice-Hall, 1992.

Cliampa, Dan. *Total Quality: A User's Guide to Implementation*. Reading, Mass.: Addison-Wesley Publishing Co., 1992.

Fuchsberg, Gilbert. "Total Quality Is Termed Only Partial Success." *Wall Street Journal*, October 1, 1992.

Gabor, Andrea. *The Man Who Discovered Quality: How W. Edwards Deming Brought the Quality Revolution to America*. New York: Penguin, 1990.

Levin, Richard I., and David S. Rubin. *Statistics for Management*, 7th ed. Upper Saddle River, N.J.: Prentice-Hall, 1998.

Pollock, Ellen Joan. "Grudgingly, Lawyers Try 'Total Quality'." *Wall Street Journal*, December 2, 1992.

CHAPTER 14

Bell, R. R., and J. M. Burnham. *Managing Productivity and Change*. Cincinnati, Ohio: South-Western Publishing Co., 1991.

Drucker, Peter E. "The Emerging Theory of Manufacturing." *Harvard Business Review*, May–June 1990.

Gunn, Thomas G. *Manufacturing for Competitive Advantage*. Cambridge, Mass.: Ballinger Publishing Co., 1987.

Johnson, D. "The Building Blocks of CIM," *Manufacturing Systems*, February 1988.

Juran, J. M. "Strategies for World-Class Quality," *Quality Progress*, March 1991.

Williamson, M. "Artificial Intelligence Takes a Stand on the Factory Floor." *Computerworld*, July 6, 1987.

Wright, J. "World Class CIM on a Small Scale." *Manufacturing Systems*, November 1989.

Index

About the Author

MICHAEL R. SUMMERS is Professor of Management Science at Pepperdine University. He is active in the Decision Sciences Institute (DSI) and the Production and Operations Management Society (POMS).

ISBN 1-56720-126-1

90000>

EAN

9 781567 201260

HARDCOVER BAR CODE